Front Office Fantasies

STUDIES IN SPORTS MEDIA

Edited by Victoria E. Johnson
and Travis Vogan

*A list of books in the series appears
at the end of this book.*

Front Office Fantasies

The Rise of Managerial Sports Media

BRANDEN BUEHLER

© 2023 by the Board of Trustees
of the University of Illinois
All rights reserved
1 2 3 4 5 C P 5 4 3 2 1
♾ This book is printed on acid-free paper.

An earlier version of chapter four was originally published as
"White-Collar Play: Reassessing Managerial Sports Games"
in *The Velvet Light Trap*, Volume 81, pp. 4–17. Copyright
© 2018 by the University of Texas Press. All rights reserved.

Library of Congress Cataloging-in-Publication Data
Names: Buehler, Branden, 1986– author.
Title: Front office fantasies : the rise of managerial
    sports media / Branden Buehler.
Description: Urbana : University of Illinois Press,
    [2023] | Series: Studies in sports media | Includes
    bibliographical references and index.
Identifiers: LCCN 2023013091 (print) | LCCN
    2023013092 (ebook) | ISBN 9780252045622 (cloth :
    acid-free paper) | ISBN 9780252087745 (paperback
    : acid-free paper) | ISBN 9780252055287 (ebook)
Subjects: LCSH: Mass media and sports—United
    States. | Television broadcasting of sports—United
    States. | Sports administration—Social aspects—
    United States. | Sports administration—Economic
    aspects—United States.
Classification: LCC GV742 .B846 2023 (print) |
    LCC GV742 (ebook) | DDC 070.4/49796—dc23/
    eng/20230523
LC record available at https://lccn.loc.gov/2023013091
LC ebook record available at https://lccn.loc.gov/2023013092

For J and Z

Contents

Acknowledgments   ix

Preface: Sporting Fantasies   xi

Introduction: "The Age of the General Manager"   1

1 The Managerial American Dream: The Administrative Fantasies of Managerial Sports Films   33

2 "He's Looking Like a Depressed Asset": The Financial Logics of Managerial Sports Talk   63

3 Datavisuality: The Quantified Aesthetic of Managerial Sports Television   103

4 White-Collar Play: Managerial Sports Games and the Modeling of Neoliberal Capitalism   141

Conclusion: The Banality of Managerial Sports Media   169

Notes   175

Bibliography   193

Index   211

Acknowledgments

This project began while I was in graduate school at the University of Southern California and so I must first thank Anikó Imre, Vicky Johnson, Virginia Kuhn, Tara McPherson, and Ellen Seiter for all their invaluable feedback and guidance during the project's initial stages. Tara was a particular source of encouragement and insight as the project first took shape.

As it developed, the project was much improved thanks to tremendously helpful comments from the series editors—Vicky Johnson and Travis Vogan—as well as from two anonymous readers. I am also thankful to Rox Samer, Raffi Sarkissian, and Brett Siegel for their feedback on individual chapters, as well as to Bryan Curtis and several members of ESPN's Stats and Information Group for sharing their time and knowledge. Jon Kendle was of great assistance during a research trip to the Ralph Wilson Jr. Research and Preservation Center. I am deeply grateful, too, to librarians at USC, SUNY Oneonta, and Seton Hall University for all their help in obtaining materials throughout the research process.

As I have continued work on the project over the past several years, I have been fortunate to have continued support from my colleagues. At SUNY Oneonta, I could not have asked for a better of set of coworkers than my fellow department members Jacqueline Bishop, Kristen Blinne, Andrew Bottomley, Nat Bouman, John Chiang, Summer Cunningham, Greg Hummel, Raúl Feliciano Ortiz, Rahul Rastogi, Karen Stewart, Gayane Torosyan, Theron Verdon, Tim Welch, and Diana Willis, while at Seton Hall, I have been so appreciative of the support from Jon Kraszewski, Bill Pace, and Tom Rondinella as program colleagues, from Dena Levine, Renee Robinson, and Cathy

Zizik as department chairs, and from Renee Robinson and Deirdre Yates as college deans.

The project has also benefited from the indirect support of so many others. While I was initially developing these ideas at USC, I was fortunate to be surrounded by so many kind and insightful graduate students, including Emma Ago, Nik Bars, Tisha Dejmanee, Nicholas Emme, Rosie Levy, Charlie Porter, Raffi Sarkissian, Rox Samer, Brett Siegel, Jeremy Tipton, Jason Voss, and Katie Walsh. Rick Jewell, meanwhile, deserves special mention for first encouraging me to write about sports media in his course on the Hollywood studio era. This project undoubtedly bears an imprint of previous academic mentors, too, so I also want to thank Amy Villarejo and Matthew Tinkcom for their indispensable guidance during my years at Cornell and Georgetown, respectively.

At the University of Illinois Press, Daniel Nasset, Maria Mendes Schaefer, Tad Ringo, and the entire publishing team have been wonderful to work with. I first described the outlines of this book to Danny many years ago and I am greatly appreciative of his continued backing of the project since those early days. I am thankful, too, for the work of copyeditor Walt Evans in readying the manuscript for publication.

I also want to acknowledge my parents, Charles Buehler and Barbara Wells, as I could not have made it to this point without their unconditional support, as well as my in-laws, Hope Druckman, Andrew Kohler, and Ted Kohler, as they have offered constant encouragement and kindness. And, finally, I want to express my everlasting gratitude to Laura Kohler—I am so incredibly fortunate to have you by my side.

Preface

Sporting Fantasies

In 2014, as I started pondering the ubiquity of sports media texts focused on executives rather than players and on roster maneuvering rather than gameplay, I became increasingly intrigued by an event I was repeatedly seeing mentioned across a range of sports media outlets—the Massachusetts Institute of Technology (MIT) Sloan Sports Analytics Conference. Although connected to an academic institution, the Sloan Conference was quickly becoming a major gathering for anyone—whether an academic, media member, or fan—interested in the quantitative analysis of sports. To that point, the conference had grown rapidly in size since its founding in 2006—advancing from a small symposium housed in a few MIT classrooms to a massive gathering necessitating sprawling convention centers.[1] Indeed, as *Wall Street Journal* reporter Jason Gay observed, the event had become something like a comic book convention but devoted to discussions of topics like statistical models of basketball lineup efficiency rather than superhero movies.[2] For my purposes, though, it was particularly notable that the Sloan Conference had become a central gathering point for sports executives, with many professional teams bringing sizable portions of their front offices to the event. Wanting to better understand who these people were and why I was seeing them across the sports media landscape, I registered for the conference and booked a ticket to Boston.

Hoping to experience the Sloan Conference as fully as possible, I arrived in Boston a day before the proceedings officially began so that I could participate in a pre-conference "hackathon" event sponsored by ESPN. As I entered the hackathon, I started walking around the room and introducing myself to the other participants, the majority of whom were young men. Some, participating in the "student" portion of the event, were undergraduates drawn from colleges around the country. Many others, participating in the "open" part of the event, had taken time off from their jobs in industries like management consulting, pharmaceuticals, and technology to come to the event. However, what appeared to unite them all—other than their seemingly coordinated choice to wear suits and the evident ability to shell out several hundred dollars in conference registration fees—was an earnest desire to make their way into a front office job.[3] Indeed, as one entrant told me, the trip to the conference had been something of an investment. Having recently lost his position at a biotechnology company, he had come to the Sloan Conference to try to finally make a long-held dream come true: to work as a sports executive. This dream pervaded the conference. Once the event began in earnest, it was a constant that every panel, no matter the topic, would feature scores of besuited young men eager to talk to anyone officially employed within the industry (my name tag—lacking a connection to any team—was constantly met with disappointed glances). In between panels, they could be seen anxiously stalking the hallways, hoping to find the conversation that might just be their way in.

That so many conference participants shared a similar managerial dream was only underscored by something that happened during the hackathon. Toward its conclusion, as entrants began presenting their work to a panel of judges, a hush grew over the room, and participants started to swap nervous glances. A new figure had entered at the back of the room and sidled up against a wall, quietly taking in the proceedings. Eyeing the figure, participants silently mouthed, "Do you see who's here?" For many of these hackathon entrants—individuals who dreamed of one day making their way into a team's front office—this silent, lurking figure was living their fantasies. This person, Daryl Morey, had worked his way up to become one of sport's power players, running the National Basketball Association's (NBA) Houston Rockets as their general manager (GM). His day-to-day life was what they strived for—negotiating trades, running models, scouting players; he had it all.

The fact it was Morey who had wandered into the room was of particular note, too. Morey's ascension to the top of the sports industry was ripe with symbolic significance, especially for conference attendees. Notably, he had made his way into the world of sport without ever playing a sport at a high level. Instead, the "quizzical, geeky" Morey had gone to college for computer science, moved on to business school at MIT (during which time he cofounded the Sloan Conference with MIT classmate Jessica Geller), and then landed at a management consulting firm.[4] That consulting job eventually allowed Morey to achieve his own long-standing dream of working in professional sports, as a consulting project led to a job with the NBA's Boston Celtics. That job, in turn, had led to his position with the Rockets.[5] For the eager participants at this hackathon, Morey was proof that fantasy sports did not have to be entirely fantasy, that the participants could still— even if they never could throw a ball particularly well or run especially fast—make it to the top of the sports world. No, finding a job in professional sports would not be easy and, yes, such a job would still require a certain background—the right school, the right connections, the right vocabulary, and so forth—but Morey, as well as a growing number of other executives like him, showed that there were routes to sports management that did not require any athletic success. This sense lingered throughout the conference. As panelists and keynote speakers repeatedly suggested, there were ways of mastering sport that did not require intimacy with what it felt like to be on the court against a heated rival or to take to the field with seconds remaining in a close game. Instead, sport could be properly understood with analytic thinking and rigorous statistical models. Advancing to the highest levels of sport, then, did not require any special physical talents; it just required the right approach.

That the hackathon participants were so familiar with Morey and that the mere sight of him at a distance could cause them to tense up suggests this managerial fantasy shared by so many at the conference—of bypassing the field and going straight to the front office—is not just a product of the sports industry. Instead, that so many have found their way to this dream reflects the central importance of sports media and its transformations of managers into stars and managerial work into white-collar paradise. Across the sports media landscape, figures like Morey have become omnipresent, whether featured as guests on sports talk radio, turned into topics of discussion on television debate shows, or even made fictional in sports films. Similarly, their everyday tasks of roster management have been frequently positioned as the make-or-break activities of sport, with actual games either abstracted or placed into the background. Taking all this managerial media in, why dream of being a pawn when you could fantasize of controlling the entire board?

The chapters that follow will tackle the ubiquity of managerial sports media from several angles—dissecting, for instance, the emergence of sports films in which the protagonists are loquacious agents rather than athletic phenoms and the popularity of sports video games that resemble mundane productivity software. But laced underneath all these analyses is a sense that something significant has shifted within the sporting landscape and made administration a potent fantasy like never before.

Preface   xiii

Front Office Fantasies

Introduction

"The Age of the General Manager"

In 2011 the film *Moneyball* became an unexpected hit—pulling in a world-wide box office of $110 million on a budget of $50 million.[1] This success was a surprise both because sports movies have recently failed to do well at the box office and because of the exact sports subject the film was dealing with: front office maneuverings. Indeed, the project had long met skepticism as it slowly lurched through the development process. Based on a 2003 Michael Lewis book of the same name, the story centers around Oakland Athletics general manager Billy Beane and his attempts to field a competitive baseball team on a bare-bones budget. Unable to rely on traditional mechanisms for success, like acquiring high-priced free agents, Beane turns to new statistical measures to find undervalued players. While the book was a best-seller, as Noel Murray of *The A. V. Club* opined in 2009, "Very little about its true story of stat-heads transforming the business of baseball screams 'movie.'"[2] Similarly, *Vulture*'s Lane Brown expressed extreme skepticism that a film studio would spend $50 million "on a film about baseball statistics."[3] Nonetheless, the film eventually made it to the screen with the front office focus still in place. And, as mentioned, the film became the rare hit sports movie, not only raking in box office dollars but also garnering six Academy Award nominations.[4]

While the success of *Moneyball* may have come as a surprise to the many film industry skeptics who had assumed asset valuation did not make for a compelling plot device, *Moneyball*'s ability to reverberate with American audiences had a certain amount of predictability. As the preface began documenting, front office executives are, in a sense, the new glamor positions of the sports media world. Sports fans, in short, no longer just yearn to soar up and down a football field or a basketball court but also dream of putting together the teams that make their way to these playing surfaces. Speaking to the fact that *Moneyball* was hardly an isolated example, 2014 saw sports film icon Kevin Costner also play a general manager, anchoring *Draft Day* as the leader of the Cleveland Browns' front office. Later that same year, Jon Hamm starred in *Million Dollar Arm*—not as a player or a coach, but rather as a smooth-talking agent scouring India for raw baseball talent. As critic Vicky Osterweil summarized at the time, "There's a new breed of sports movie in town." She continued, "These films celebrate the real heroes of sports, the real heroes of any workplace: the bosses."[5]

Sports movies have hardly been the only instances of sports media texts focusing on the front office. Turning to video games, it might be observed that one of the most routinely popular sports games franchises across the world is *Football Manager,* which places its players in charge of a soccer team, and in the process largely eschews sporting action in favor of duties like payroll accounting. Other massively popular franchises, including *FIFA, Madden,* and *NBA 2K,* also include managerial modes. *Madden,* for example, has included an administrative mode that asks players to consider a team's finances and marketing operations. The game mode has even asked players to set the price of stadium concessions and team merchandise like hats and sweatshirts. Perhaps even more significant than the introduction of managerial modes to sports video games, though, has been the ever-increasing popularity of fantasy sports that place participants in control of virtual rosters of athletes. According to the Fantasy Sports and Gaming Association, an estimated 62.5 million people now play fantasy sports in the United States and Canada—up from 12.6 million in 2005.[6]

Looking to other forms of sports media, it can also be observed that sports television is full of front office executives and discussions of their maneuvers, with managerial events like the National Football League (NFL) and National Basketball Association (NBA) entry drafts even becoming major television attractions. Indeed, draft coverage can outdraw major live game telecasts.[7] Sports radio and audio media have also turned their interest to off-field maneuverings. Examining the rankings of the most popular sports podcasts, one can continually find numerous podcasts devoted to fantasy sports. As the NFL draft approaches every year, draft-focused podcasts also soar up the rankings. Moreover, front office executives are regular guests on several top-ranking podcasts, such as *The Lowe Post* and *The Woj Pod.* Perhaps even more notable, though, is how frequently these audio texts integrate managerial tasks into their regular programming. For example, one of the most consistently dominant podcasts throughout the medium's history has been *The Bill Simmons Podcast.* Simmons often discusses leagues' drafts, free agency periods, and trade activities on his podcast. Indeed, Simmons has even dubbed himself the "Picasso of the Trade Machine," referring to an ESPN web tool that allows fans to simulate NBA trades.

These many examples all lend credence to Neal Pollack's argument on *Slate* that we are increasingly living in "the age of the general manager." As he writes, "If you don't care about buying, selling, and trading, the sports world has much less to offer you these days."[8] In this project, I offer a critique of this state of affairs, arguing that the centering of the front office evident in ever more sports media texts speaks to a new set of sporting fantasies that highlight the unique pleasures of management. These managerial fantasies, in turn, speak to an assortment of broader societal phenomena, including managerialism, financialization, and quantification. Indeed, as individual chapters will document, the texts of managerial sports media serve as perhaps the clearest cultural manifestations of many of these phenomena and how they intersect with issues of power. Before proceeding to the ideological workings of sports media's managerial fixation, though, this project opens below with an examination of the roots of this fixation, providing necessary context for the cultural probes that follow.

The Origins of Managerial Sports Media

If one is to accept that sports media is showing signs of a wide-ranging managerial fixation—a fixation so wide-ranging that few realms of the sports media landscape have been left untouched—it becomes apparent that such a fixation cannot have a simple, one-dimensional explanation. With so many texts across so many media forms bearing traces of "the age of the general manager," it would be impossible to pin the managerial interest to the maneuverings of any single network, movie studio, or other media entity. Similarly, it would be difficult to trace the managerial fixation to any single cultural or societal explanation. With that in mind, this chapter begins the work of explaining managerial sports media by offering a multi-faceted account that spans multiple industries and considers several interlocking cultural and societal transformations.

Before moving into these explanations, though, a few brief qualifiers are necessary. First, it must be acknowledged that sports media's interest in management is not entirely novel. Sports teams, of course, have long employed administrators, and their administrative maneuvers have long appeared in both real-world media coverage of sports and fictional narratives set in the sporting universe.[9] One can observe, for instance, the many blaring headlines that surrounded Babe Ruth's move from the Boston Red Sox to the New York

Introduction   3

Yankees in 1920 or the prominent role for front office executive Branch Rickey in the 1950 biopic *The Jackie Robinson Story*. This book, though, concentrates on the intensity of the contemporary managerial fixation and, accordingly, this section will focus on explicating the contextual factors that have helped produce this recent intensity. With that said, this book will frequently return to the longer historical trajectory of managerial sports media—noting, for example, how the recent wave of managerial sports films was preceded by other films interested in the business of sports, such as *Number One* (1969) and *North Dallas Forty* (1979), or how contemporary managerial sports games have roots in the tabletop sports simulations that grew popular in the mid-twentieth century.

Second, it should be noted this book is primarily focused on the recent managerial fixation within American sports media. Accordingly, the following section will highlight factors that account, in particular, for the content of American media texts. With that said, sports media's managerial fixation is very much a global phenomenon. As mentioned, for example, managerial sports games like *Football Manager* are internationally popular, while European broadcasters like Sky can treat soccer transfer deadlines with much the same fervor as American broadcasters covering drafts and free agency periods. Unsurprisingly, then, while the explanations in this section are focused on addressing American sports media, those explanations are not necessarily unique to the American context. Indeed, scholars have documented how several of the factors cited below—like the intensifying search for streaming video content and the move of sports teams to an "analytical and rational" management style—are applicable well beyond the United States.[10]

Moreover, in concentrating on American sports media, this book mostly highlights media centered around men's sports and, accordingly, the explanations below are also largely focused on men's sports. On the most basic level, this focus reflects the deeply skewed nature of the American sports media landscape. With men's sports receiving a highly disproportionate amount of attention relative to women's sports—not just in television and radio coverage, but also in film and video game treatments of sport—there are many more managerial texts related to men's sports than to women's sports.[11] Indeed, managerial media play a role in this continuing imbalance, as media companies have often chosen to add new coverage of administrative maneuvers within men's sports rather than expand their coverage of women's sports. There are also more elaborate conjunctural reasons for the preponderance of managerial sports texts related to men's sports. For instance, one point that will be stressed below is that managerial texts often revolve around player movement, with free agency a particular subject of interest. As a result of

4   Introduction

the continued underinvestment in women's sports, the professionalization of women's sports has occurred on a delayed timeline relative to men's sports and, accordingly, free agency has also come later to women's sports than men's sports. The National Women's Soccer League (NWSL), for example, only began phasing in a collectively bargained free agency system for its 2023 season. Even with these sorts of caveats in mind, it should be noted that the managerial fixation has also begun extending, if to a lesser degree, to media coverage of women's sports—ESPN, for instance, began carrying the Women's National Basketball Association (WNBA) draft in 2001 and added a WNBA free agency special in 2022—and many of the phenomena discussed below, like financialization and quantification, are very much germane to managerial texts revolving around women's sports.

Finally, it must be said that explanations for the precise contours of sports media's managerial fixation need to remain specific to the exact texts and industries at hand. For instance, sports television's recent interest in quantitative metrics—the subject of this book's third chapter—is partially rooted in factors particular to the sports television industry, such as the introduction of new graphics technologies, that are not directly relevant to the recent strain of sports films featuring player agents—one of the subjects of this book's first chapter. Nonetheless, there are broader explanations that cut across the entirety of managerial sports media. Thus, while the data-driven coverage of sports television cannot be understood without delving into the particulars of the sports television industry, that coverage is also enmeshed in phenomena that extend beyond sports television and, accordingly, have played a role in transforming many other aspects of sports media.

Managerial Sports Media as a Sports Media Phenomenon

In accounting for the current spread of managerial sports media, some of the most rudimentary explanations lie within sports media industries. After all, administrative content can only exist in the world with the efforts of these industries—putting, for instance, executive-laden films into theaters or lengthy free agency specials on television. As a starting point, it can be observed that the ubiquity of managerial sports media, particularly within radio and television, is closely related to media companies' interest in turning major men's sports into topics of year-round coverage. Notably, the massively popular NFL only plays games for five months of the year. The seasons of other prominent leagues like the NBA, National Hockey League (NHL), and Major League Baseball (MLB), meanwhile, each extend over seven months of the year. Thus, by focusing on transactions—many of which occur during leagues' off-seasons—media companies have looked to fill their programming schedules with NFL, NBA, NHL, and MLB content even after players and coaches have wrapped up their years and retreated to the golf course. On a related note, a managerial focus provides a way for media companies—or even individuals with fledgling podcasts—to cover popular leagues even if they do not hold rights to broadcast a league's games. This, arguably, is how the managerial mode began its rise in prominence, as the NFL draft's introduction to television emerged mainly out of necessity.

When ESPN launched in 1979, it declared a bold intention to be the first cable network devoted entirely to sports. However, it was initially hampered by a relative lack of subscribers and money. Thus, the channel was hard-pressed to find many sports to televise when it launched. Indeed, an early promotional brochure touted ESPN's ability to bring viewers sports like "Professional Karate," "Horse Show Jumping," and "Pro Celebrity Golf."[12] The channel, then, was eager to get a piece of popular sports leagues however it could. To that end, it looked for events that had long been considered undesirable by the major networks—or, as the promotional brochure put it, live events that "used to be considered avant-garde in the industry," like the "NFL player draft."[13] Indeed, the draft was considered such an undesirable (or "avant-garde") property that anecdotes have the league's then-commissioner, Pete Rozelle, responding to ESPN's initial proposals to televise the draft by asking, "Why would you want to do that?"[14] Furthermore, the league's owners unanimously voted against the network's initial offer to broadcast the draft, not eager to place any of its proceedings on the fledgling network. Fred Gaudelli, a former ESPN producer, reflected, "Nobody knew what ESPN was about. Why would [the NFL want] to put its brand on their air?"[15] Moreover, getting the draft television-ready seemed more trouble than it was worth. Jim Steeg, the NFL's vice president of special events at the time, later commented, "It seemed like a pain in the neck to set all this up for something that didn't seem to be a very popular event."[16] However, ESPN's then-president, Chet Simmons, eventually convinced Rozelle that the draft had significant television potential. After Rozelle sold that potential to the league's owners, ESPN covered its first NFL draft in April 1980.[17]

Several decades later, similar content dilemmas continue to occur across the sports media landscape. For instance, staying within sports television, recent years have seen the launch of many new national cable sports networks, like CBS Sports Network, FS1/FS2, the Golf Channel, and the Tennis Channel. In addition, there are now also several league-owned networks, such as the MLB Network, NBA TV, the NFL Network, and the NHL Network, as well as a panoply of college-focused channels, including the ACC Network, the Big Ten Network, the Pac-12 Network, and the SEC Network. Significantly, too, there are many regional channels, some of them team-owned, like the Yankees Entertainment and Sports Network (YES) and the Mid-Atlantic Sports Network (MASN). Moreover, recent years have also seen an explosion in streaming services with significant sports components, like ESPN+, Paramount+, and Peacock. Amid the many programming strategies these outlets have utilized to fill their programming schedules—like airing alternative and niche sports, commissioning documentaries, and so forth—managerial content has emerged as a staple, with transactional topics rolled into a wide range of studio programming.[18] As in the case of ESPN and NFL draft coverage, a mere attachment to popular events—even just a discursive one—can stand in when live game coverage of those events is not an option. The reliance on managerial content is hardly unique to sports television, either. For example, as the number of sports podcasts has exploded over the course of the medium's short history, many of these podcasts have filled their schedules with lengthy discussions of even the most minor of transactions.

Managerial content, too, often has the added benefit of being relatively cheap. Returning to the subject of sports television, for example, as more and more outlets have vied for the rights to the same limited pool of popular live sporting events, the fees to these events have increased dramatically. Because of these escalating fees, a frequent question within the television industry has been whether there is a "sports media bubble," with rights fees perhaps outpacing the actual value of these properties.[19] This question has been given added urgency over the last several years, as more and more consumers have decided to cut their cable subscriptions in favor of streaming plans. ESPN, for instance, could be found in 100 million homes in 2011 but was down to seventy-four million homes by 2022.[20] NBC, meanwhile, decided to entirely shutter its sports cable channel NBCSN in 2021.[21] With such trends in mind, sports media reporter John Ourand has suggested that outlets "are becoming more judicious about where they spend their money," including by occasionally preferring "cheaper studio programming" over more expensive live events.[22] Thus, studio programming frequently concerned with managerial minutiae, as in a debate show like ESPN's *Around the Horn* (2002–), would seem to hold ever more appeal. The popularity of managerial sports programming on television, then, recalls the rise of reality television programming in the 2000s. As Ted Magder documents, the growth of the reality genre came as part of a "general effort to reduce production costs and financial risk."[23] And, as Chad Raphael points out, such an effort was similarly precipitated by the explosion in the number of television outlets—an explosion that di-

Introduction   7

luted audiences and advertising revenues and, in turn, led to pressures to cut programming costs.[24]

Sports media's managerial focus also appears to be particularly well-suited to an era of media convergence. In effect, administrative content becomes part of a feedback loop between internet outlets, radio and audio media, and television. For example, ESPN's reporters will often break transactional news on Twitter, elaborate on a television show like *SportsCenter* (1979–), write a brief story for the ESPN website, and follow up again on Twitter and on podcasts. "Insider" journalists who specialize in transactional minutiae, like ESPN's Adam Schefter and Adrian Wojnarowski, will even ostentatiously read text messages and use social media platforms while on television—signaling that important information is currently being exchanged or that critical news may be breaking online. Sports media columnist Bryan Curtis, who has written at length on the subject of managerial sports media and the rise of "insider" journalists both for *Grantland* and *The Ringer,* jokes in an interview with me that looking at a phone while on air "is the new power in media. . . . If you're allowed to do that, that means you're really powerful."[25] Many of the concerns of managerial media—information about contract terms, trade negotiations, and so forth—are, to repeat, not beholden to the same sorts of rights agreements as are broadcasted games. Accordingly, this information can be endlessly circulated and amplified between platforms. Moreover, Curtis implies that programming focused on transactions can increase interest in other programming, including live game broadcasts.[26] Debate shows that devote programming space to speculating over a player's upcoming free agency, for instance, might fuel interest in that player's performance in an upcoming game. As Curtis notes, too, such speculation gives fans fodder for second-screen engagement, as they may watch a game on one screen while also taking to social media platforms like Twitter to discuss the implications of that game on free agency.[27] Indeed, managerial content is so well-suited to convergent media that administrative content stretches into video games and film, though in fictional forms. Video game series like *Madden* and *NBA 2K,* for instance, have incorporated simulated social media feeds into their game modes, in the process spotlighting artificially generated tweets from the "insider" journalists like Schefter. Schefter, too, was even written into the film *Draft Day*.

The following section will delve further into the mechanics of the sports industry. Here, though, it might be briefly noted that sports media entities, like podcast and television networks, do not operate in isolation. Instead, sports teams and leagues also have an active role in the workings of the sports media industry and, significantly, also have a vested interest in making their organizations subjects of fascination throughout the entire course of the year and encouraging administrative content. Notably, for instance, the rights agreements between leagues and television networks can include agreements to program additional, year-round content meant to keep the leagues as visible as possible. That leagues' desires to remain visible plays a direct role in fueling administrative media content is further illustrated by leagues' scheduling decisions. The NFL, for example, has intentionally positioned itself to have managerial "events" scattered throughout the league's off-season: a scouting combine in February, free agency and an annual owners meeting in March, the draft in late April/early May, and then mini-camps and preseason training sessions (OTAs) later in May. Thus, on both the league's outlets as well as other outlets that cover the league, there is a steady stream of new NFL content to circulate throughout the year, even if that content might entail little more than news about a prospect's hand size or a player's contract renegotiations.

It is not just in the interest of sports organizations to keep attention on a sport throughout the year, but also in the interest of players. As Curtis explains, it is "better for marketing opportunities and fame . . . if you don't disappear for six months of the year."[28] Players, then, also have reason to draw attention to administrative maneuvers and, in so doing, intensify off-season coverage. To illustrate this point, Curtis mentions the 2015 free agency of Los Angeles Clippers center DeAndre Jordan. Early in the free agency period, Jordan came to an initial agreement with the Dallas Mavericks. After rethinking this agreement, Jordan wavered and contacted the Clippers about the possibility of staying in Los Angeles. This indecision set off an "emoji war" that became a major sports media news item.[29] In brief, Dallas Mavericks player Chandler Parsons tweeted an emoji of a plane—appearing to signal he was traveling to meet with Jordan to convince him to commit to the Mavericks. Next, Clippers guard J. J. Redick tweeted an emoji of a car—indicating he was also on the way to see Jordan—which was then followed by Clippers forward Blake Griffin tweeting emojis of a plane, helicopter, and car—an intimation that he was ending his vacation in Hawaii and heading to Jordan's home. More and more players—and teams—joined the emoji "battle," which eventually took to players' Instagram accounts. In a case like this, transactional content did not just serve the interest of the media organizations (by providing them content to discuss across media forms) and the NBA (by keeping media attention on the league during the long off-season), but also players (by raising or maintaining their profiles, even while some were on vacation).

The ascent of administrative content might also be traced to the desire by media companies to tap into perceived audience demand for this content. The

Introduction   9

roots of such demand invite speculation, and, to that end, the next section will discuss how changes in labor relations between athletes and sports leagues may have shifted the nature of sports fandom. Moreover, subsequent chapters will touch on the appeal of specific forms of managerial sports media, as in the fourth chapter's exploration of the resonance of managerial sports games. Theorizing broadly here, though, Curtis speculates administrative sports content is popular because it appeals to all fans—not just those of winning teams.[30] Even perennially losing teams, after all, engage in trades, contract signings, and other transactions. Relatedly, Curtis proposes that part of the appeal of so much managerial content might be that it is frequently oriented toward the future, thus allowing audiences to creatively exercise their imaginations in speculating—often hopefully—what would unfold, for instance, if their favorite team acquired a star player. For example, writing on the increasing popularity of NBA trade rumors, Curtis comments, "It's about the *possibility* of what *might* happen on a court in the future. . . . Oddly, that's what makes it fun."[31] The second chapter, on managerial sports talk, will return to this future orientation at length.

Lingering on the topic of imagination, another reason audiences might be interested in managerial work is that many fans may find it relatively easy to picture doing that work themselves. After all, much of the work of a front office executive—reviewing spreadsheets, sending emails, and so on—is the same sort of work so many other individuals perform in their daily lives. As Curtis suggests—and as the preface began exploring—this familiarity seems to spur administrative fantasies. "We're not really going to play centerfield for the Yankees or quarterback for the Patriots," he remarks, "but we can imagine sitting in an office and making phone calls."[32] As the preface noted, too, these managerial fantasies have seemingly been given even more life by a new wave of executives—to be further discussed below—who have arrived to their front office roles without having played sport at a high level or even having worked in sports before.

Curtis, too, theorizes that individuals desire to know what is going on behind the scenes in any industry and has connected sports media "insiders" like Schefter and Wojnarowski to film industry "insiders" like Nikki Finke.[33] Such a connection suggests another general theory for fans' apparent interest in managerial sports media: the universal appeal of gossip. To that point, Lawrence Wenner argues the "sports press provides a socially sanctioned gossip sheet for men in America, a place where a great deal of conjecture is placed upon 'heroes' and events of little worldly import."[34] Wenner's argument is about sports journalism, generally, but this sentiment seems particularly true of managerial sports media focused on transactions. As Curtis explains, transaction-focused journalism is heavy on rumor and hearsay. "We like to gossip," he declares. "An Adrian Wojnarowski tweet is the *People* magazine that we otherwise wouldn't allow ourselves to be seen with."[35] Suppose this comparison was further developed, with connections drawn between sports media and other realms of the media landscape. In that case, it is significant that the focus on transactions allows athletes (the "characters" of sports media) to stay in audiences' lives for the entire year. Moreover, it links seasons together—providing sports a sense of seriality. Curtis argues that transactions can even produce more intriguing "narratives" than those found in the course of game action.[36] He returns to the DeAndre Jordan example. Curtis argues that the relatively low-scoring Jordan is probably not the most fascinating NBA player for basketball fans. However, his free agency period was full of twists and turns, including the aforementioned "emoji war." Curtis argues that sports "don't have naturally occurring soap operas" but implies that episodes like Jordan's free agency can come relatively close.[37]

Broad speculation over audience demand for managerial sports content might also single out, amid the wider ubiquity of managerial sports media, the particularly dramatic growth of fantasy sports over the last few decades and the potential relationship between that growth and interest in other managerial texts. In brief, as individuals create and maintain virtual rosters of athletes, it can be imperative to be up to date on the latest administrative minutiae—immediately knowing, for instance, if a free agent has been signed to replace an injured player—and to closely follow the nuances of depth charts across a sport. With that in mind, many fans would seem to have an interest not just in the growing amounts of programming explicitly devoted to fantasy sports, but also in the broader realm of managerial content—following and tracking, for instance, Schefter's transactional news and speculation across television shows, podcasts, and social media. Taking another speculative leap, it might also be suggested that fantasy sports have made fans more and more familiar with the ins and outs of administrative maneuvers and, perhaps, primed them for other managerial texts more focused on administrators than athletes, as in managerial sports films like *Draft Day* and *Moneyball*. Alongside the growth in fantasy sports, one might also call particular attention to the increasing legalization of sports gambling. Again, there would seem to be a potential relationship between this phenomenon and interest in managerial sports media, for as individuals place wagers on sporting events, it can be advantageous to closely follow the latest administrative developments. The growth of fantasy sports and sports betting triggers follow-up questions, however. For instance, is it just the case that surging participation in fantasy sports has precipitated demand for other managerial texts (for example, ESPN's coverage of NFL free agency), or is it also the case that those other managerial texts (like the free agency coverage) have played a role in increasing the popularity of fantasy sports? It may be impossible, though, to fully address these sorts of questions of cause and effect. Instead, it would seem sports betting, fantasy sports, and other managerial media have all fed into one another.

The questions regarding the intertwined relationship between sports betting, fantasy sports, and other managerial media speak to a similar question that can be used to wrap up this section: is managerial content more of a product of media industry trends, like the increasing number of sports media outlets hungry for cheap programming, or more of a product of audience demand? Or, to put it in other words, is the interest in administrators and their work among sports fans an independent phenomenon or a media creation? Taking a stance on this question, Curtis suggests that the "desire" for managerial content has primarily been produced by media companies, commenting that "writers and broadcasters largely created or helped to lead people to" what he terms "transaction culture."[38] As an example, he points to the NBA's annual trade deadline. Major media companies like ESPN, he observes, "have done a really good job of conditioning people to think that the trade deadline is a climactic event"—a "conditioning" evident in the countless articles, podcasts, and television features leading up to the deadline. Despite the hype for a recent NBA trade deadline, though, Curtis recently looked back and noticed that "basically nothing happened that appreciably changed the trajectory of the NBA season or postseason."[39] For Curtis, this discrepancy between hype and reality highlights just how constructed managerial "events" can be and how successfully fan interest can be fabricated. But as Curtis admits, trying to separate industrial maneuverings from audience interest is bound to be a fruitless exercise. Rather, they might instead be understood as existing in something of a feedback loop—fueling each other with such regularity that managerial content has become inescapable.

Managerial Sports Media as a Sports Industry Phenomenon

An examination of sports media industries points us toward several reasons why managerial sports media has taken root with such intensity. The ubiquity of administrative content cannot be explained, for instance, without considering the ongoing hunt for alternative, non-event programming across sports media outlets. However, an analysis of sports media industries only takes us so far in accounting for the content of managerial sports media.

Notably, the content of managerial sports media is not invented out of whole cloth. Instead, managerial sports texts are grounded in the maneuverings of the sports industry and, accordingly, need to be contextualized along those lines.

As a starting point, one might begin with Curtis's straightforward observation that the coverage of transactions—a staple of managerial sports media—relies, of course, on the existence of transactions. And, as he suggests, there are now many more transactions than there were just a few decades prior.[40] This increase, though, is not a product of random chance but rather a reflection of recent changes in labor relations. It must first be acknowledged that transactions are not new to sports. One might again note, for instance, Babe Ruth's famous move from the Boston Red Sox to the New York Yankees in 1920. However, player movement within the major men's sports leagues today is also different than it was one hundred years ago. Most significantly, free agency—a primary subject for managerial sports media—is a relatively new development for these leagues. Whereas players were once bound to their original teams for the entirety of their careers (regardless of their desires), they now have increased opportunities to negotiate with other teams as their careers progress.

The example of baseball is broadly illustrative of how free agency came to be a significant component of the North American sports landscape. For most of MLB's long history, the movement of players between teams was tightly restricted by team owners.[41] A crucial part of this control was the reserve system that allowed teams to retain players' rights permanently and, accordingly, pay them below-market salaries. Over the 1960s and 1970s, however, players and their newly recognized union, the Major League Baseball Players Association (MLBPA), increasingly mobilized against this status quo. One of the most visible episodes in this movement came in 1970, when star Curt Flood, with support of the MLBPA, sued the league, suggesting the reserve system violated antitrust regulations. Although the U.S. Supreme Court eventually dismissed the case, labor historian Daniel A. Gilbert argues that Flood's lawsuit was a landmark moment that began to both sway public opinion and help "develop a consensus among players that the reserve system needed modification."[42] Notably, too, Flood's case underscored power dynamics that will be recurrent themes across this book. Flood elaborated, for instance, on the dehumanizing effects of the league's labor system, writing that he felt like "a piece of property to be bought and sold irrespective of [his] wishes," while Gerald Early highlights the many racial overtones of Flood's lawsuit, noting, for example, how the case underscored the paternalistic treatment of Black athletes like Flood by both management and the press.[43]

Introduction   13

Flood's lawsuit—despite ending in dismissal—helped set the stage for what would follow within the sport of baseball several years later. First, a neutral arbitration process—a process that had been gradually won via collective action through the MLBPA—ruled that several players could become free agents. Next, in 1976, a new collective bargaining agreement finally codified free agency more broadly, establishing that players with six years of experience would be able to negotiate with other teams across the league. Meanwhile, other men's sports leagues in North America slowly moved toward their own versions of free agency, with Joshua Mendelsohn highlighting a broader pattern across major men's sports of player unions forming in the 1960s and then in the 1970s "going after the same main goal, free agency."[44] To that point, the same year Flood filed his lawsuit against MLB, basketball star Oscar Robertson and the NBA Players Association (NBPA) filed an antitrust suit against the NBA that eventually led, several years later, to the end of the NBA's reserve system and the introduction of the league's first, limited version of free agency.

That the gradual introduction—and, in subsequent decades, expansion—of free agency has been pivotal in fostering managerial sports media can be illustrated by the existence of programming like "The Decision," a much-watched 2010 ESPN special in which superstar basketball player LeBron James announced where he would sign his next contract. Indeed, in his book about the NBA's labor battles, *Hard Labor,* longtime basketball journalist Sam Smith draws a direct connection between the NBA players' fight for free agency and "The Decision."[45] As Smith suggests, a program like "The Decision"—while firmly rooted in ESPN's desire for ratings—would have been impossible without the players' hard-fought efforts to achieve greater freedom of movement, for if players could not dictate where and under what terms they would play, there would be much less interest in what would happen when their contracts expired. "The Decision" is only the most visible example of the importance of free agency to managerial sports media. Across coverage of the major North American men's sports leagues, free agency has become a significant topic of discussion. Speculation over the future destinations of particularly notable free agents like Tom Brady (NFL), Kevin Durant (NBA), Bryce Harper (MLB), and John Tavares (NHL) can last months or even years. Illustrating the importance of this free agency content, discussion about Brady's free agency was one of the primary ways television, radio, and podcast networks compensated for the loss of live sporting events in 2020 during the COVID-19 pandemic. ESPN, for instance, used Brady's free agency to anchor news shows like *SportsCenter,* morning shows like *Get Up* (2018–), and debate shows like *First Take* (2007–).

Returning to the subject of audience demand for managerial content, scholars have suggested the introduction of free agency also significantly reconfigured how fans relate to sport and, in the process, spurred increasing fan investment in administration. Focusing on baseball, for instance, historian Krister Swanson argues the labor battles that led to the introduction and expansion of free agency also produced a growing awareness of baseball's economic operations, with fans increasingly immersed in media coverage of player-management relations and related subjects like revenue sources and contract terms—a stark change, Swanson writes, from earlier eras in which team owners had successfully cultivated a perception that the sport should be viewed more as a "sacred institution" than as a business.[46] Moreover, Swanson suggests that as free agency triggered increased player movement within the sport, fans sought ways to adjust to the new levels of roster flux. As Swanson argues, then, fans became increasingly interested in player personnel decisions—adopting, he writes, "a growing appreciation for the significance of shrewd business and player personnel moves by team management."[47] Relatedly, Andrew J. Ploeg posits the introduction of free agency in baseball was a key contributor to the emergence of Rotisserie League Baseball (Roto) in 1980—a fantasy baseball league often cited as a key landmark in the rapid rise of fantasy sports over the past few decades. More specifically, Ploeg argues that the roster turnover produced by free agency "initiated a shift in baseball fandom from a reliance on stability, consistency, and community to a negotiation of uncertainty, variability, and individuality."[48] Such a shift in fandom, Ploeg writes, set the stage for Roto, for one notable way fans sought to "negotiate" this new volatility was to vicariously manage roster fluctuations themselves by adopting the perspective of a team executive.

The rise of free agency goes a long way toward explaining how exactly the growing number of transactions has enabled managerial sports media. However, it must also be noted that it is not simply the existence of *more* transactions that has undergirded managerial media, but also *more complex* transactions. In a series of academic articles about the responsibilities of general managers, Christopher Deubert and Glenn Wong detail how the job has grown increasingly complicated across the major North American men's leagues. Significantly, the evolving collective bargaining agreements that have codified free agency have also introduced more and more intricacies into roster management. They mention in the case of the NBA, for instance, the "increasing complexities" related to the league's salary cap—a collectively negotiated limit on how much money individual teams can spend on player contracts.[49] Similarly, Mendelsohn observes that the league's original cap structure—itself part of an "enormously complex" labor agreement—now seems "quaint" given the many nuances of the modern cap.[50] For example, NBA front offices must consider baroque rules about exceptions to the cap and how to balance salaries in trades. The NBA is not alone in witnessing these "increasing" complexities. MLB executives, for instance, must weigh "complicated rules" around mechanisms like waivers and options, while NFL executives must juggle various forms of guaranteed and unguaranteed compensation.[51] Moreover, as Wong and Deubert suggest and as texts like *Moneyball* further detail, player evaluation is increasingly centered around statistical analyses that have demanded more and more technical skills.[52]

Perhaps counterintuitively, the increased complexity of sports management has provided additional fodder for managerial sports media. Rather than glossing over minutiae, managerial sports texts delve into administrivia for all it is worth. Radio and television talk shows, for instance, often wade not just into which players a team might sign as part of free agency but also under which terms. Indeed, basketball talk shows like ESPN's *The Jump* (2016–2021) and *NBA Today* (2021–) have gotten extended mileage out of discussing the NBA's byzantine roster rules—explaining, for instance, what it might mean for a team to use a mid-level salary exception or to offer a "supermax" contract extension. One might point, for example, to a brief *Jump* segment in which Wojnarowski quickly broke down the details of player Andre Iguodala's contract situation—a segment in which he touched on the financial terms of Iguodala's deal, various dates within the NBA's trade calendar, the need for teams to balance salaries in trade proposals, and the possibility of Iguodala's contract being bought out. As chapter 3 details at length, advanced statistical analysis is also an increasing focus for managerial sports media. *The Jump,* for example, even broadcast episodes live from the MIT Sloan Sports Analytics Conference.

The increasing quantity and complexity of transactions partially explains the rise of managerial sports media by speaking to its content. Still, more might be said about the figures who dominate managerial sports media. As mentioned above, administrative figures—including current and former executives—are increasingly ubiquitous. On a basic level, this ubiquity can be explained by the growing quantity and complexity of transactions, as these figures are primarily employed to analyze these transactions. With that said, there is more to this heightened visibility, as the heightened status of managerial figures within sports media also speaks to their heightened position within the sports landscape, more broadly.

One might first observe the increasingly prominent role of sports agents within the sports industry—a prominence signaled not only by the financial clout of major agencies like Creative Artists Agency (CAA) but also by the

16   Introduction

cultural visibility of agents via appearances on radio and television and via fictional representations in television programs like *Arliss* (HBO, 1996–2002) and *Ballers* (HBO, 2015–2019) and films like *Jerry Maguire* (1996), *Million Dollar Arm* (2014), and *High Flying Bird* (2019) (films discussed at length in the next chapter). According to Lisa Pike Masteralexis, agents—intermediaries who assist and represent players in contract negotiations as well as other financial arrangements—long had a limited role within the sports landscape, their existence serving more as "the exception not the rule."[53] However, that situation began to change in the wake of the labor battles of the 1960s, '70s, and '80s. More specifically, as collective bargaining agreements evolved and revenues ballooned, the stakes of contract negotiations grew higher and demanded additional expertise. Indeed, agents often arrive at negotiations armed with their own statistical analyses. Moreover, with salaries continuing to rise, agents have also taken on a range of new duties, becoming "responsible for tax and estate planning, investment advice, and providing other financial management and service options."[54] Perhaps unsurprisingly, agents are increasingly being asked to apply these skills in leading front offices, as exemplified by the Los Angeles Lakers hiring former agent Rob Pelinka as their general manager in 2017 and the New York Knicks hiring former agent Leon Rose as their president in 2020.[55]

Also significant for managerial sports media has been the heightened status of team executives themselves. Returning to Wong and Deubert's analyses of front offices, what it means to work for a team has evolved over the last several decades. They note, for instance, how NBA front offices used to be relatively small operations, with Boston Celtics head coach Red Auerbach even famously serving as "a one-man front office"—not just coaching the team, but also handling "drafts, scouting, travel arrangements, and contract negotiations."[56] More recently, though, NBA GMs have "had more difficulty wearing all the hats that Auerbach famously wore," as NBA front offices have greatly expanded and now play host to a wide range of personnel—including not just public-facing GMs but also additional executives like salary cap specialists and analytics experts.[57] These developments have been mirrored in other sports. Deubert, Wong, and Daniel Hatman note, for example, that NFL GMs "oversee a large, complex network of individuals working in a variety of fields."[58] With that in mind, they draw parallels between NFL GMs and corporate executives in other industries, observing that NFL GMs are often even tasked with overseeing seemingly unrelated departments like "finance, information technology, and marketing."[59] They conclude, then, "The role of the NFL GM is complicated, multi-faceted, and about as stressful as any job on earth."[60]

As Wong and Deubert explain, the growth in front office personnel—and the increasing complexity and visibility of the job of the GM—reflects the fact that a league like the NBA has become "a more lucrative and financially complicated environment."[61] As suggested throughout this chapter, the business of sports—largely thanks to growing media contracts—is increasingly big business. The NFL and NBA's annual television rights, for instance, are now worth billions of dollars per year.[62] Accordingly, teams now have price tags that also stretch into the billions.[63] These sorts of financial terms have changed the ramifications of team management—ensuring that executives must be able to handle the "magnitude" of the job and, accordingly, do not cost their owners financially in terms of local media rights, attendance, sponsorship deals, or a range of other factors that influence a team's bottom line.[64] As Deubert, Wong, and Hatman write of NFL GMs, front office executives "are clearly responsible for managing high stakes organizations."[65]

The importance of the bottom line is further reflected in the ways major sports have been reconceptualized as abstract financial assets enmeshed in broader financial networks. Sports business journalist Brendan Coffey notes that while sports teams "have long been a billionaires' playground," the landscape of sports ownership has recently evolved to accommodate the fact that the valuations of major sports teams have continued to balloon.[66] Major sports have not only seen an influx of owners drawn from new financial spheres, like private equity, but also drawn increasing interest from institutional investors with financial backing from sources like pension plans and sovereign wealth funds.[67] As financial reporter Sonali Basak commented in the wake of private equity firms taking stakes in NBA teams like the Golden State Warriors and Sacramento Kings, sports teams appear to represent "the next asset class"—offering, as other journalists have pointed out, appealing tax write-offs, sizable appreciations in value, and valuations relatively independent of other investments.[68]

The shifting nature of team ownership helps explain which types of executives are increasingly trusted to protect these "assets" and, accordingly, which figures are increasingly at the forefront of managerial sports media. When, for instance, the Philadelphia 76ers were purchased by an ownership group led by private equity billionaire Josh Harris in 2011, Harris and his co-owners—also drawn from the world of finance—eventually looked for a new GM comfortable with the types of approaches common in their industry. They turned, then, to Sam Hinkie, who before joining the front office of the Houston Rockets had gone to business school and worked in management consulting and private equity. As journalist Pablo Torre summarizes, Hinkie's background endeared the owners to him. "As a veteran of finance,"

Torre writes, Hinkie was attractively "fluent in the dispassionate language of expected value and probability."[69] Writer Yaron Weitzman suggests this shared background even helped facilitate Hinkie's approach to team building, with Harris and the other owners endorsing Hinkie's unconventional methods. Infamously, Hinkie intentionally bottomed out the team to stockpile as many high draft picks as possible—in the process trading away veteran players and churning through large numbers of young prospects. In sum, Weitzman concludes, Hinkie ran "a private-equity-like playbook—take over a distressed asset; tear everything down."[70] Hinkie's former boss with the Rockets, Daryl Morey—one of the most visible executives within managerial sports media— followed a similar path to team management. After business school and a stint working as a consultant, Morey was hired by the Boston Celtics to help with their business operations. In that role, he eventually attracted the attention of Rockets owner Leslie Alexander, a Wall Street investor, who wanted, as Michael Lewis details, to "rethink the game" using new technologies and metrics.[71] Morey, with his background in business, fit that desire.

Hinkie and Morey, though, represent just a few of the many recent examples of executives moving from other industries to sport. In *Astroball*, journalist Ben Reiter documents the turnaround of the Houston Astros as they went from perennial cellar-dwellers to World Series champions. As Reiter documents, the turnaround was largely led by financiers-turned-sports executives, with Astros owner Jim Crane, the head of an investment management firm, turning to Jeff Luhnow, a St. Louis Cardinals executive from the worlds of management consulting and Silicon Valley, to lead the team's front office. Luhnow, in turn, filled the front office with others of a similar type. Reiter mentions, for instance, the rise of the Astros assistant general manager, Brandon Taubman, who came to the Astros from a financial firm in which he had been an "expert" in derivatives.[72] Again, it is worth emphasizing the familiarity of this story. Staying within baseball, one might also point to the rise of managerial figures like Los Angeles Dodgers executive Andrew Friedman (formerly employed by an investment bank and a private equity firm) and Tampa Bay Rays executive Matthew Silverman (formerly employed by an investment bank). The recent trend across the sport, writers Ben Lindbergh and Sam Miller summarize, is "twenty- and thirtysomethings with Wall Street experience replacing weather-beaten general managers who came up as players and scouts."[73]

Returning to the idea that Hinkie brought with him, a "private-equity-like" approach to running a team, it is helpful here to turn to Karen Ho's ethnography of Wall Street investment banks. In her work, Ho argues that Wall Street has developed its own distinctive organizational culture.[74] Significantly, as

Introduction   19

figures like Hinkie and Luhnow have taken leadership roles across major sports, aspects of this culture have seemingly followed suit. Indeed, in noting the rise of front office executives like Luhnow within baseball, journalist Joon Lee observes the accompanying rise of a "Wall Street culture."[75] Perhaps most noticeably, teams have increasingly mimicked the "culture of smartness" prevalent on Wall Street.[76] As Ho writes, Wall Street firms recruit heavily from hyper-elite institutions like Harvard and Princeton and then draw on the cachet of these schools to mark themselves as extraordinary and, in turn, to legitimate their advice and worldviews. Of late, sports teams have also begun filling their ranks with the same sorts of recruits. To that point, Lee documents how the percentage of MLB front offices being led by Ivy League graduates has skyrocketed—having increased from 3 percent in 2001 to 43 percent in 2020.[77] Notably, too, front offices have also apparently replicated the patterns of exclusion Ho observes within Wall Street. Lee notes, for instance, that as baseball teams have increasingly pulled from the Ivy League, they have inherited those institutions' "diversity and classism problems," as in the effects of legacy admission processes that benefit wealthy and white applicants.[78]

Together, the trends cited above clarify that the rise of managerial sports media might, to a large degree, be considered a media phenomenon rooted in the operations and decision making of sports media organizations, but that a media-based account of the managerial fixation only extends so far. More specifically, a media-based account fails to account for the exact contours of managerial sports media—why certain types of content (like free agency specials) proliferate, why certain faces (like Daryl Morey's) appear so frequently, and so forth. Just as the sports media landscape has evolved over the last several decades, so has the major sports landscape. However, as the following section documents, these evolutions cannot be understood in isolation and require further contextualization.

Managerial Sports Media as a Societal Phenomenon

The above sections demonstrate that sports media's managerial interest can only be fully understood by considering changes in sports media industries and parallel changes in how major sports operate. Free agency coverage, for instance, can only exist with . . . free agency. However, before concluding this survey of managerial sports media's roots, it must be emphasized that both the sports media and sports industries do not exist at a remove from wider societal trends. On perhaps the broadest level, the increasing importance

20   Introduction

of front office executives—and the accompanying popularity of managerial sports media—reflects the increased stature of managerial classes and the accordant hold of managerialism. This argument is perhaps counterintuitive. In the 1980s, the shareholder value principle—which stresses the need for corporations to prioritize their stock performance—became dominant within financial discourses. As part of this shift, financiers and corporate leaders repeatedly touted the importance of trimming unnecessary layers of management from corporate structures. Political economist David Gordon cites, for instance, consultant Peter Drucker's claim that management had become "overstaffed to the point of obesity" and General Electric CEO Jack Welch's professed desire to end the practice of "hiring people just to read reports of people who had been hired just to write reports."[79] Similarly, sociologist Adam Goldstein documents how infamous businessman Carl Icahn "decried the 'incompetent, inbred management of many of our major corporations' and described his task as eliminating 'layers of bureaucrats reporting to bureaucrats.'"[80] Over the last several decades, then, one might have expected to see management in decline. As Gordon, Goldstein, and other scholars have observed, however, the shareholder value era has instead witnessed just the opposite trend, with the number of managers—and their pay levels—continuing to grow from the mid-1980s through today. Accordingly, Goldstein concludes, "The rise of financial capitalism has actually reinforced key dynamics of the managerialist order, enlarging the managerial class and heightening its members' ability to capture organizational resources."[81]

As suggested by Goldstein's reference to the "managerialist order," the recognition that the number of managers has continued to grow in recent decades lends credence to the idea that the ideology of managerialism has further and further entrenched itself within American society. According to Thomas Klikauer, managerialism can best be understood as a project that not only elevates the importance of managers—framing them, Peter Fleming argues, as "superhuman individuals"—but also gospelizes their ability to better any organization, whether a Fortune 500 technology company or a non-profit conservation group.[82] Klikauer writes, "Managerialism's perilous central doctrine is that differences between a university and a car company are less important than their similarities and that the performance of all organizations can be optimized by the application of generic management skills and knowledge."[83] Similarly, Fleming writes managerialism "fanatically holds to the belief that managing people is a transferable skill that can be tradable and cross-referable regardless of the organizational context that is ostensibly being managed"—a philosophy that manifests itself in "captains of industry" leading universities without ever having taught a class or avia-

Introduction   21

tion executives being placed in charge of hospitals.[84] As Klikauer, Fleming, and other scholars note, business schools have been particularly important sites for this ideological project, not only inculcating the "generic management skills and knowledge," but also spreading the idea that this skillset is universally applicable.

As the above section clarifies, major sports—and managerial sports media, in turn—are wrapped up in the prevalence of managerialism. To repeat, the size of front offices has ballooned over the past several decades, with more and more executives flooding the managerial hierarchies atop professional sport. Meanwhile, new managerial figures have also emerged in sites like sports agencies. To repeat, too, the sports industry has increasingly turned to the same sort of "Ivy League–educated, analytically based, PowerPoint-savvy individuals" elevated in a range of other industries, like consulting and finance.[85] Many of these "analytically based" individuals even arrive with business school credentials, like Morey, an MBA from MIT, and Hinkie, an MBA from Stanford. In turn, these executives and managerial sports media work not just to stress the credibility and wisdom of front office personnel but also to impart the same sorts of "generic management skills and knowledge" that have been applied across any number of disparate realms. The tenets of managerialism will come under closer scrutiny in several of the following chapters, with the first chapter arguing that managerial sports films heroize and elevate sports administrators, and the second and third chapters suggesting that some of the managerial class's "generic" management knowledge has found its way into sports talk radio and television.

Related to the "generic management skills and knowledge," the particular breed of managerialism exemplified by major sports is inseparable from the phenomenon of financialization, which has entailed the creep of finance into ever more realms of society. Although it is hardly new for major sports to be considered big business and, accordingly, for owners to conceive of teams as just one part of their broader financial portfolios, the accelerating reconceptualization of teams primarily as liquid financial assets—and the related installation of financially minded executives into seats of managerial power—is a clear indicator of the growing encroachment of finance into sport. Particularly notable for this project, though, is what Max Haiven has described as the broader infiltration of "the logics, codes, value paradigms, speculative ethos, measurements and metaphors of the financial sector . . . into other (non-financial) economic and social spheres."[86] Significantly, the language and logics of finance have hardly remained confined to macro discussions of team and league valuations. Instead, these logics have bled into how teams are managed on a day-to-day basis, with executives hunting for leverage and talking of their players in the language of "assets" and "stocks." The second chapter, focused on sports talk radio and television, investigates this bleed of the financial from front offices into sporting discourse, with players framed as speculative "investments" to be shrewdly managed.

Financialization has, in turn, been linked to the increased fetishization of quantification and "data-driven decision making." Across a wide variety of industries—from agriculture to health care to transportation—"analytics" and "big data" have become popular buzzwords, with managers preaching their adherence to allegedly objective quantitative metrics. As made famous by cultural texts like *Moneyball,* the sports industry has been no exception to this trend toward quantification. When, for instance, financially oriented executives like Morey have taken over teams, they have steered hard toward quantitative metrics, including those driven by big data systems, in ruthless quests for efficiency both on and off the playing surface. Managerial sports texts, in turn, have reflected this trend in further integrating and promoting these sorts of metrics. On any number of basketball podcasts, for instance, listeners are apt to hear hosts discuss player efficiency ratings and usage numbers, while baseball telecasts have increasingly incorporated advanced statistics like OPS (On-base Plus Slugging) and WAR (Wins Above Replacement). Indeed, several networks have introduced alternative telecasts specifically devoted to statistical analysis. The third chapter, on the use of quantitative metrics in sports television, returns to this quantification trend at length.

Another relevant concept here is neoliberalism. Although neoliberalism is occasionally denounced as an overly repeated buzzword, the term continues to hold great utility in describing a set of influential ideas meant to push back against the welfare state, economic regulation, and labor unions.[87] Indeed, the sprawling effects of neoliberal ideology have already been lurking in the background throughout this chapter, as exemplified by the growth of media rights fees—growth that has, in turn, spurred the increasing valuations of teams, changes in ownership, and so forth—being partially rooted in the deregulation of cable television.[88] Notably, one key argument in many analyses of neoliberalism is that as the welfare state and labor unions morph and recede as a result of neoliberal attacks, citizens find themselves left to their own devices to weather the ebbs and flows of capitalism. Individuals, then, are meant to take responsibility for their own fate and to become "active" and "resourceful."[89] As Brenda Weber explains, a citizen must become an "entrepreneur of the self," maximizing themselves so that they can become "competitive within a larger global marketplace."[90] The fourth chapter, on managerial sports games, addresses this aspect of neoliberalism at length,

Introduction   23

as several scholars have cited these games as particularly overt promoters of neoliberal principles in encouraging players to, for instance, adopt a self-optimizing calculative rationality.

Phenomena like managerialism, quantification, and neoliberalism also point to ongoing changes in the nature of work. The last several decades have witnessed a significant decline in American manufacturing employment.[91] In parallel, employment in other sectors has boomed, with anthropologist David Graeber observing, for instance, that recent years have witnessed a "ballooning . . . of the administrative sector," as exemplified by the introduction and growth of industries like financial services, human resources, and corporate law.[92] The expansion of sports team front offices—and the increased visibility of the front office personnel across sports media—serves as a reminder, then, not just of the pervasiveness of managerialism but also of these broader shifts associated with postindustrialization. As suggested above, for instance, the daily minutiae of sports management—from juggling emails to tracking numbers in dense spreadsheets—closely mirrors the stereotypical digital work of the new "knowledge economy." Indeed, the fourth chapter, in examining the mundane interfaces of popular managerial sports games like *Football Manager* and *Out of the Park Baseball,* argues that audiences' engagement with the "neoliberal fantasies" of these managerial texts can only be properly understood by taking into account the contemporary digital workplace.

All these phenomena, too, have played a role in shifting the contours of hegemonic masculinity. As, for instance, the nature of work has changed over the past few decades, hegemonic masculinity has, in tandem, incorporated qualities often associated with postindustrial labor, like technical expertise. To that point, sociologist Lori Kendall draws on gender theorist Raewyn Connell's observation that terms like "nerd" have traditionally been used to mark certain men as removed from what Connell has referred to as the masculine "circle of legitimacy."[93] However, as Kendall observes, the growing role of computing technology in work and home life has meant increasing respect for the technical skills commonly associated with "geeks" and "nerds." As she writes, then, "Since the 1980s, the previous liminal masculine identity of the nerd has been rehabilitated and partly incorporated into hegemonic masculinity."[94] Indeed, media scholars have highlighted how this "rehabilitation" has played out in popular culture, with Anastasia Salter and Bridget Blodgett noting, for example, how television shows like *The Big Bang Theory* (CBS, 2007–2019) and *Chuck* (NBC, 2007–2012) have given new "shine and depth" to geeks, and Heather Mendick et al. highlighting the recent cultural valorization of "geek entrepreneurs," with figures like Tony Stark/Iron Man—a tycoon-cum-prodigy-cum-inventor—in the Marvel films representing the "newly hegemonic" status of qualities like "genius" and "innovation."[95] Although, as T. L. Taylor observes, "geek masculinity" has long been conceived in opposition to a more traditionally hegemonic "sporting masculinity" valorizing physical ability—witness the popularity of the "nerd vs. jock" trope—one can observe a parallel elevation of technical savvy within major sports and, in turn, managerial sports media.[96] For instance, in both fiction and nonfiction texts, the new analytically minded executives have often been lauded for their math wizardry and "outside-the-box" thinking. In fact, popular texts like *Moneyball* have made quantitative "disruption" central to their heroic narratives. As several chapters throughout this project will explore, managerial sports texts reflect hegemonic masculinity stretching—often with tension—beyond the athleticism associated with the playing surface to incorporate the technical competence increasingly associated with the front office. Notably, too, the chapters will examine how these changes have worked to legitimate unequal gender relations.

Of particular interest for this project will be considering how depictions of a reconfigured hegemonic masculinity have been racialized, as managerial sports texts have often suggested changes to hegemonic masculinity might work, in particular, to remasculinize white men. White masculinity has long been associated with anxieties around a feared loss of its many privileges—including in cultural texts that center white-collar administrators, as in Sloan Wilson's 1955 tale of the "feminizing threat of conformity" in the postwar era, *The Man in the Gray Flannel Suit*—but the remasculinization evidenced in managerial sports media might be best understood as especially enmeshed in cultural and economic anxieties that have emerged in recent decades.[97] Focusing on the media reverberations of these anxieties, Amanda Lotz notes, for example, the preponderance of cable television shows featuring white men grappling with the "realignment of gender norms" in the wake of neoliberalism, postindustrialization, and second-wave feminism, like *Breaking Bad* (AMC, 2008–2013) and *The Sopranos* (HBO, 1999–2007), while Taylor Nygaard and Jorie Lagerwey highlight a wave of television comedies, such as *Togetherness* (HBO, 2015–2016) and *You're the Worst* (FX/FXX, 2014–2019), appearing in the wake of the Great Recession that focused on floundering white characters "losing access to the jobs, housing, and relationships they thought were their automatic due."[98] Similar concerns are front and center in managerial texts like *Million Dollar Arm* and, accordingly, sports executives have come to serve as additional symbols of feelings of white masculine precarity.

Speaking, though, to how managerial sports texts address these feelings of precarity, more related context involves recent conservative backlashes to popular feminism and Barack Obama's presidency, as well as the political rise of Donald Trump.[99] Kyle Kusz notes, for example, how Trump has conjured fantasies of "white male omnipotence" that respond to "white male status anxieties."[100] As Kusz notes, too, the sporting landscape has been important terrain in the construction of these power fantasies—highlighting, for example, how Tom Brady has become another potent symbol of "a brash, guilt-free, successful, non-deferential, unconstrained, and unapologetic way of being white and male."[101] With that in mind, the many white men spotlighted by managerial sports media might be understood as not only symbolizing an imagined white masculine precarity but also showing how these anxieties fuel fantasies of white masculine omnipotence, with executives representing, like Trump and Brady, "white masculinities deserving of public respect and reverence because they are masters of their own respective universes."[102] Indeed, in a film like *Draft Day,* the administrative figure straddles both these functions at once—simultaneously standing in for fears of lost status as well as fantasies of managerial expertise being used to assert a new form of dominance.

That the present ubiquity of managerial sports media is partially rooted in factors extending beyond sport and sports media is underscored by the fact that a recent cultural interest in administration is not confined to sports media. For example, in probing the media reverberations of the Great Recession, Diane Negra and Yvonne Tasker note the appearance of corporate melodramas like *Up in the Air* (2009) and *Company Men* (2010) that use administrative figures to render the corporate workplace "both a site of power and authority and fundamentally incompatible with American manhood."[103] Aaron Heresco observes, meanwhile, that financial television networks like Fox Business regularly treat CEOs as "rock stars" to be "admired and emulated."[104] Reality television, too, has been a recent site of intense administrative interest, as in popular shows like *The Apprentice* (NBC, 2004–2017), *Shark Tank* (ABC, 2009–), and *Undercover Boss* (CBS, 2010–). One might call attention, for example, to the huge number of "troubleshooter" programs—perhaps the quintessential embodiment of the managerialist idea that "superhuman" managers can be "parachuted into almost any situation with little experiential knowledge"—that feature seasoned managers offering their advice to a wide variety of business owners on how to be successful administrators.[105] In CNBC's *The Profit* (2013–2021), for instance, corporate executive Marcus Lemonis arrives each episode to a new struggling business to preach his mantra of "people, process, product"—urging flailing administrators to improve, for example, their accounting processes so they can better quantify their businesses. Moreover, managerial sports games like *Football Manager* and *Out of the Park Baseball* are far from alone in asking gamers to supervise virtual employees and balance imagined budgets, as exemplified by the popularity of other business simulation games like *Roller Coaster Tycoon*. As this project examines sports media's managerial interest, it will frequently reference these other managerial texts to help illuminate sports media's entwinement in wider phenomena like managerialism and financialization—comparisons that make clear that the manager is a broadly resonant cultural icon. Such iconic status underscores the importance of analyzing the spread of managerial sports media—one of the most visible indicators of the wider managerial fixation—in attempting to understand the current conjuncture.

The Many Manifestations of Managerial Sports Media

Sports media is besotted with managerial figures and managerial activities—an infatuation that, in turn, both reflects and drives significant transformations in culture and society. There have been few cultural texts, for instance, that have more enthusiastically promoted the wisdom of the managerial class than films like *Moneyball* and *Draft Day* or that have more widely circulated big data mythology than telecasts devoted to the statistical analysis of sport. However, any analysis of managerial sports media's entanglement with these broader phenomena—entanglements that also speak to managerial sports media's imbrication with issues of power related to race, class, gender, and sexuality—needs to consider the specific contours of these texts. Accordingly, each of the following chapters is concentrated on a particular set of managerial texts. Such focus allows for closer probes of the specific connections between managerial sports media and the cultural and societal shifts in which these texts are enmeshed.

In starting to address the particulars of sports media's managerial fixation, the first chapter focuses on narrative sports films. As several media scholars have observed, the sports film genre has long revolved around the "American Dream" mythology, figuring the world as a merit-based, level playing field in which hard-working underdogs typically emerge as sporting champions who use their athletic success to elevate their economic and social standings. This chapter employs textual analysis to examine how the recent wave of managerial sports films, including *Moneyball, Draft Day,* and *Million Dollar Arm,* refigures the narratives and ideologies of the sports film genre, thereby transforming the traditional "Athletic American Dream" into a "Managerial American Dream." To start, the chapter lays out the parameters of the managerial sports film subgenre, explaining how these films

Introduction   27

have reworked the traditional sports film narrative. More specifically, the chapter argues that these films have largely retained the familiar underdog narrative arc in which hard work leads to victory but have reframed that arc to highlight managerial work and managerial figures. As exemplified by a film like *Draft Day,* the conflicts and triumphs of these new sports films are no longer confined to the playing field. Instead, they are increasingly set in office environments in which a conference call can have as dramatic consequences as a walk-off grand slam. Moreover, the protagonists are no longer familiar athletic figures like the washed-up star looking for one last shot at glory or the promising young prospect looking for their big break. Indeed, the protagonists of managerial sports films are not athletes at all.

As the chapter further argues, the reconfiguration of the genre's traditional formulas has significant reverberations for its ideological workings. The reorientation of the sports film around administration has promoted managerialism by valorizing the rewards of bureaucratic work and refigured how the sports film treats race, class, gender, and sexuality. More specifically, the chapter suggests managerial sports films continue the sports film's long-held interest in remasculinizing straight white men in the face of perceived threats to their status but have updated that ideological project to respond, in particular, to anxieties around white-collar work. Throughout the subgenre, films propose that straight white men are uniquely well-adapted to handle the demands of white-collar work—expertly balancing the "aggressive" version of masculinity more typically promoted by the genre with a new, "civilized" version of masculinity required by office work. As the chapter argues, this balanced masculinity represents a twist on the genre's standard template, in which straight white men remasculinized by embracing a traditional, physical mode of masculinity and, often, besting athletes of color on this terrain. In the new strain of managerial sports films, to be solely confined to the physical realm is to remain limited in one's masculinity and, almost always, it is characters of color who are left behind on the playing surface while white men take up new seats of power in the front office.

The second chapter turns the project's attention to real-world coverage of sports administration, focusing on the pervasiveness of managerial content within sports talk radio and television. In examining the ubiquity of bureaucratic matters in sports talk—exemplified by the lengthy discussions of trades, free agency signings, and other transactional maneuvers that appear across countless studio television programs and drivetime radio shows—the chapter argues that this content is frequently oriented within a financialized frame. Not only do sports commentators regularly draw on financial language in discussing managerial maneuvers—witness the constant use of terminology like "assets," "investment," and "stocks"—but also financial *logics* that orient the world of sport around the same financial rationalities that govern ever more parts of everyday life. Within sports talk, administrators—and audiences at home—are advised to approach sports like a shrewd investor, carefully balancing risk amid an ever-changing market. Accordingly, sports talk has become one of the clearest indicators of the spread of finance into ever more facets of everyday life. While much of what happens within the sporting landscape is only tangentially connected to the world of finance, sports talk's consistent calls to treat sport primarily as a site of speculative assets and moving markets has meant that sports talk programming and financial talk programming have grown increasingly similar—all the way down to ticking clocks that mark the end of trading activity.

The financialization of sports talk also points to clear throughlines in how managerial sports texts are enmeshed in issues of race and gender, as sports talk's financial logics not only further normalize the place of finance in everyday life but also work to again remasculinize white men. Like managerial sports films, sports talk has consistently elevated the status of administrators—largely a collection of white men—at the expense of athletes, in this case by suggesting that the financially oriented work of these administrators makes them the true stars of the sporting world, while athletes exist largely as their manipulatable commodities. Like managerial sports films, sports talk has also positioned the work of these administrators as normatively masculine, again suggesting that sporting masculinity is no longer solely rooted in traditionally valued attributes like athleticism. However, within sports talk, financial logics take center stage in this process of masculinization, as these logics connect front office work to several qualities that are newly ascendant within hegemonic masculinity, such as educational achievement and technical expertise.

In discussing the financial logics of sports talk, chapter 2 alludes to the key place of a calculative rationality within managerial sports media. Chapter 3 expands on this idea in further expounding on the place of quantification within managerial sports media. In recent years, a growing number of executives across all the major North American sports leagues have become smitten with analytics, employing advanced statistical measures to evaluate players and guide their decision making (a trend evidenced in the rising prominence of the Sloan Conference discussed in the preface). As sports media has pivoted toward management, then, it is no surprise that it has also become increasingly data driven. The third chapter documents how this data fixation has begun to alter the form and content of sports television—a phenomenon the chapter terms "datavisuality."

Introduction   29

As it analyzes datavisuality, the third chapter does not just summarize what it has meant for sports television to become data-driven but also examines the specific industrial roots of this phenomenon. First, the chapter details how the sports graphics industry has recently developed new technological tools that have enabled broadcasters to place data anywhere and everywhere on the television screen. Second, the chapter considers why broadcasters have decided to employ the new tools developed by the sports graphic industry. The chapter focuses on ESPN to answer this question, drawing on interviews with several of its employees to explore the company's increasing interest in data-driven storytelling. As these interviews suggest, ESPN views data-driven storytelling as a way to keep up with broader trends in the sports industry and, in the process, differentiate itself from a growing slate of competitors. Chapter 3 also analyzes the wider sociopolitical ramifications of the datavisuality phenomenon. For example, the chapter explains how datavisuality has entailed an increasingly intertwined relationship between sports media and big data, as the sports television industry has begun to use many big data tools also employed by teams and leagues. Turning toward the field of critical data studies, the chapter questions the epistemological consequences of this intertwining, suggesting that datavisuality risks reinforcing the problematic notion that big data is better data.

Providing a final case study of managerial sports media, the fourth chapter scrutinizes the popularity of digital sports games, including both video games and fantasy leagues, that allow players to take on administrative roles. As the chapter highlights, something of a critical consensus has started to emerge around these managerial sports games. In brief, scholars have consistently suggested that managerial sports games, in placing individuals in control of virtual rosters of athletes, offer "neoliberal fantasies" that encourage an instrumental, dehumanized view of sport that treats athletes as little more than arrays of numerical player ratings. This line of criticism, notably, recalls critiques offered in this book's earlier chapters.

While arguing that the existing scholarship around managerial sports games importantly calls attention to the neoliberal principles that undergird these games, the chapter seeks to complement this analysis by further considering how players might engage with these games, particularly by weighing how these games fit within everyday life amid neoliberal capitalism. To that end, the first half of the chapter focuses on how managerial sports games model the workings of contemporary sport, in the process arguing that these games offer particularly explicit portraits of how sport has transformed in recent decades in attempting to simulate, for instance, sport's globalized financial flows. Suggesting that this sort of modeling can invite critical reflection on contemporary sport, the chapter draws attention

30   Introduction

to several examples of "nonnormative" gameplay, as in players who have experimented with the games' demands for financial optimization. The second half of the chapter shifts its focus to how managerial sports games also offer models of contemporary work, highlighting that the games frequently rely on stark user interfaces meant to replicate office productivity software like the Microsoft Office suite. Given these work-like interfaces, the chapter suggests the experience of navigating a managerial sports game must inevitably echo what many players encounter in their everyday work lives. Accordingly, the chapter argues, managerial sports games may permit digital laborers opportunities not just to experience an alluring sense of agency, as many other games also allow, but also to experience that sense of control in the very same workplace environments in which that control may often go lacking amid bureaucratic dysfunction and administrative dictates.[106] Managerial sports games, then, may be uniquely resonant against the background of the frequently felt "bullshit" of working life.[107]

In closing the book, the conclusion briefly considers an aspect of managerial sports media lurking beneath the analyses offered in the previous chapters: its banality. As the conclusion suggests, administrative content has become something like the white noise of the sports media landscape—endlessly circulating at a low, empty hum. This banality, the conclusion argues, is key to understanding managerial texts. The marginality of so much administrative content fuels its creation, as the close attention to contract numbers and trade terms can preclude broader contextual coverage that might risk alienating the athletes, teams, and leagues that serve as business partners to media companies. As the conclusion suggests, then, meaningful alternatives to managerial sports media—including versions of sports media that might escape or subvert the instrumentality and hyperrationality of the managerial mode—may have to come from outside the mainstream sports media apparatus.

Related to the banality of managerial sports media, sports media texts—and, in particular, many of the seemingly mundane examples considered in this project, like daily studio shows and regular-season event telecasts—are often dismissed by cultural critics as lowbrow fare not particularly ripe for close consideration. This low status would seem, in turn, to contribute to sports media's continued underrepresentation in both popular media criticism and scholarship.[108] However, in demonstrating how sports media industries and texts are enmeshed in significant cultural, economic, political, and social phenomena like financialization and managerialism, this book establishes that careful considerations of sports media are integral to fully understanding the contemporary media landscape. Indeed, as many of these examples demonstrate, key portions of culture and society only come fully into focus once the role of sports media is taken into account.

1

The Managerial American Dream

The Administrative Fantasies of Managerial Sports Films

The formula for a traditional American sports film is familiar: underdog athletes striving to prove their doubters wrong; momentous, climactic matches that pit these plucky protagonists against their biggest rivals; endings that—win or lose—validate the underdog's pursuit of victory. Over the last few decades, however, these narrative conventions are increasingly in question. Significantly, athletes have started to lose their place at the heart of the genre. Instead, a new wave of sports films has begun focusing on the exploits of the sports world's administrators. Kicking off with *Jerry Maguire* (1996), Cameron Crowe's film about an idealistic sports agent, this trend has since continued with the films *Moneyball* (2011), *Draft Day* (2014), *Million Dollar Arm* (2014), and *High Flying Bird* (2019). In each of these films, the protagonist is a managerial figure seemingly more at home in a conference room than on a playing surface.

In this chapter, I explore the sports film's reorientation away from the playing surface and toward the front office, analyzing what it has meant for the genre to see its usual iconography—including those familiar sights of bats, balls, and locker rooms—fading away in favor of a new set of recurring sights and sounds revolving around office furniture, tailored suits, and beeping cell phones. First, I delve into the generic conventions of this new category of managerial sports films, examining their fit within the genre's traditional template and, in the process, offering explanations for their origins. Second, I build on this generic analysis to further probe the ideological content of managerial sports films. As I argue in this section, in reorienting the genre toward managerial figures and managerial work, these films do not just promote the gospel of managerialism—valorizing a new version of the "American Dream" that closes not in on-field victory, but rather in managerial success—but also continue the genre's conservative racial and gender politics through an idealized version of white masculinity oriented around white-collar work. Finally, I close the chapter by considering what it might mean to resist this managerialist project, using *High Flying Bird* to demonstrate how a film might instead use management as a gateway to critique.

The Rise of the Managerial Sports Film

Before attempting to lay out the contours of the managerial sports film, it would be helpful to briefly discuss the sports film genre, more generally. First, it should be acknowledged that the "sports film" genre as it is commonly understood today was not in place as a category for much of American film history. That is to say, while sports-related films have long had a key place in Hollywood—see, for instance, classic silent films like Charlie Chaplin's boxing short *The Champion* (1915) and Harold Lloyd's football feature *The Freshman* (1925)—sports-related films were long grouped into other genres. In the studio era, for instance, movies were often categorized by specific sport or grouped by their other narrative conventions.[1] Although this generic haziness has not entirely subsided—witness, for instance, the continued usage of a sport-specific label like the "boxing film" in the critical discourse around films like *Creed* (2015) and *Southpaw* (2015)—in recent decades the "sports film" has grown into a more salient genre. To that point, Seán Crosson argues, "Increasingly a sports film genre is being recognized," while Bruce Babington notes, "The category 'sports film' has become naturalised and uncontentious."[2] As Crosson and Babington further suggest, the growing acceptance of the generic category indicates a shared understanding of an overlapping set of conventions—conventions hinted at in the opening of this chapter and further fleshed out in a growing body of scholarship around the genre.

According to Lester Friedman, the sports film can—like other film genres—be defined based on recurring narratives, characters, and iconography. In terms of narrative arcs, Friedman argues for several common types, including structures like "individual salvation/redemption/renewal," in which characters redeem themselves through sport, "team unity," in which divided teammates work to overcome their differences, and "miracle wins," in which underdogs triumph against the odds.[3] Other scholars have also emphasized the genre's repeating plotlines. Katharina Bonzel, for instance, notes that the genre is hardly complete without "the plot point of 'the big game,'" while Crosson similarly identifies "the big game, race or fight finish" as perhaps the most repeated element of the genre.[4] These familiar narrative arcs then bleed into the genre's typical character types. Unsurprisingly, for example, several scholars mention the recurring presence of what Crosson describes as "a marginalized or 'underdog' individual, or team."[5] Finally, the genre plays host to a recurring set of sights and sounds. To that point, Friedman notes elements such as uniforms and sporting equipment, as well as sounds like a basketball swishing through a net, while Bonzel similarly points to "team jerseys, sporting paraphernalia, and the locker room."[6] These conventional sights and sounds are also accompanied by oft-repeated cinematographic choices, like the use of slow-motion to accentuate critical moments of sporting action.

While the sports film—and all these familiar conventions—has increasingly been recognized as a distinct genre over the last few decades, this period has also witnessed those conventions become increasingly contested. As David Sutera details in an exploration of what he terms the "post-classical Hollywood sports business film," in the 1960s and 1970s, sports films started to grow increasingly interested in the business of sports—something that had long been on the margins of the genre's typical template.[7] Sutera documents, for instance, the gradual appearance of films like *Number One* (1969), which delves into the financial future of a fading superstar athlete, and *North Dallas Forty* (1979), a critique of professional football that explores the sport's entwinement with corporate America. As Sutera further details, this interest in the business side of sports continued to accelerate in the following decades, as exemplified by films like *Bull Durham* (1988) and *Major League* (1989), both of which address the disposability of athletes in the contemporary sports landscape. Perhaps most significantly, though, in the past few decades, Sutera argues, the genre has come to increasingly center what he dubs the "non-athlete sports protagonist"—characters who are "representative of the business side of sports," as illustrated by films like *Jerry Maguire*, which stars Tom Cruise as a sports agent, *Any Given Sunday* (1999), which features Al Pacino as a professional football coach, and *Trouble with the Curve* (2012), which revolves around Clint Eastwood as a baseball scout.[8] In the process, the outlines of the genre have begun to shift. As Sutera notes, for instance, these new sports business films—particularly those focusing on non-athletes—do not only significantly modify the genre's character types but also other aspects of the genre, including iconography. For example, sports business films are more likely to take place in settings "such as offices and board rooms rather than in sports stadiums, arenas, or playing fields typical of classical era sports film."[9] These sorts of shifts in mind, one might even suggest that the sports film has started to hybridize with the genre that film scholar Jack Boozer has dubbed the "business career movie"—a category of films based around managerial work and career trajectories, as exemplified by films like *Executive Suite* (1954) and *Wall Street* (1987).[10]

Amid the non-athlete protagonists increasingly common to the sports film—coaches, owners, scouts, and so forth—there is one type of character that is particularly novel for the genre: the administrator. The films mentioned at the start of the chapter—*Jerry Maguire, Moneyball, Draft Day, Million Dollar Arm,* and *High Flying Bird*—are not just notable for delving into the business of sports but also for doing so through the perspective of the managers positioned—sometimes uncomfortably—between professional sport's workers (athletes) and owners. These administrative characters, then, embody professional sport's enlarged bureaucracy and all its intermediary functions. *Draft Day*—and its star—is emblematic of this new perspective. As Sutera points out, *Draft Day*'s star, Kevin Costner, has a long history with the sports film, including star performances in genre mainstays like *Bull Durham, Field of Dreams* (1989), and *Tin Cup* (1996).[11] Indeed, Friedman notes, Costner has starred in so many sports films that he has become part of the genre's iconography.[12] In almost all his classic sports performances, Costner appears as an athlete—a fact that aligns with the genre's traditional interest in athlete protagonists. For instance, in *Bull Durham,* Costner plays an aging baseball catcher tasked with mentoring a young pitcher, while in *Tin Cup,* he plays a washed-up golfer looking to regain his form. In *Draft Day,* though, this model shifts. Costner is no longer an athlete in this role, but rather a general manager tasked with serving as a middle layer between a demanding owner and the team's many players, coaches, and other staff members. Accordingly, the terrain of the genre also changes. Costner's character is not personally interested in throwing touchdowns or blitzing quarterbacks, but rather in the day-to-day responsibilities of a white-collar manager: making phone calls, leading meetings, and such.

That the managerial sports film has emerged as a growing subgenre reflects the fact that film genres have long been flexible—adapting to changes in the world around them. As Friedman notes, "Genres are not static entities." He continues, "Quite to the contrary, they are fluid, open-ended, and responsive."[13] In terms of that responsiveness, it is significant that the status of the broader sports film genre has flagged within Hollywood in recent years. Although there have been a few modest theatrical successes—including films like *42* (2013), *Creed* (2015), and *Ford v. Ferrari* (2019)—the reputation of the genre within the industry has sagged. Notably, for instance, the genre has been affected by the broader decline of mid-budget studio filmmaking.

Disney, for example, was once a prolific producer and distributor of sports films, but in recent years has largely moved away from mid-priced genre filmmaking in favor of tentpole films from franchise properties like Marvel and *Star Wars*.[14] Relatedly, the genre has been squeezed by a greater prioritization of international audiences, with sports films—particularly those featuring sports like baseball and American football—viewed as primarily a domestic phenomenon. Summarizing the industry perspective, Mike Fleming Jr. comments in *Deadline*, "The trouble with jock films . . . is they do little business overseas."[15] The weakening status of the sports film has seemingly led to experimentation with content. *Million Dollar Arm*, for example, was viewed as a way of possibly boosting the viability of the genre within the international marketplace, with its tale of a baseball agent scouting for talent in India viewed as having potential appeal to audiences outside the United States.[16] It can be noted, too, that managerial sports films have the alluring potential to be cheaper to produce than traditional sports films, as managerial sports films do not necessarily need to worry about carefully choreographing action scenes or filling stadiums with extras. As a case in point, *High Flying Bird*'s complete lack of game action likely aided its ability to be produced on a reported micro-budget of two million dollars.[17]

Just as significant as generic responsiveness to industrial context, though, is responsiveness to broader societal contexts. As Thomas Schatz argues, Hollywood genres like the western have long evolved in response to "the changing beliefs and attitudes of contemporary American society."[18] The sports film is no different, and the managerial sports film represents just the most recent evolution of the genre. Most significant for the sports film is how the sporting landscape has changed over time. Sutera rightly points to the influence of the Curt Flood legal case and the rise of free agency in helping to explain the genre's increasing fascination with the business side of sports, but as the introduction explained, the Flood case represents just the tip of the iceberg in explaining how the sports world has changed over the last several decades. As mentioned, for instance, recent years have witnessed the rising prominence of sports agents, which helps explain their appearance as protagonists in *Jerry Maguire*, *Million Dollar Arm*, and *High Flying Bird*. Similarly, the escalating attention paid to the NFL draft, as illustrated by its transformation into a premiere television spectacle, helps explain the appearance of a sports film, *Draft Day*, based solely around that event. Of course, too, the genre's evolution is shaped by broader ideological currents. Sutera specifically highlights the role of neoliberalism—how it fuels, for instance, sports business films' occasional interest in subjects like deindustrialization and downsizing workforces—but as the rest of this chapter will document, the genre's shift away from its usual conventions is also shaped by other related ideologies, as well, such as managerialism. These broader ideological currents help explain why the sports film's evolutions accord with similar movements in other genres. Mark Houssart notes, for instance, a wider filmic turn that has seen corporate managers transform from despicable villains to sympathetic heroes.[19]

While the emergence of the administrative protagonist represents new terrain for sports films—with Bonzel even definitively declaring that *Jerry Maguire* and *Draft Day* do not fit within the genre—managerial sports films still resemble traditional sports films in crucial ways.[20] They often, for instance, work toward the big climactic game that has long been one of the genre's primary hallmarks. *Jerry Maguire,* for example, builds to a significant game that will determine the contract terms for Maguire's one client, while *Moneyball's* climax is structured around the team's maintenance of a lengthy winning streak. Importantly, too, while the genre's traditional iconography may fade into the background, it does not entirely disappear. *High Flying Bird,* for instance, may set much of its action in office suites, but the film is still full of basketballs and basketball courts. Similarly, *Moneyball* may be about roster management, but the familiar baseball fields and locker rooms are never far away. In most shots, these are still clearly films about sports set in the sports world. Perhaps more significantly, though, managerial sports films may not center their narratives around athlete protagonists, but they still retain a consistent and robust interest in plots that see the underdog triumphing against "seemingly overwhelming odds."[21] The marginalized agent protagonist of *Million Dollar Arm,* for instance, shows the familiar "obsessive determination, personal sacrifices, and gritty hard work" in looking for baseball prospects in the unconventional location of India, while the similarly obsessive executives of *Moneyball* look to atypical statistical methods to triumph over their better-funded opponents.[22]

The continued place of underdog narratives within managerial sports films ensures that they continue to speak to an essential aspect of the broader sports film genre that has not yet been mentioned: its close relationship with the "American Dream" mythology. Indeed, the relationship between the sports film and the American Dream has been one of the most studied aspects of the genre, appearing in most scholarly examinations of its ideological foundations. With that in mind, the next section will focus its attention on that relationship, analyzing how managerial sports films refigure the American Dream with a new managerialist thrust.

From the Athletic American Dream to the Managerial American Dream

The Sports Film and the American Dream

The "American Dream" has long been at the heart of American culture and society, with historian Jim Cullen even referring to it as an omnipresent "national motto" that forms "a major element of [American] national identity."[23] Perhaps as a result of its longevity and its prominence, the concept can also be, as Bonzel notes, somewhat hazy.[24] Indeed, Cullen suggests that while the term may be "a kind of lingua franca" that is widely understood, it is also cloaked in an ambiguity that reflects the many contexts in which the concept is employed. "There is no *one* American Dream," he thus suggests. "Instead, there are many American *Dreams*."[25] Nonetheless, one can try to pin down recurring elements. Friedman, while again noting that the American Dream is a "slippery and multilayered ideological construct," summarizes key principles at its center: "The United States was conceived of and actualizes a meritocracy, a level playing field overflowing with boundless opportunities to succeed. If you work hard, follow the rules, exert discipline, and undertake self-sacrifice, you can attain your highest aspirations: you can make the dream flesh."[26] Even more succinctly, Cullen offers, "Anything is possible if you want it badly enough."[27]

The American Dream concept has been at the heart of sports film scholarship because, as Andrew Miller suggests, the genre has long been one of the biggest propagators of its aspirational mythology. Indeed, speaking to Cullen's contention that "there are many American *Dreams*," Miller argues that the genre has employed the American Dream concept so much that it has formed its own wildly popular version of the myth: the "Athletic American Dream." According to Miller, the Athletic American Dream dates to the genre's origins in the silent era, with some of the earliest sports films—like football film *The Half Back* (1917) and baseball film *The Busher* (1919)—not just featuring eventual genre staples like images of athletic activity and plotlines that build to big climactic games, but also emphasizing a clear ideological message that "hard work, strong moral character, and a commitment to fair play" lead to success.[28] As Miller notes, too, this success is often achieved not just on the playing field, but also off it, with the athlete protagonists parlaying their athletic accomplishments into greater social and economic status. In the ensuing decades, this message continued to solidify. Miller points, for instance, to films like *Knute Rockne, All American* (1940) and *Pride of the*

Yankees (1942) as featuring dedicated athlete protagonists who achieve both sporting success and economic and social success.[29] The genre, Miller thus summarizes, "coalesces around underdog-to-champion, hard-work-leads-to-victory narratives" that—like the American Dream mythology, more generally—gloss over any systemic barriers.[30] Indeed, much of the American Dream mythology revolves around its availability to anyone—no matter their background.

As Miller and other scholars point out, the genre's treatment of the American Dream is a vision not just of social and economic advancement but also of masculinization. That is to say, the genre has not only long marginalized women—typically positioning them in secondary support roles—but also offered a fantasy of becoming "the ideal American man."[31] This ideal man, Miller explains, demonstrates athletic prowess and plays sports the right way. He sacrifices his individuality for the betterment of his team, for instance, and always perseveres through adversity. Often, too, his sporting accomplishments are paired with heterosexual romantic triumphs. Miller notes, for example, how in films like *The Freshman* (1925) and *The Gladiator* (1938), the protagonists use sports to "become real men with real girlfriends."[32] Friedman, meanwhile, adds that sports films "foreground an 'aggressive masculinity'"—prioritizing grittiness and physical strength, not to mention the ability to be violent when necessary.[33] Bonzel, too, notes this retrograde aggressive masculinity in analyzing the American Dream's presence in the *Rocky* series. As she explains, the protagonist of the series, Rocky Balboa (Sylvester Stallone), embodies a rugged masculinity built around "self-reliance and toughness"—as clearly illustrated by the culturally ubiquitous images of Rocky bloodying his hands while training in a meat locker.[34]

The genre's vision of the American Dream does not just promote retrograde gender ideals but also is regressive in its treatment of race. On the most basic level, almost every film mentioned in this section—from *The Half Back* to *The Pride of the Yankees* to *Rocky*—features a white protagonist. This skewed representation fits with the sports film's historical norms, as the genre has long centered on the aspirations of white athletes. Aaron Baker notes, for instance, that during the classical Hollywood period, Black characters primarily appeared either in supporting roles or as obstacles for white protagonists to overcome on the way to achieving their dreams.[35] These sorts of representations have hardly disappeared in more recent decades. To that point, Bonzel mentions how *Rocky III* (1982) heroizes Rocky by pitting him against Black boxer Clubber Lang (Mr. T). Lang, Bonzel explains, is established as a foil by being stereotypically depicted as "sexually aggressive, even predatory," as in a scene where Lang hurls lewd comments at Rocky's wife,

Adrian.[36] Bonzel here quotes Melvin Burke Donalson, who argues that Lang "represents the urban savage, the brute"—thereby, again, reinforcing that Lang primarily exists as an obstacle for Rocky to inspirationally overcome to further his American Dream.[37] As a large number of scholars have further documented, the genre's treatment of race also intersects with its treatment of gender, with the genre having long been a site specifically dedicated to shoring up white masculinity. Several scholars have argued, for instance, that the *Rocky* franchise serves, as Babington suggests, as "a fantasy of American white working-class assertion against perceived disenfranchisement by a multicultural society."[38] *Rocky*'s American Dream, then, is not just about elevating a form of masculinity centered around self-reliance and toughness, but also, as Victoria Elmwood writes of the franchise's first film, "the remasculinization of white men."[39]

More recently, the genre has featured more protagonists of color, as exemplified by films like *Coach Carter* (2005), *The Express* (2008), *42* (2013), *Creed,* and *Race* (2016). However, the genre's increasing diversity has not necessarily meant that the form has moved dramatically forward in its racial politics. Significantly, the genre's continued centering of the American Dream means that systemic barriers continue to be underemphasized, with the primary determinant for protagonists' success still often rooted in their ability to work hard and persevere through adversity. Bonzel argues, for instance, that *Creed* may offer a "positive representation of black masculinity," but that it also "contributes to the myth of the achievability of the American dream despite systemic disadvantages for black people . . . putting responsibility solely into the hands of the individual."[40] Similarly, Kyle Kusz suggests *Coach Carter*'s treatment of urban education valorizes the transformative influence of the eponymous Coach Carter (Samuel L. Jackson) while eliding discussion of "such influential social forces and conditions as de facto racial segregation, institutionalized racism, and systemic class divisions."[41] As Kusz points out, too, the familiar white protagonists have hardly disappeared from the genre. Indeed, Kusz argues that the early 2000s witnessed a prominent strain of sports films starring "white everymen," as in *Dodgeball: A True Underdog Story* (2004), *Miracle* (2004), and *Cinderella Man* (2005).[42]

In summary, then, as much as the sports film has been about "big games" and dramatic halftime speeches, it has also been about reaffirming the American Dream—repeatedly telling stories about (primarily straight white male) athletes finding success by working hard and self-sacrificing. The following section, then, investigates how much that Dream mythology holds once several critical elements of the genre—including the presence of the ubiquitous athlete-heroes—are refigured as part of the managerial sports film.

Forming the Managerial American Dream

In the traditional sports film, the American Dream revolves around athletic performance. It is no coincidence, after all, that Miller terms the genre's version of the myth the "*Athletic* American Dream." It is not just that sports films almost always feature athlete protagonists aspiring toward athletic success, but also that the genre emphasizes athletic activity as essential to those aspirations. Across countless films, protagonists show their dedication through long, grueling practice sessions in which they sweat and, as *Rocky* demonstrates, bleed. Indeed, one of the genre's signature elements is the training montage that documents the hours and hours of work the athlete protagonist devotes to improving their athletic skills and stamina. The genre's "big games" are also key sites for the athletes to demonstrate their toughness and perseverance—perhaps, for instance, rebounding from a devastating body blow or storming back from a large deficit. Of course, too, it is on the field/court/rink/and so forth where athletes find many of the rewards of the American Dream—the athlete's hard work so often paying off in a victory or, at least, a loss that feels like a victory.

Largely drained of the genre's familiar athletic action—the exhausting practices, the knockdown punches, the game-winning touchdowns, and such—it would initially seem that the managerial sports film would have difficulty retaining the genre's vision of the American Dream. However, the managerial sports film retains more of that myth than might otherwise be expected. As already mentioned, for instance, it keeps the striving, hard-working underdog. The protagonists of *Jerry Maguire* and *Million Dollar Arm,* for example, are both sports agents who have started their own small agencies after leaving larger, more prestigious firms. Both must labor, then, to regain their prior statures without the impressive resources and reputations of their former employers. Similarly, the front-office executives of *Moneyball* must strain to outcompete their deep-pocketed rivals. On a basic level, too, these films largely retain the ethical dimensions of the genre's American Dream. Jerry Maguire, for instance, is presented as an admirable underdog not just because he is willing to outwork his competitors but also because he retains the "strong moral character" long characteristic of the genre's protagonists.[43] The film posits that, unlike other sports agents, Maguire pursues the profession the right way—not emptily chasing dollar signs, but rather valuing his clients as individuals and fully investing in their lives and dreams. And, of course, these films hold onto the genre's triumphant endings. *Jerry Maguire,* for instance, closes with Maguire's client, Rod Tidwell

(Cuba Gooding Jr.), receiving the lucrative contract he has long sought and then tearfully praising Maguire.

While the general outlines of the sports film's version of the American Dream remain within the managerial sports film—thereby ensuring that these films align with the broader mythos of the genre—there are, of course, significant ramifications to the decentering of athlete protagonists. Most obviously, if the traditional sports film suggests that athletic performance is key to obtaining the American Dream, then the managerial sports film, in deemphasizing athletic action, instead posits that a different sort of performance—administrative performance—is key to the American Dream. One can start by noting the activities that audiences see the protagonists do. In brief, what unites the protagonists of managerial sports films is administrative work. Rather than training in meat lockers or playing in crowded stadiums, the stars of managerial sports films hold meetings and make calls. Even more specifically, though, it can be said they engage in acts of management. In other words, they plan, set objectives, write mission statements, coordinate resources, communicate with their superiors, delegate tasks to subordinates, and so forth. Take, for instance, the responsibilities of protagonist Sonny Weaver Jr. (Kevin Costner) in *Draft Day*. Over the course of the film, Weaver, the general manager of the Cleveland Browns, liaises with his boss (the team's owner), meets with employees to discuss the team's strategy, converses with his managerial counterparts at other teams, and so on. Although the specific nature of these conversations—game attendance, roster moves, and the like—are particular to the world of professional sports, the rough outlines of Weaver's day likely resemble that of so many other administrators across so many various industries.

Particularly significant here is the framing of these bureaucratic responsibilities. Rather than suggesting that these sorts of mundane tasks—meetings, phone calls, and so on—are numbing office drudgery, managerial sports films instead suggest that administrative duties can be as exciting as anything on the playing surface. As *Draft Day*'s Weaver negotiates a trade with his counterpart in Jacksonville over speakerphone, the scene grows tense, with the film score dropping out and frequent cutaways being made to nervous onlookers and a ticking clock (figures 1.1a-b). In many ways, it is equivalent to the stereotypical sports film scene in which time winds down as the underdog team runs their big play while tense fans bite their lips. Notably, these managerial tasks also net the protagonists their happy endings. For instance, in Weaver's case, his shrewd ability to navigate between the competing needs and interests of his team's owner, his subordinates, and his counterparts leads

FIGURES 1.1A-B: Sonny Weaver Jr. (Kevin Costner) negotiating a trade while a clock ticks down in *Draft Day*.

him to a successful draft that pleases all and, seemingly, reinforces his job security. In emphasizing the excitement and rewards of managerial duties, managerial sports films paint a rosy picture of administrative work—both meaningful on a daily basis and a means toward a happy, comfortable life.

In replacing the Athletic American Dream with a Managerial American Dream that valorizes both the material and immaterial rewards of managerial work, managerial sports films align with the broader shift toward the managerialism described in the introduction. To repeat, managerialism is an ideological project that works to bolster the status of managerial figures, with managers elevated into a socially powerful group supposedly blessed with exclusive knowledge of how to best run organizations. It is notable, then, that the administrative protagonists of managerial sports films are all, in brief, impressively capable—admirably combining qualities like assertiveness, creativity, and flexibility. Taken together, the films suggest there is something special about administrators. However, what is unique about managerial sports films—particularly in comparison to the sports radio and television programming to be discussed in the next chapter—is that they do not just posit that managers are exceptional, but also suggest that management is something to aspire to. Such aspirations form an implicit base for managerialist ideologies—establishing the idea that becoming a manager is fulfilling a fantasy. They suggest, in essence, that those who have climbed into these roles can be viewed as all the more special.

Beyond reinforcing managerialism, other ramifications of the decentering of athletic protagonists become clear if one further unpacks the relationship of managerial sports films to race, class, gender, and sexuality. As mentioned above, the sports film's version of the American Dream has typically not just been a tale of athletic triumph but also of class ascension. To that point, the genre's protagonists usually hail from the working class, with the genre's narratives then so often figured around upward class mobility, if not dramatic escapes, as Friedman writes, from "lives of poverty and stagnation."[44] A film like *Rudy* (1993) is typical. Throughout the film, the working-class background of Rudy Ruettiger (Sean Astin), an undersized football player who dreams of playing for the University of Notre Dame, looms large. At several points in the film, for instance, the film goes inside the steel mill where Rudy's friends and family and, eventually, Rudy work. Indeed, it is a deadly accident at the steel mill that inspires Rudy to finally act on his dream and begin working toward admission to Notre Dame—though not before receiving a lecture from his father that "Notre Dame is for rich kids . . . not for us." Needless to say, Rudy goes on to prove his father wrong, earning admission to Notre Dame and eventually suiting up for its football team. As Miller notes, a college degree often works as a symbol of class elevation within the sports film genre. So, it is significant that *Rudy* ends with an epilogue noting that the protagonist successfully graduated from Notre Dame and that several of his younger brothers would follow his lead by also earning college degrees.[45]

On the other hand, managerial sports films essentially remove the working-class trappings of the genre. Suffice to say, there are no steel mills in movies like *High Flying Bird*. Instead, managerial sports films primarily operate in upper-middle-class/upper-class environments. Whereas *Rudy* begins with a sweeping wide shot that shows the working-class neighborhoods and smokestacks of Joliet, Illinois, *Million Dollar Arm* opens in the sizable, well-appointed office of sports agent J. B. Bernstein (Jon Hamm). As *Million Dollar Arm* proceeds, we then see Bernstein hop in his Porsche and, soon after, retreat to his large, modern Los Angeles home. Underscoring all this signaling of Bernstein's upper-class status is that Bernstein is played by Jon Hamm, most famous for his depiction of the suave advertising executive Don Draper in *Mad Men* (AMC, 2007–2015). Similar representations pervade the other managerial sports films. *Draft Day,* for instance, also begins by giving the audience a taste of the protagonist's comfortable, upper-class life by opening in Weaver's spacious, contemporary home, full of floor-to-ceiling windows and stylish, modern furniture (figures 1.2a-c).

Fitting, though, with the retention of the broader genre's underdog trajectory, managerial sports films are not absent class anxiety. *Million Dollar Arm* may open with scenes that quickly introduce Bernstein's high-class living, but it also quickly establishes that Bernstein may be at risk of losing that lifestyle. While Bernstein is sitting in his Porsche, for instance, the audience learns that he is behind on rent for his office space. Not long after, the audience also learns that his fledgling sports agency is on the brink of dissolving. A similar path is charted in *Jerry Maguire.* At the opening of the film, Maguire is living lavishly. He wears expensive suits, works in a stylish office, lives in a beachfront condo, and travels in first-class comfort. However, once Maguire is fired from the powerful sports agency that has afforded him these luxuries, his lifestyle comes into question. Meanwhile, in *Draft Day* and *Moneyball,* the executive protagonists labor while under the constant threat of losing their jobs. In *Draft Day,* for instance, after Weaver departs his stylish, modern home, he tunes in to a sports talk radio host ominously predicting Weaver will "be gone" if he does not turn the team around and then soon after sees the words "Fire Sonny" written onto a dirty car window. Next, Weaver meets with his boss, team owner Anthony Molina (Frank Langella). Molina immediately puts heavy pressure on Weaver, laying out his priorities—and the stakes—for the team's draft. "I need you to make a splash, Sonny. We need to sell tickets." He continues, "If you can't do it, then I have to do it, and I don't want to have to do that." As if the implication was not explicit enough, Weaver replies, "Just to be clear here, you're threatening to fire me, right?" This subject returns over the course of the movie, with Weaver lamenting that a poor draft will undoubtedly lead to his termination. A similar fear hangs over *Moneyball.* As the protagonist of the film, Oakland Athletics general manager Billy Beane (Brad Pitt), discusses the team's unconventional roster strategy with the team's assistant general manager, he summarizes, "If this thing we're doing doesn't work . . . neither of us have jobs." As J. D. Connor argues, then, the movie's happy ending is not about the team beating out its rivals or Beane triumphantly parlaying his success with the Athletics into a

FIGURES 1.2A-C: Weaver begins the day in his well-appointed home in *Draft Day*.

bigger and better position. Instead, "The happy ending, for Beane, [is] winning enough games that he can keep his job."[46]

Significantly, then, managerial sports films reorient one of the critical tenets of the Athletic American Dream. These films are not about class *ascension* but rather about class *maintenance*. As exemplified by the ending of *Moneyball*, these films do not see their heroic protagonists using sports as a springboard toward greater social and economic status. Instead, these protagonists have already achieved a great deal of status—living comfortably while working in high-prestige jobs. Instead, then, these protagonists are underdogs because they have to claw to maintain that status. That the class dynamics of the genre have shifted aligns with broader societal shifts. As scholars of work and labor have documented, employment has become less secure in recent decades. Indeed, economic historian Wayne Lewchuk terms this "the era of Increased Precarious Employment."[47] This era is most visibly exemplified by the rise of the gig economy, but the precariousness extends far beyond this new category of informal employment. More broadly, workers have seen their wages stagnate, their benefits atrophy, and their ties to their employers grow increasingly tenuous. This marks a notable shift from the postwar era, in which employers prioritized stable workforces and, accordingly, invested in worker retention. Instead, employers now lust after the "nimbleness" of a highly flexible "lean" workforce, with workers thus seen, as sociologist Erin Hatton describes, as "profit-limiting liabilities rather than profit-boosting assets."[48] Accordingly, as business historian Louis Hyman summarizes, "In ever more insidious ways, employers have found means to make workers disposable."[49]

As these scholars have noted, the shift toward precariousness has mainly been ideological. Over the second half of the twentieth century, they note, a combination of interests, including temporary employment agencies and management consultants, worked to propagate the idea that, as Hyman explains, "no one had a right to job security" and that businesses were well-served to reconceive of their workforces as drains on company profits.[50] Indeed, Hatton writes, these campaigns "had a powerful impact on the cultural battlefield, helping establish a new morality of business."[51] Speaking to this dramatic cultural impact, a looming sense of precariousness pervades a significant slice of recent film and television. For instance, media scholar Nick Couldry argues that popular reality television shows like *The Apprentice* and *Big Brother* closely reflect the workings of the harsh neoliberal workplace, spotlighting dynamics like the need for workers/contestants to submit to a higher external authority.[52] In the American version of *The Apprentice,* for example, Donald Trump presides over a series of challenges that pit aspiring corporate executives against each other—the one winner receiving the chance to work for Trump's company, and the many losers each being coldly dismissed with the statement, "You're fired." In fact, this ritual "firing" is the signature element of the show, with NBC even using the tagline "Who will be the first to get fired?" in their promotional materials. Turning to more examples of precariousness filtering into popular media, Diane Negra and Yvonne Tasker note the preponderance of cultural texts produced in the wake of the Great Recession dealing with themes like unemployment and austerity, while Taylor Nygaard and Jordie Lagerwey highlight the many recent television comedies in which characters grapple with diminishing access to employment and home ownership.[53] There are even signs of this precariousness in other sports-related films, with movies like *The Wrestler* (2008) and *Foxcatcher* (2014) also emphasizing "downward mobility" rather than the traditional American Dream narrative.[54] Given these sorts of examples, is it not surprising that managerial sports films have also incorporated a sense of economic vulnerability into their familiar narrative template. In this new context in which employers have turned "'good' jobs into 'bad' ones (and bad jobs into worse ones)," aspirations of moving up in the world are—both in perception and in reality—increasingly unrealistic.[55] The protagonists of films like *Draft Day* and *Moneyball* may have entered the vaunted managerial caste yet—like so many workers anxiously hanging tight to their uncertain jobs—all they can do is hope to cling to what they have, hoping not to be the next in an endless wave of downsizing. The American Dream, then, becomes one of not backsliding further down the class ladder, and there are perhaps no clearer exemplars of this diminished fantasy than protagonists who apparently—by way of their modern homes and expensive cars—have so much to lose.

The sports film's shift toward management does not just reconfigure how its version of the American Dream addresses class dynamics but also, relatedly, how it approaches race, gender, and sexuality. As mentioned above, the genre has long revolved around white masculinity. The American Dream, it suggests, is a fantasy in which straight white men turn to conventional forms of masculinity to better their lives. Again, this ideological project comes into question with managerial sports films deemphasizing athletic action. The retrograde form of masculinity typically offered by the genre has long used that athletic action as its bedrock—essentially associating manliness with physicality by way of the endurance and strength displayed during physically grueling training sessions and exhausting contests against athletic rivals. The protagonists of managerial sports films, on the other hand, show little of that physicality in performing administrative tasks like running conference calls and office meetings. Indeed, while the valorized athletic protagonist more typical of the sports film is, like the action star, partially defined through a spectacular, impressively hardened body that is flaunted during those training sessions and big games, the bodies of managerial protagonists are little seen, often being hidden under suits and other business attire.[56]

However, it would be a mistake to assume that managerial sports films reject entirely the model of masculinity typically offered by the genre. While managerial sports films may deemphasize physical activities, they nonetheless continue the genre's ideological project, as Kusz describes it, of shoring up white masculinity in the face of threats to the "normative and dominant place for straight white men in American culture and society."[57] As he details in noting the glorification of white everymen in turn-of-the-century sports films like *Dodgeball*, sports films should be understood as "'social and political allegories articulating deeply-rooted fears, desires, and visions' of contemporary American white men produced from their unstable social positions in an economically precarious, more diverse and increasingly globalized America."[58] In thinking through how those "fears, desires, and visions" are articulated by managerial sports films, it might be first noted that these films are broadly situated among the recent feelings/claims of white masculine precarity referenced in the introduction. Here it might be noted, for instance, that the cultural texts mentioned above that have grappled with the aftereffects of the Great Recession have frequently—with little regard for continued inequalities that disadvantage women and people of color—positioned white men as the foremost victims of the economic calamity. The precarious protagonists of managerial sports films—particularly the films produced in the wake of the recession, like *Million Dollar Arm* and *Draft Day*—might be understood, then, as fitting within the wider post-recession trope Negra and Tasker identify of "male injury in which white men are positioned as both sign and symptom of economic contraction."[59] With that said, managerial sports films' recurring glorification of administration also points to a more specific set of "fears, desires, and visions" unique to the subgenre, with these films offering a portrait of white masculinity that, in particular, responds to anxieties that have surrounded white-collar work.

For decades, corporate work has fostered fears that office workers—and, in particular, straight white men office workers—are becoming dangerously alienated from their labor and emasculated, as famously expressed by cultural texts like C. Wright Mills's *White Collar* (1951), Sloan Wilson's *The Man in the Gray Flannel Suit* (1955), and William Whyte's *The Organization Man* (1956). Such fears have hardly subsided in recent decades. Several scholars, for instance, have documented the ways gendered anxieties surrounding white-collar work underscored the flood of what Latham Hunter terms "office movies" in the 1980s and '90s. Hunter describes how these films, such as *Falling Down* (1993) and *American Beauty* (1999), figured white-collar work "as site and/or symptom of a widespread male-specific social affliction."[60] As a case in point, the comedy *Office Space* (1999) suggests corporate office work is mostly meaningless, bureaucratic monotony and that men would be better served by exiting for blue-collar work, as exemplified by protagonist Peter Gibbons (Ron Livingston) happily departing the software industry for a job in construction. Contemporary television has also suggested that white-collar work leads to disaffection and emasculation. For example, Adam Berg, Andrew D. Linden, and Jamie Schultz have critically examined the gender politics of the reality television program *White Collar Brawlers* (Esquire Network, 2013–2014). Each week, *White Collar Brawlers* immersed two white-collar workers into the sport of boxing, subjecting them to several weeks of training before pitting them against each other in a climactic match. As Berg, Linden, and Schultz write, the show repeatedly implied that white-collar men lack "masculinity-establishing attributes" such as "physicality, self-mastery, tenacity, violence, and individualism."[61] However, boxing was offered as a solution to this crisis. Taking advantage of the sport's "pugilistic capital," the show posited that white-collar workers could finally "achieve ideal masculinity—to become 'real men.'"[62]

In analyzing the wave of white-collar movies in the 1980s and '90s, Karen Lee Ashcraft and Lisa A. Flores suggest these films address a critical tension in white-collar masculinity. According to Ashcraft and Flores, men in white-collar professions are expected to "simultaneously perform accountability to conflicting expectations for civilized and primitive selves in public and private arenas"—a tricky balancing act that asks for attributes like care and trust to be carefully weighed against features like aggressiveness and control.[63] Implicit in the challenge of this balancing act is the fear that corporate life risks over-civilization and emasculation. White-collar masculinity, they summarize, "is susceptible to feminization, given its reputed lack of physicality and bureaucratic sterility, suppression of the body, self-imposed discipline, and obligatory ingratiation."[64] And, as they and other scholars like Tasker have noted, these perceived risks have only increased in recent decades as more and more women have entered the corporate workforce.[65] Ashcraft and Flores further argue that films have not only dramatized these anxieties but also proposed solutions for white-collar men struggling with the need to balance competing masculinities. *Fight Club* (1999), for instance, suggests that "men must rediscover the primitive" that has been stripped out by the impotence and materialism of white-collar lifestyles, but also that "primitive habits must be curbed by civilized norms," lest they spiral out of control.[66]

These tensions between "civilized" and "primitive" masculinities form an unspoken base to the Managerial American Dream. The administrative protagonists of managerial sports films operate at a remove from the physical realm of the playing field and, accordingly, are at the same risk of perceived emasculation as the fictional white-collar figures analyzed by the scholars mentioned above. Indeed, as the points above about class stagnation indicate, the protagonists of managerial sports films are particularly primed to be viewed as victims of changing workplace culture, as they are repeatedly positioned as maintaining a loose grip on their comfortable lifestyles. In approaching these gendered anxieties around white-collar work, though, managerial sports films take a different tack than the "office movies" mentioned above. That is to say, unlike films like *Office Space,* which suggest white-collar workers are wasting away in their unfulfilling corporate jobs and need to retake control by altogether rejecting the feminizing constraints of office work, managerial sports films instead suggest that conventional forms of masculinity can be fully reclaimed within white-collar professions. This departure from other white-collar films would seem to have its origins in the sports film genre, for it is significant that while managerial sports films may deemphasize physical prowess in favor of administrative expertise, they continue to hold onto the genre's traditional "aggressive masculinity" that valorizes the competitiveness, toughness, and risk taking of underdogs in the face of steep challenges.

This aggressive masculinity is on full display in *Draft Day.* Throughout the film, the protagonist Weaver acts swiftly and decisively. He is always on the front foot—confidently sparring with other members of the organization and refusing to back down in negotiations. He never flinches, either, at the riskiness of his maneuvers—and, indeed, they are quite risky if one compares his fictional roster moves to ones that might take place in reality.[67] This daringness is not only praised in the film—the team's owner, for example, enthusiastically salutes Weaver's "balls" in the wake of Weaver's confrontational, unorthodox draft day maneuvers—but was also glorified in the film's marketing materials, with the trailer declaring, "You can trust the experts, you can go by the book, or you can make history." Such aggressiveness is apparent in the other managerial sports films, too. *Moneyball,* of course, revolves around Beane's willingness to boldly defy the traditional norms of his sport, while *Million Dollar Arm* applauds Bernstein for audaciously staking his professional future on the untried strategy of scouting for baseball talent in India, and *Jerry Maguire* portrays Maguire as a maverick who enterprisingly redefines his entire white-collar profession. These managerial protagonists, then, may not superficially resemble traditional protagonists like Rocky Balboa—never shirtlessly lifting weights or furiously pummeling cow carcasses in meat lockers, for instance—but they nonetheless stand as symbols of individual agency who hold onto the "self-reliance and toughness" long characteristic of the genre.

Fitting with the dualism of white-collar films mentioned above, though, managerial sports films balance this aggressiveness with what might be termed a "civilized" restraint—a dimension of masculinity less typically associated with the genre. As managerial sports films suggest—in line with Ashcraft and Flores's analysis—this "'civilized/primitive' masculinity" leads to its protagonists' ability to thrive both as white-collar workers and as men. One can analyze, for instance, the trajectory of Jerry Maguire. As mentioned, Maguire is portrayed as boldly assertive—rebelling against the mandates of his sizable corporate employer and then, upon his firing, displaying an entrepreneurial streak in starting his own sports agency. Kusz highlights, however, that much of the narrative is concerned with Maguire struggling to "constitute a 'kinder and gentler' masculinity" that allows him to be not only a better father and husband, but also a better agent.[68]

Similar traits are on display in the other managerial sports films, as well. *Draft Day* protagonist Weaver may be depicted as a hard-driving, confident risk taker who, as the film's marketing tells us, proudly goes against "the book," but he also exemplifies the ability to switch to something like a "soft, sensitive" masculinity when appropriate.[69] To that end, the film repeatedly emphasizes Weaver's ability to listen, court, and empathize. Weaver, for instance, copes with his owner boss's large ego by tactfully reassuring him, and investigates prospects' potential by attentively conversing with them about their lives and dreams. Notably, too, Weaver's balanced masculinity is defined against a more regressive form of masculinity offered by his subordinates. At one point in the film, for instance, Weaver walks in on his scouting staff using a laptop to ogle a prospect's romantic partners while engaging in misogynistic banter. Weaver immediately shuts the laptop and gives his staff an exasperated expression. After one scout continues to press the issue, Weaver slams his fist on the table and snaps, "I'm trying very hard to not completely lose my shit"—a forceful retort that not only signals Weaver's singular focus but also indicates Weaver has moved to the top of the administrative pyramid by not engaging in the sort of overt sexism that has more typically marked the sports film.[70] In his analysis of the broader genre, Baker remarks that sports films "often foreground dominant masculinity, yet they also show how it has been refigured (and sometimes does not stand up) over time in response to changes in American society."[71] Such an observation in mind, it is perhaps not surprising that managerial sports films have brought the wider genre a reworked version of its idealized masculinity that reflects gendered anxieties about deindustrialization—suggesting straight white men, rather than flagging in the face of the new demands of postindustrial work, are instead able to uniquely adapt and thrive in this environment.

To that last point, it must also be emphasized that the "civilized/primitive" dualism on display in managerial sports films is limited in its availability. The films continually equate, for instance, this idealized, balanced masculinity with heterosexuality. The managerial successes of the protagonists of *Draft Day* and *Million Dollar Arm,* for example, intersect with heterosexual romances, and both films conclude with the sports film's familiar "heterosexual union."[72] Meanwhile, in their analysis of white-collar films, Ashcraft and Flores emphasize that these texts specifically present a vision of "white/collar masculinity." As they argue, the films only allow white men the flexibility to balance the complex demands of civilized/primitive masculinity. Managerial sports films work in a similar vein—implicitly suggesting that only white men can successfully navigate the tensions inherent in white-collar work and turn the office place into a site of masculine empowerment. To begin, it can be noted that—continuing with the sports film's more extended history—the protagonists of managerial sports films are almost all white men. Meanwhile—again fitting with the genre's historical norms—women and characters of color are positioned mainly in secondary supporting roles in which their narrative purposes are to help the protagonists realize their goals. This is perhaps most famously exemplified by *Jerry Maguire,* as Maguire's wife Dorothy Boyd (Renée Zellweger) and his Black client Rod Tidwell continually help Maguire on his journey toward self-discovery and white-collar success. Boyd, for instance, assumes what Sutera terms a *"femina domestica* role" in assisting Maguire by performing "the traditional unpaid domestic duties ascribed to women."[73] At the same time, Tidwell continually offers Maguire nuggets of wisdom, as in the need to reach for a harmonious "kwan" that balances "love, respect, community," and financial well-being. Similarly, in *Draft Day,* the only woman who features prominently, salary cap analyst Ali Parker (Jennifer Garner), primarily functions as a romantic interest and supportive sounding board for Weaver; her own administrative expertise is rendered largely incidental. Meanwhile, the only prominent character of color in *Draft Day,* draft prospect Vontae Mack (Chadwick Boseman), seems to mostly exist as a symbol of family-oriented virtuousness both to reinforce Weaver's sensitivity in valuing these attributes more than his shallow subordinates and, in turn, to confirm the savviness of Weaver's aggressive maneuvers to pick Mack rather than other, more touted prospects.[74] *Moneyball,* meanwhile, is almost entirely absent of any speaking characters who are not white men.

Notably, too, characters of color are not just placed into supporting roles but are also often framed less as individuals than as objects over whom the white administrative figures can exercise control. Indeed, this sort of racially skewed power has long been a criticism directed at managerial sports media. As will be further explored in coming chapters, scholars like Andrew Baerg and Thomas Oates have noted, for instance, how sports television and digital sports games vicariously position their audiences—mostly, according to industry statistics, white men—as exercising control over athletes of color. Managerial sports films rely on a similar dynamic. Throughout *Draft Day*, for instance, the film continually highlights how Weaver holds Mack's professional fate in his hand. Moreover, over the course of the film, Mack has to repeatedly convince Weaver that he is worth drafting. In *Moneyball*, meanwhile, one pivotal scene depicts Beane negotiating a trade for pitcher Ricardo Rincón. Throughout the scene, Rincón is but a name to be bandied about—to be, in Beane's phrasing, bought, sold, and profited upon. Furthermore, *Million Dollar Arm* acts, in the words of film critic Joe Morgenstern, "as a parable of colonial exploitation," with Bernstein imagining India as an "untapped market" and a fresh pool of human capital that he might be the first to cash in on.[75] This sense of Indian athletes as a new sort of, in Bernstein's phrasing, "investment" trickles down to the film's formal choices. For example, as Bernstein arrives to an athletic facility in Lucknow to scout for talent, the film employs multiple point-of-view shots of Bernstein coolly gazing out over fields of athletes—a formal strategy that recalls Richard Dyer's observation that perspective shots have so often been used to "reproduce racial power relations" in showing a "white male character scrutinising, appraising and savouring."[76] Here, the shots reinforce the idea the Indian athletes are merely lying in wait—anticipating the moment the enterprising Bernstein will capitalize on their raw abilities.[77] The administrative heroes of managerial sports films may be middle managers who are precariously subject to the whims of others, but, speaking again to the films' continuing valorization of an aggressive masculinity, the films suggest that their protagonists—and even supporting front office characters, like *Moneyball*'s assistant general manager Peter Brand (Jonah Hill)—retain the critical ability to control others, particularly athletes of color.

Because it is almost solely straight white men whom the films allow to satisfyingly fulfill the "elusive quest for an ideal blend of control and excess," they seemingly imply that this balance is out of reach for others.[78] It is a twist on the genre's traditional model, in which straight white men remasculinized by embracing a traditional, physical mode of sporting masculinity and, often, besting athletes of color on this terrain. In the new strain of managerial sports films, to be solely confined to the physical realm is to remain limited in one's masculinity. And, again and again, it is characters of color who are left behind on the playing surface while white men display a new idealized masculinity as they take up a new seat of power in the front office—a power made absolutely clear when they reshape the lives and careers of athletes in brief phone calls with other white men. Kusz notes that as the sports film has entered the new millennium, it has retained a distinctly "regressive racial and gender politics."[79] As the preceding paragraphs make clear, this generic regressiveness extends to the managerial sports films, which, yet again, primarily work to "re-secure a normative and dominant place for straight white men in American culture and society in the present and into the future."[80]

Taken together, managerial sports films offer a cohesive vision of a revised American Dream. In this new American Dream—a Managerial American Dream rather than an Athletic American Dream—one can again fantasize of using sports as a gateway to prosperity, but this imagined success is transformed. Rather than finding success on the field, the protagonists of managerial sports films find their success in conference rooms and corner offices. This revision suggests that administrative work, rather than a bureaucratic slog, can be exciting and rewarding. As the films imply, those rewards are not just material—allowing administrators to cling (if barely) to a comfortable lifestyle—but also immaterial, as white-collar work allows its participants (if straight white men) to embody a fulfilling version of contemporary masculinity. In documenting the place of the American Dream within American culture, Cullen notes that the idea at its core—the search for a "better and richer and fuller" life—has changed over time as different definitions of "better," "richer," and "fuller" have arisen and competed for dominance.[81] The rise of the Managerial American Dream reinforces this argument, suggesting that while the American Dream remains a key myth in American culture, the outlines of that myth are far from static.

Questioning the Managerial American Dream

In occasionally highlighting the precariousness of modern life—with workers clinging to tenuous jobs under the watchful eyes of demanding bosses—one can see glimpses of how the managerial sports film might begin to gesture toward a critique of contemporary capitalism. However, as is probably clear from the simultaneous valorization of administrative work and "white/collar masculinity," the version of the American Dream offered by managerial sports films—the Managerial American Dream—is hardly a revolutionary vision. These are films primarily about heroic straight cisgender white men upholding the capitalist status quo by successfully negotiating their privileged—if precarious—place between professional sport's workers and owners. In his analysis of *Moneyball*, Connor makes this conservativism clear. As he writes, *Moneyball* is, at its heart, a story about a group of managers figuring out a novel way—vis-à-vis statistical analysis—to underpay athletes for their labor. As mentioned, the film's celebratory resolution salutes Beane for that managerial accomplishment. Connor notes, then, that the film's happy ending is "decidedly *not* [about] the players discovering they are undervalued and successfully demanding their rightful compensation." He continues, "This relationship looks like exploitation, and in *Moneyball*, we are supposed to root for it."[82] Similar analysis could also be applied to the other managerial sports films. *Draft Day*, for instance, valorizes Weaver for shrewdly navigating the NFL's draft process—a process that has long been criticized both for restricting the freedom for athletes to choose where they play and for depressing athletes' salaries.

Notably, though, the version of *Moneyball* that made its way to theaters was not the version initially envisioned. Initially, the project was to be directed in quite a different fashion by Steven Soderbergh, a director known for his diverse body of work spanning from *Sex, Lies, and Videotape* (1989) to *Ocean's Eleven* (2001) to *Che* (2008). As Connor details, Soderbergh's version was inspired by the film *Reds* (1981), Warren Beatty's biopic of Russian Revolution chronicler John Reed, and meant to incorporate interviews with actual baseball players and managers.[83] While Soderbergh's unconventional approaches eventually scared off *Moneyball*'s producers and he subsequently exited the film, he ultimately returned to this hybrid method with another managerial sports film: *High Flying Bird*.[84] Throughout *High Flying Bird*, Soderbergh weaves together the fictional story of Black sports agent Ray Burke (André Holland) with black-and-white interviews conducted with several NBA players, including stars like Donovan Mitchell and Karl-Anthony Towns (figure 1.3). It is a formal experiment in a genre not known for its formal adventurousness—intentionally breaking the traditional filmic spell in which a narrative unfolds as invisibly as possible.

According to Soderbergh, *High Flying Bird*'s atypical interview segments were essential to the film's attempt to capture the reality of professional sporting life:

> There's something really compelling, I think, about these real players describing their experiences. And it really hit home that these guys are under enormous pressure, you know, to perform, and to conform. And that their lives are not entirely their own.[85]

Managerial Sports Films 57

FIGURE 1.3: Interviews with NBA players like Donovan Mitchell appear throughout *High Flying Bird*.

This last sentiment—that the players' lives are not entirely their own—is a driving message in the film. To summarize *High Flying Bird*'s plot with a bit more depth, the film follows Burke's efforts to navigate a professional basketball lockout that has placed both him and his clients in financial peril. In an attempt to speed the end of the lockout, Burke lays the groundwork for a one-on-one game between two young players—an event that eventually goes viral and signals to the league's owners that players have the power to garner attention and money beyond the league's traditional structures. As Burke comments in a press conference held after the game, "It was the beginning of change. Change of this game that's been played behind the game. [It] was just a glimmer, a lightning flash of what could be the beginning of a whole new industry." It becomes possible to imagine, in other words, professional basketball outside the auspices of a league like the NBA—to imagine, as Samantha N. Sheppard explains in an examination of the film, "the absence of owners, player's associations, and even agents exploiting players in their prime earning years," thereby making "way for a player-controlled economy of the sport."[86]

In her analysis, Sheppard argues that *High Flying Bird* "rebels against 'playing the game' on sports culture's hegemonic terms," even suggesting the film "becomes an anti-sports film."[87] Building on that analysis, here it can be suggested that *High Flying Bird* might be considered, in particular, an anti-managerial sports film. In critiquing the "game that's been played behind the game," *High Flying Bird*—even though it again centers on a managerial figure—serves as an implicit critique to many of the elements of the Managerial American Dream. Managerial sports films have not just posited that sporting power resides in front offices where white men dictate the fates of athletes of color but also suggested that this front office power is to be valorized. The front-office workers in films like *Draft Day* and *Moneyball* are savvy and charismatic—exemplifying a new idealized version of masculinity. On the other hand, *High Flying Bird* implies that front-office workers, rather than the new heroes of the sporting landscape, are instead part of a parasitic, restrictive sporting apparatus that contributes little in profiting off the labor of Black athletes.

To that point, it might be mentioned that the sports teams found throughout most managerial sports films are depicted as being rigidly hierarchical—placing members of the organization into a strictly vertical chain of command that locates all power in the front office. In *Draft Day,* for instance, Weaver is—quite proudly—in complete control of the team. At one point, for example, the team's head coach confronts Weaver, wanting to know why Weaver has made a trade without first consulting him. "Did you think," the coach asks, "it might be important to discuss this decision with me first?" Weaver responds harshly, "No. It's my call." Not long after, Weaver is confronted by the team's quarterback, who, like the coach, is upset he has been left out of Weaver's plans. Responding to the player's request to now be traded, Weaver replies, "If I trade you, I trade you; if I don't, I don't." Continuing, Weaver spits, "Don't bother me with your shit." As suggested by these sorts of scenes, workers in most managerial sports films are meant to be obedient, and decisions are not to be questioned or challenged. Indeed, managerial sports films frequently suggest that audiences should admire these administrative figures for taking on the challenge of single-handedly leading their organizations in the face of the constant annoyances presented by unruly coaches and athletes. It is notable, then, that *High Flying Bird,* in gesturing toward a player-controlled version of the sport, rejects this top-down model that the other managerial sports films implicitly promote. The film stresses, for instance, that the rigid hierarchy found in a film like *Draft Day* goes hand-in-hand with exploitation, suggesting throughout that the NBA's athletes are the reason for the league's prosperity and are not valued accordingly. Moreover, as the section above suggested, it underscores that this exploitation is highly racialized, with the league's predominantly Black workforce denied their fair share of power and resources by the league's mostly white owners and administrators.

In pointing toward the exploitation inherent throughout the NBA and other sports organizations, *High Flying Bird* digs further into the power structures of modern sport than the other managerial sports films. For instance, while team owners are occasionally present in the other films, they often exist in the background. This backgrounding has the effect of amplifying the importance of the administrative workers at the hearts of these films—suggesting that while demanding owners may dangerously lurk somewhere within the waters of the sports landscape, it is the managerial protagonists who take the truly consequential actions. Indeed, in *Moneyball,* one might be mistaken for assuming Beane—for all his mentions of potentially being fired if he underperforms—has total control of the team's operations, as Oakland's owner makes but two small appearances.[88] In this way, managerial sports films become part of a larger project to obscure the power of team owners—a project most clearly signaled by the centering of league commissioners, rather than team owners, in a substantial portion of media coverage of league maneuvers.[89] *High Flying Bird* does not participate in this illusion, instead making it clear that it is team owners who have historically dictated the terms of the "game that's been played behind the game." To that end, it makes an owner a primary character in the film and implies that this figure, New York owner David Seton (Kyle MacLachlan), is the driving force behind the league's finances, most notably by controlling the league's television contracts. In this way, *High Flying Bird*'s depiction of ownership is less connected to the other managerial sports films than to more traditional iterations of the broader sports film genre. For example, genre classics like *Slap Shot* (1977), *Major League* (1989), and *Any Given Sunday* (1999) all make team owners central to their plots and, as part of this plotting, depict them as the power centers of the sports business.

Notably, though, *High Flying Bird* is not only interested in highlighting where power resides in contemporary sport but also how that power is exercised. To that end, then, it is significant that *High Flying Bird* follows the lead of these previous sports films like *Slap Shot* and *Major League* not just in spotlighting the role of team owners but also in painting owners as indifferent to the lives of the athletes on their teams and, accordingly, all too willing to use and exploit athletes as little more than financial assets. In *Slap Shot,* for instance, as team owner Anita McCambridge (Kathryn Walker) prepares to fold the hockey team at the film's center to take a beneficial tax write-off, the team's player-coach Reggie Dunlop (Paul Newman) implores her, "We're human beings, you know." McCambridge's eventual reply is to tell Dunlop, "I don't think you understand finance." *High Flying Bird* brings this critique of capitalist sport into the contemporary era—suggesting that as modern sport has become even more financialized, this cold, calculated logic has, unsurprisingly, held firm. For instance, as team owner Seton finalizes the league's new broadcasting deal and looks to end the lockout, he glibly comments to the head of the players' union, "I believe in family. This team's my family. I need us to be one big family again." Seton, the film makes

60   CHAPTER ONE

clear, views the players primarily as profit centers—family only in so far as they support the team's bottom line and do not demand more than what he deems their "fair" share of the league's revenue.

High Flying Bird's examination of the power structures of modern sport does not stop at critiquing the parasitic nature of sporting infrastructures but instead extends into reestablishing the central importance of athletes. Early in *High Flying Bird,* Burke passes an unknown package to one of his clients, calling the mysterious gift "a bible." At the end of the film, it is revealed that the package contains sociologist Harry Edwards's influential 1969 text *The Revolt of the Black Athlete,* an analysis of the activism of Black athletes like Tommie Smith and John Carlos. As the film closes, too, we see Burke heading into a meeting with Edwards. The emphasis on Edwards and his influential work signals, of course, the film's broader political project, emphasizing, much as Edwards does in his book, that Black athletes are exploited by the racist power structures of modern sport, but it also serves to highlight the opposite workings of the other managerial sports films and, in particular, their centering of administrators. Athlete activism, in brief, is supported by the acknowledgment of the centrality of athletes to sport—that athletes are not, as Edwards writes in *The Revolt of the Black Athlete,* disposable "machines," but rather the very heart of sport; that a sport belongs to its athletes instead of the tangential forces that exist to profit from competition.[90] Seen in this light, the sports film's traditional focus on athlete protagonists appears almost radical. For all the conservative tendencies of the genre, as in the aforementioned focus on straight white men, the conventional foregrounding of athletes instead of coaches, executives, owners, and so forth, has highlighted that sport revolves around its athletes. On the other hand, most managerial sports films suggest that athletes exist on the margins of sport—mere assets to be signed, swapped, and cut. In this conception of the sporting landscape, the thoughts and concerns of athletes are irrelevant; their collective power is—and should be—minimal, lest that collective power interferes with the authority of the white men working in the front office. Even while starring another managerial figure, *High Flying Bird* rejects this vision of the sporting world, as clearly signaled by the frequent inclusion of the voices of NBA players like Mitchell and Towns.[91]

In direct contrast with *Moneyball,* then, *High Flying Bird* asks its viewers not to celebrate sporting exploitation, but rather to question it—interrogating what forces have most benefited from the transformation of professional sport into a financial behemoth and, accordingly, seriously considering Burke's dream of a system that puts "the control back in the hands of those behind the ball instead of those up in the skybox." While other managerial sports films essentially promote a refigured version of the American Dream that both valorizes white-collar administrative work and simultaneously reaffirms sport as a site for white men to demonstrate authority, *High Flying Bird* instead suggests this vision is perhaps closer to the "American nightmare" that Edwards, drawing on Malcolm X, highlights in *The Revolt of the Black Athlete*—an upsetting fantasy of racialized control.[92]

2

"He's Looking Like a Depressed Asset"

The Financial Logics of Managerial Sports Talk

As documented in the previous chapter, sports media is increasingly full of fictionalized depictions of administrators and administrative work. Sports media's managerial fixation, though, is hardly limited to the heroization of imagined bureaucrats. As I will detail in this and coming chapters, sports media's managerial fixation also extends into the coverage of real-world sporting events. Taking first steps into this real-world managerial coverage, this chapter will focus on the pronounced managerial streak within sports talk programming—a loosely defined genre encompassing radio, podcast, and television programming devoted to discussions of sports rather than live event coverage. Within sports talk, administrative figures and administrative work are almost as ubiquitous as in managerial sports films, with commentators spending endless hours debating the performances of front office executives and, in turn, proffering what they would do if they were instead in control. Along the way, discussions tread deeply into contract terms, salary cap rules, trade mechanics, and any other manner of administrative minutiae.

As the mention of contracts and salary caps suggests, the content of managerial sports talk is heavily financial. In discussing administrative matters, conversations often revolve around issues of money management, delving into topics like the size of players' contracts and teams' financial flexibility. As I argue in this chapter, though, managerial sports talk's entwinement with finance goes beyond a shift in subject matter. Rather, I contend that managerial sports talk illustrates that for sports media to adopt a managerial lens also entails an imbrication in the *logics* of finance—positioning the sports world not just as a site of athletic skill, geographic loyalties, lengthy traditions, and other qualities more popularly associated with sport, but also as a site of investment and risk management. In the process, these financial logics again fuel a broader ideological project that extends across all managerial sports media, with a centering of administrators and administrative work—in this case, through the lens of finance—both reordering and reinforcing white hegemonic masculinity.

Defining Managerial Sports Talk

Before delving into the financial logics of managerial sports talk, it is first necessary to clarify what exactly distinguishes this subset of sports talk—to explain, in other words, what makes managerial sports talk distinct from the rest of sports talk programming, just as the previous chapter detailed what distinguishes managerial sports films from traditional sports films. A quick detour into the broader background of sports talk provides helpful context. For many sports fans, sports radio and television is likely synonymous with live event programming. However, sports radio and television is a vast and crowded space in which live event broadcasts figure but one part. For example, while live event telecasts may dominate year-end sports television rating numbers, the typical daily schedule of a channel like ESPN is primarily composed of studio shows like *First Take* (2007–), *Get Up* (2018–), and *SportsCenter* (1979–). Similarly, sports radio schedules are typically dominated by formats like call-in shows rather than live coverage of games. Meanwhile, podcasts are absent live sports coverage by their very nature.

Although sports radio and television may be primarily associated with live game coverage, there is a long history of sports broadcasters relying on alternative, non-live event sports programming, stretching back to examples like the sports television anthology shows *Wide World of Sports* (ABC, 1961–1998) and *CBS Sports Spectacular* (CBS, 1960–).[1] With that said, industry demand for non-live event programming has only amplified in recent decades, with that demand primarily fueled by the significantly increased number of sports broadcasting outlets. Sports television programming, for instance, was once limited to occasional appearances on over-the-air broadcasters like ABC and NBC. The 1980s and 1990s, however, witnessed the arrival of more and more cable television outlets entirely devoted to sports programming. The success of ESPN in the 1980s, for instance, not only beget many additional ESPN channels in the 1990s and 2000s, including ESPN2, ESPNU, ESPN Classic, ESPN Deportes, and ESPNEWS, but also helped spur the creation of a wide range of other sports cable outlets, such as the National College Sports Network, the Outdoor Life Network, and Speed.[2] More recently, as the fate of legacy television has increasingly come into question, there has also been a rise in online sports streaming services, including mainstream services like ESPN+ and niche-based services like FloSports.[3] Meanwhile, there has also been a relatively recent explosion in sports radio, with all-sports radio first taking hold in 1987 with the launch of New York City's WFAN and then quickly becoming a popular template in markets across the country.[4] Indeed, Jorge Mariscal comments that all-sports radio "spread like an unchecked virus" in the 1980s and 1990s as the industry deregulated and AM stations looked for new formats while music formats departed for FM frequencies.[5] Recent years, too, have seen the emergence of the podcasting medium and the creation of ever more sports-oriented podcasts.

As the number of sports broadcasting outlets has boomed over the last several decades, there has been an accompanying demand for content to fill all these new programming schedules. In particular, sports broadcasters have looked for cheap content to fill these open hours. While outlets have occasionally turned to sporting events without significant rights fees—see, for instance, ESPN's early programming schedules, full of niche sports like miniature golf—perhaps the most popular solution to this desire for inexpensive programming has been to turn to talk programming.[6] ESPN, for instance, has long filled its programming schedules with studio shows based around discussions of sports. The highlight show *SportsCenter,* for example, has been a fixture on its schedule since the channel's launch. Other sports television networks have adopted similar strategies. William Kunz notes, for instance, how sports leagues debuting their own cable channels in the 1990s and 2000s primarily relied on studio shows to fill their schedules.[7] He observes, for example, how the MLB Network scheduled hours and hours of the studio show *MLB Tonight* upon the channel's launch in 2009.[8] Relatedly, as the number of sports radio stations has exploded over the past few decades, sports talk formats have also formed the base of those schedules, with Mariscal commenting that sports talk had strong appeal "as a low-cost programming option."[9] As a case in point, as WFAN premiered the all-sports radio format in the late 1980s, Paul Gullifor argues its much-imitated "recipe for success" consisted of a shrewd combination of play-by-play coverage of local teams like the New York Mets and hours-upon-hours of talk programs such as the afternoon-drive show *Mike and the Mad Dog* (1989–2008).[10]

As countless hours of discussion-based shows have filled ever more hours of sports programming, broadcasters have deployed a wide variety of talk formats. *SportsCenter* and many other television imitators have, for instance, become known for recapping recent sporting events, mainly focusing on highlights. More recently, several sports television broadcasters have introduced morning sports talk shows, meant, like general interest morning shows *Good Morning America* (ABC, 1975–) and *Today* (NBC, 1952–), to help viewers start their day by casting a wide net in covering a diverse range of topics with a mixture of headlines and light analysis. A large number of other popular television studio shows, such as *First Take* and *Pardon the Interruption* (ESPN, 2001–), have instead focused on back-and-forth debates, while several others, like *The Rich Eisen Show* (2014–) and *The Dan Patrick Show* (1999–), are radio show simulcasts that mix analysis, debate, and guest interviews, while many others still act as shoulder programming in directly accompanying live game broadcasts. Meanwhile, there are also significant variations in focus. For example, shows on national broadcasters like ESPN and FS1 ostensibly attempt to cover the entire international sporting world. In contrast, shows on local and regional outlets, like the New England Sports Network (NESN) in New England and the MSG Network in the Mid-Atlantic, tend to focus more specifically on the teams in their local markets. Additionally, while some programs, like ESPN talk shows *NFL Live* (2002–) and *NBA Today* (2021–), emphasize a single sports league, others discuss topics from a wider variety of major sports. Sports radio shows and sports podcasts, too, employ a broad range of discussion-based formats. Some sports talk radio shows, for instance, are closely associated with audience call-in segments, in which listeners call in to the show and converse with the hosts. In contrast, others eschew call-in segments to instead focus on interviews with athletes and journalists. As in the case of sports television, too, many sports radio shows act as shoulder programming, and there are also variations in focus, both in terms of sport and in terms of the split between nationally syndicated coverage and local coverage.

Managerial sports talk, as a type of sports talk, is not a distinct genre of sports broadcasting that can be tidily slotted into the above breakdown of talk formats. Unlike the managerial sports film, then, managerial sports talk does not feature clear categorical boundaries. Rather, it can best be understood as a set of tendencies that frequently emerges across these many talk formats— a cluster of emphases, in other words, prone to appear everywhere from debate programs to morning shows to postgame recaps. More specifically, managerial sports talk can be understood as a set of tendencies centering on both administrators and the work they perform. To begin, this managerial streak has entailed a prominent place for managerial figures. For example, the performance of specific front office executives has become a common point of discussion during sports talk shows, and these same executives have also become frequent guests on these programs. In addition to the interest in current executives, former executives are also increasingly ubiquitous across a wide variety of sports talk programming, frequently being positioned as "ex-

66   CHAPTER TWO

perts" in administrative maneuvers. For example, ESPN's talk programming regularly features appearances from figures such as Bobby Marks, formerly an executive for the NBA's Brooklyn Nets, and Louis Riddick, formerly an executive for several NFL teams.

Next, sports talk's managerial streak has meant a conspicuous place for transactions, whether those transactions are completed, in-process, rumored, or purely imagined. Most noticeably, this interest in transactions has entailed ever-expanding coverage of events like free agency periods and trade deadlines. These transactional events do not just produce their own subcategories of talk programming—as in ESPN's occasional NBA free agency specials or the MLB Network's seasonal *Hot Stove* (2009–) morning show—but also are discussed in great depth within any number of other talk programs. A morning show like FS1's *First Things First* (2017–), for example, might sprinkle in segments about an MLB free agent signing or an NBA trade amid a range of other topics. A primary responsibility for former front office executives like Marks and Riddick is to add context to these events, explaining, for instance, how teams might fit player contracts under a league's salary cap (figure 2.1). Indeed, these personalities are frequently asked by talk show hosts to handle "front office questions" or to put "a general manager hat back on." The increasing coverage of transactions has also entailed a growing role for "insider" journalists who traffic almost solely in transactional news and speculation. These "insiders," like ESPN's Adam Schefter and Adrian Wojnarowski, Fox's Ken Rosenthal, NFL Network's Ian Rapoport, and Stadium's Shams Charania, have become some of the most well-known personalities for their respective networks. Rapoport, for example, can be found on NFL Network talk programming throughout the year, providing constant updates on items like contract negotiations and trade terms.

Finally, sports talk's managerial streak has entailed a great interest in player evaluation—a natural accompaniment to the increased interest in transactions. This interest is most clearly evident in the expanded coverage of events like entry drafts, pro days, and scouting combines, with much discussion centered around prospects' strengths, weaknesses, and overall potential to thrive as professionals. The expanded interest in player evaluation is also illustrated by the growing role for prospect evaluation "experts" like ESPN's Jonathan Givony and Todd McShay.[11] To that point, McShay has not just appeared regularly on the network's many outlets in the annual lead-up to the NFL draft but has also popped up on ESPN college football programming throughout the season, intermittently discussing players' NFL draft prospects. Notably, though, player evaluation is not limited to discussions of prospects, as commentators also constantly evaluate current professionals,

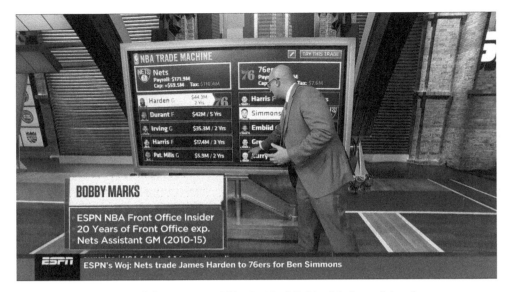

FIGURE 2.1: ESPN's "NBA Front Office Insider" Bobby Marks explains the financial details of an NBA trade during an episode of *NBA Today*.

assessing their recent play and future potential. For this chapter, it is particularly significant that the emphasis in these discussions is often financial, with player evaluations frequently judged through the lens of a player's contract (whether a player is, for instance, "living up" to the size of their contract) or their "trade value" (whether, for example, a player's recent poor play might harm the team's ability to trade them).

As suggested by these features, sports talk's managerial streak is most pronounced during the portions of the sporting calendar when transactions occur most frequently, as around drafts, league meetings, and trade deadlines. Of course, it would make sense that broadcasters are more likely to discuss transactions when there are more transactions to consider, but there is an additional broadcasting logic to this temporal rhythm. In brief, many transactions happen during leagues' off-seasons. During off-seasons, broadcasters are also without games from those leagues to either broadcast or discuss—a particularly pressing concern for broadcasters like the MLB Network or the NFL Network primarily devoted to a single league. Thus, sports talk programs looking for ways to stay connected to the major men's sports leagues—instead, it might be noted, of expanding their coverage of other subjects, including women's sports—are apt to feature extended discussions of transactional minutiae like contract negotiations, draft pick swaps, and so on. That said, managerial sports talk is hardly confined to lulls in the sporting calendar. As a case in point, amid the 2021 NBA Playoffs—ostensibly the climactic high point of the league's season—sports talk programs frequently pivoted away from discussions of those playoff games and turned instead to transactional topics. As an example of such a pivot, in the wake of the Philadelphia 76ers' exit from the playoffs, the future of Philadelphia player Ben Simmons became a frequent subject of conversation across a large number of sports talk programs, with many commentators suggesting it was time for the team to trade Simmons and, accordingly, going deep into his contract terms and potential trade partners. In fact, conversations about "fake trades" involving Simmons occasionally served as the lead topic on sports talk programs.

Notably, the interest in transactions and player evaluation also spreads into sports talk programming primarily concerned with gambling and fantasy sports. However, the interest in transactions and player evaluation manifests slightly differently in discussions of betting and fantasy. For instance, in gambling segments, commentators are apt to focus on how viewers can exploit knowledge about players and roster transactions for financial gain, perhaps turning insights about a team's off-season maneuvers into a smartly placed bet. In fantasy segments, meanwhile, commentators emphasize how knowledge of players and transactions can translate into success in fantasy competitions. For instance, ESPN's fantasy programming frequently connects contract negotiations and trades with fantasy scoring and rankings. Significantly, fantasy shows are also interested in transactions centered not around "real world" teams and leagues but rather around hypothetical fantasy scenarios—asking, for example, whether it might make sense for fantasy owners to add and drop certain players from their fantasy rosters. Here, the interest in managerial activities spreads to the audience's virtual administrative work, thus speaking to their ability to replicate many of the maneuvers that actual front office executives perform.

In summary, while not a distinct genre, managerial sports talk nonetheless features explicit overlapping attributes—entailing an interest in both administrative figures and the work they perform. However, how managerial sports talk approaches these figures and subjects has not yet been outlined. How, for instance, are transactions discussed? How are players evaluated? What is the expertise on offer from these past and present administrators? As I will argue in the next section, it is not just the personnel and subject matter—contract negotiations, trade rumors, and so forth—that define managerial sports talk, but also its values and rationalities; its ways of suggesting, in other words, how one should carry themselves in a sporting universe defined by its administrative operations.

Managerial Sports Talk's Financial Values

In probing the values and rationalities of managerial sports talk, it is helpful to start on the surface, paying attention to its linguistic tropes. Language, after all, is indicative of how people understand and describe the world around them. Given its overlapping attributes, it is unsurprising that managerial sports talk features a shared set of keywords. Commentators will often, for instance, employ a similar vocabulary in referring to transactional mechanics. Audiences must quickly come to learn, then, what is meant by terms like "cap space" (how much money a team has available to spend under a league's salary cap), "roster bonus" (a contractually defined payment that a player earns for being on a team's roster on a specific date), and "trade exception" (a sort of voucher that allows NBA teams to exceed the league's salary cap). While, as might be expected, much of the linguistic overlap within managerial sports talk is specific to the world of sports and, in particular, the nuances of its administrative operations, if one listens and watches sports talk with enough frequency, they might notice language from another realm also appearing with great regularity. More specifically, one might notice that these analyses of administrative minutiae are frequently discussed using terminology more typically associated with the world of investment and banking. Player transactions, for instance, are often discussed in terms of trade and free agent "markets" or "marketplaces." Relatedly, players are frequently described as "assets," "investments," and "stocks"—assets, investments, and stocks that, accordingly, can be "undervalued" or "overvalued." Indeed, broadcasters might even express a desire to "buy shares" in a player. On and on, the financial terminology goes—"blue-chip," "bullish," "bearish," "dealing," "hedging," "holding," "shorting," "going long on," and so on.

That managerial sports talk so regularly employs the language of investment and banking suggests a particular orientation to the world, with sport rhetorically collapsing into finance. This language highlights the ongoing fusing of sport and finance discussed in the introduction, with teams becoming popular financial investments and financially oriented owners turning to MBAs with backgrounds in consulting and finance to manage their teams. Noting, however, that sports talk borrows the lexicon of finance in discussing managerial maneuvers only gets us so far in analyzing the values and rationalities of managerial sports talk. To understand how this sport/finance entanglement functions, we need to explore how these terms are used and the meanings within—thereby coming to represent not just the importation of financial terminology into sports talk, but also with that terminology, the importation of financial *logics*. Such an inquiry quickly brings this analysis into conversation with the growing amount of scholarship around the concept of financialization. Financialization, in brief, is a term generally used to describe, as Philip Mader, Daniel Mertens, and Natascha van der Zwan write, the "vastly expanded role played by finance in contemporary politics, economy, and society."[12] As this broad definition suggests, scholarship around this concept is diverse in nature, including explorations of topics ranging from corporate ideology to state monetary policy. Particularly important for this chapter, though, are the analyses that have focused on what has been termed the "financialization of everyday life," and even more particularly, those that have emphasized "the adoption of 'financialized' subjectivities" in daily routines—noting, for instance, how the ubiquity of financial mechanisms like credit cards, mortgages, and student loans has not only further entwined individuals' lives with the workings of the financial industry, but also reshaped how individuals view the world.[13] Such scholarship is perhaps most famously exemplified by the work of sociologist Randy Martin. Martin argues that all manner of individuals—not just those in the financial world—are being offered the "invitation to live by finance."[14] As he elaborates, this invitation entails importing logics from financial markets into "all domains of life."[15] Similarly, Rob Aitken contends, "Those of us who have not often imagined our lives in relation to the world of high finance are now increasingly asked to make connections to finance, to rework ourselves as investors in our own lives."[16]

In documenting how financialized subjectivities are created and shaped, several scholars have emphasized the role of cultural texts. Unsurprisingly, a particular interest has been financial texts that offer relatively direct lessons on operating in an increasingly financialized society. In his analysis of the financialization of daily life, for instance, Martin closely analyzes texts like financial self-help books, advertisements for financial service firms, and financial education software. These sorts of texts, Martin argues, act as "primers" for financialization, both selling and teaching principles like risk management.[17] As another example, Daniel Fridman has examined the best-selling self-help texts of financial "guru" Robert Kiyosaki, suggesting these texts encourage readers to learn to "calculate as an investor" and, in turn, transform how they see the world—developing an "entrepreneurial spirit" that frees them to take risks and become responsible for their economic fates.[18] Into this category of analysis, one might also place examinations of financial television. Aaron Heresco, for instance, suggests that CNBC represents a full-throated embodiment of the financialization of American life—even becoming "a window into the soul of finance."[19] Accordingly, he writes, the outlet plays a crucial role in creating financialized subjects who embrace, for instance, a calculative rationality. In a related argument, Diane Cormany writes that financial news outlets, including CNBC, affectively align with financialization—prioritizing a sense of urgent movement that matches the financial industry's desire for constant churn.[20]

While it is not surprising that financial texts have been a primary focus of analysis for scholars interested in the widening spread of financial logics and values, one can also see financialization operating through cultural texts at a further remove from the financial industry. To that point, Max Haiven argues, "The financial sector influences and transforms culture and social life beyond its formal borders," elaborating that "traces and resonances of financialization" can be found "beyond the realm of banking, personal finance, economic discourse and other zones where we might expect to find it."[21] Indeed, Haiven has analyzed the influence of financialization in sites like the Pokémon franchise, which he argues acts as a tool for children to learn the ethos and skills required in a financialized society.[22] In a related vein, several literary scholars have noted connections between financialization and developments within contemporary literature, with Torsten Andreasen, Mikkel Krause Frantzen, and Frederik Tygstrup even highlighting the appearance of a "finance fiction" genre grappling with how to "describe the working of present-day financial activity and its influence on the way we live now."[23] Particularly significant for this chapter, several media scholars have also found traces of financialization in popular film and television. For instance, Laurie Ouellette and James Hay draw on Martin in arguing that television plays a vital role in the financialization of everyday life, acting as a "financial planner and advisor" in teaching viewers how to order their financial lives successfully.[24] Notably, they do not just emphasize the importance of financial news and analysis shows in offering these financial lessons but also highlight the significant role of reality television programs like *Wife Swap* (ABC/Paramount Network, 2004–2020) and game shows like *Deal or No Deal* (NBC/CNBC, 2005–2019).

Superficially, managerial sports talk may seem like an awkward fit alongside these other texts analyzed in the context of financialization, given that many of them are either about the world of finance or offer direct lessons to their audiences about how to thrive amid the conditions of financialization. Much of CNBC's programming, for instance, is touted as providing fairly straightforward financial advice. A show like *Fast Money* (2006–), for example, is billed as giving "you the information normally reserved for the Wall Street trading floor, enabling you to make decisions that can make you money," while *Mad Money* (2005–) is described as taking "you inside the mind of Jim Cramer, one of Wall Street's most respected and successful money managers, as he acts as your personal guide through the confusing jungle of Wall Street investing to help you make money." Even reality television programs and game shows, though at an ostensible remove from the day-to-day workings of the financial industry, can offer viewers relatively direct financial instruction. In analyzing *Wife Swap,* for instance, Ouellette and Hay dissect an episode in which it is suggested that a mother "unable to control her shopping impulses" learn from another mother who has a strict financial regimen.[25]

While managerial sports talk may not provide explicit advice to audiences about which stocks to buy or how to responsibly balance their household budgets, its adoption of financial language indicates it has become another site in which to examine the "traces and instantiations of the logic of finance where one would not have searched for them in the first place."[26] Indeed, such language points to managerial sports talk being an obvious sign of what Haiven refers to as "the expansion and infiltration of the themes, ideas, tropes, measurements, metaphors and influence" of finance "into spheres seemingly in no way related to the core operations of the financial economy."[27] How, though, this "expansion and infiltration" works—bringing not just the language of finance into sports talk but also its values and rationalities—needs further investigation. The rest of this section, then, will probe three specific clusters of financial vocabulary—centered around the language of investment, market movement, and risk management—that have emerged within managerial sports talk. An examination of these linguistic clusters indicates that the rhetorical collapse of sport/finance points to the deep embedding of financial *logics* within sports media. Accordingly, managerial sports talk is hardly an outlier among the aforementioned cultural texts. Instead, managerial sports talk becomes another critical site in which to document the ongoing financialization of culture and society.

Sport as "Investment"

To illustrate how managerial sports talk's financial terminology suggests a particular orientation to the world—a financialized orientation—one might start by looking more closely at the pervasiveness of the language of "investment" within managerial sports talk. Sports talk commentators often describe all manner of administrative minutiae—future draft picks, salary cap space, and so forth—using terms like "capital," "holdings," and "war chests." Particularly noticeable is how frequently players are termed "assets," "investments," and "stocks." Like assets, then, players are said to appreciate and depreciate in "value"—becoming relative "busts" or, as Thomas Oates notes in the context of NFL draft discourse, "bargains." Relatedly, then, teams might "buy low" on a player when their perceived value is higher than the "asking price" or "sell high" if it seems like their value may have peaked. Speaking to these sorts of discursive tropes, as the future of Ben Simmons became a frequent topic of conversation amid the 2021 NBA Playoffs, both Simmons and other NBA players were constantly referred to as "assets." For example, on ESPN's *Keyshawn, JWill & Zubin* podcast (2020–2021), co-host Keyshawn Johnson repeatedly called Simmons a desirable "asset" despite his playoff struggles. Simmons, Johnson opined, was "an asset that people would take." He later elaborated, putting himself in the position of the 76ers: "I've got an asset, and I can move that asset to get something in return." He continued, "It's not like the dude can't play basketball anymore. . . . You figure out whomever you can get for that asset that you have." On another ESPN program, *SportsCenter,* analyst Stephen A. Smith employed similar language in imploring the 76ers to trade Simmons, commenting, "What you need to do is use him to get viable assets, like [Golden State Warriors player] Andrew Wiggins." Meanwhile, on Spotify's *Ringer NBA Show* (2016–), commentator Wosny Lambre turned to this lexicon in suggesting that Simmons's poor playoff performances had harmed his value. "He's looking like a depressed asset right now," Lambre declared.

Unsurprisingly, investment is a central theme in the scholarly work examining the financialization of everyday life, with scholars pointing out the increasing role of investment products in many individuals' lives and the increasing hold of investment as a cultural imaginary. For instance, sociologist Gerald Davis argues, "In twenty-first-century America, investment became the dominant metaphor to understand the individual's place in society and a guide to making one's way in a new economy."[28] Referring to the United States as a "portfolio society," Davis elaborates that "investor-citizens" are increasingly tasked with managing diverse collections of financial assets—from 401(k) retirement accounts to 529 college savings plans to health savings accounts—and, accordingly, asked to view more and more of society through the lens of investment.[29] Even "friends, families, and neighborhoods," he contends, "are now 'social capital,' investments that might pay off down the road."[30] Fitting with such arguments, scholars have suggested that cultural texts evidence traces of this increasing call for individuals to view themselves as investors. One area of interest, for instance, has been the way the growing securitization of homes is both reflected and shaped by popular television. Hay, for example, documents the rise of what he terms "realty TV," which he defines as "a vein of Reality TV programs oriented toward the virtues, pleasures, and rewards of capitalizing on home improvement and investment."[31]

He details, for instance, how the cable channel HGTV, in tandem with the broader societal reconceptualization of home mortgages as financial assets, gradually reoriented its programming away from an emphasis on the home as a site of personal expression to instead frame it as a site of financial investment. In a related vein, Shawn Shimpach argues that within HGTV programming, "The home is slyly presented as a site of financialization, the place in which it pays to invest," noting, to that point, the frequent use of graphics detailing how much a house may have increased in value by way of a home improvement project.[32] With this context in mind, the ubiquitous language of investment within managerial sports talk can be understood as being part and parcel of this broader elevation of investment into the "dominant metaphor" for understanding society. Managerial sports talk beckons individuals to adapt the lens of investment further, viewing the world of sports, like so many other areas of society—education, housing, retirement, and such—as a site of speculation. Perhaps most obviously, discussions treating players as "assets" and "stocks" suggest that these individuals are not just athletes, but also financial resources—implying that players can, like investments, be purchased, held, and traded, all the while (hopefully) providing positive returns to the teams that control them. Indeed, the language of "control" is ubiquitous in sports talk, as in teams having "control" over their players while they are under contract. The language of "assets" and "stocks" also hints at a revised, financialized orientation toward the temporality of sport. As Carolyn Hardin summarizes, financialization is often said to reposition the future into the present. As an example of this "future-in-present temporality," Hardin examines the shift from traditional retirement pensions to 401(k) investment plans.[33] As she writes, 401(k) investment has meant "bringing the future time of retirement into the present," with workers constantly having to distribute and manage their retirement funds in the present.[34] A similar "future-in-present" orientation comes to bear when players are figured simultaneously as athletes and financial resources. That is to say, as players become speculative "assets," audiences are encouraged to be mindful of both a player's present performance on the playing surface and how that performance is affecting the player's future value. Under this logic, an excellent performance is not just exciting because it might provide aesthetic enjoyment or contribute to a team's victory but also because it may help the player appreciate in value and, in turn, facilitate a future transaction. Alternatively, poor performances—or injuries, personal strife, and the like—can be viewed as weakening a player's value and, in the process, limiting a team's future options. Indeed, this pattern is evident in the discourse around Simmons, with his playoff struggles continually filtered through the lens of his trade value. With such a lens in place, visions of the present and the future collapse into one another, blurring the distinction between.

If the language of "assets" and "investments" suggests that the sports world is full of athletes-cum-investments, it also implies that sport is replete with investors to manage all these athlete assets. Here, then, managerial sports talk's centering of administrators becomes significant. If athletes are figured as speculative financial assets, these administrative figures are typically positioned as the speculators seeking positive returns on the investments. To that point, as discussions of Ben Simmons began to fill sports talk amid the 2021 NBA Playoffs, commentary often turned to 76ers executive Daryl Morey and his responsibility to properly manage the Simmons asset. On *SportsCenter,* for instance, reporter Brian Windhorst declared that Morey needed "to protect [Simmons's] value." As the "market" for Simmons developed, Windhorst elaborated, Morey would "have to be very careful . . . not to show his hand and potentially give away [the team's] position." On the Philadelphia sports radio show *The Sports Bash with Mike Gill,* host Gill and guest Paul Hudrick also implored Morey to be cautious, with Hudrick suggesting Morey not "sell [Simmons] for pennies on a dollar while his value is at his absolute lowest." They expressed faith in Morey, however. Hudrick effusively commented, "Daryl Morey is one of the most creative executives we've ever seen in the NBA—the things he's done, the ways he's able to maneuver."

Managerial sports talk's suggestion that front-office executives act as the investors of the sports world hints at parallels with financial news media. In their analyses of CNBC programming, both Cormany and Heresco highlight the frequent references to and interviews with investors, CEOs, and other financiers. According to Heresco, the spotlighting of these investor figures "creates and perpetuates a culture of finance, one based on myths of heroic investors and rock-star financial performers who should be admired and emulated." Indeed, Heresco notes that in "idolizing these financial heroes," some CNBC programming even suggests "follow these individuals into investments."[35] There is a similar element of mythologization within managerial sports talk. As mentioned, executives are frequent guests within managerial sports talk and regular topics of conversation. Moreover, while the front offices of professional sports teams are, invariably, staffed by many employees, including scouts, data analysts, salary cap specialists, and a range of other personnel, part of the reason that many front-office executives have become well-known names among sports fans is that managerial sports talk frequently elides the role of all these front-office workers, preferring instead to equate the entire front office with specific executives. Indeed, much like star athletes, many executives are even discussed on a first-name basis. Thus, transactions and player evaluation are often discussed not as the activities of teams but rather as the activities of these seemingly all-powerful, decisive individuals. For example, on a 2019 episode of ESPN's basketball talk show *The Jump* (2016–2021), New Orleans Pelicans executive David Griffin was singled out for his "great work" during the league's offseason, while a celebratory discussion of the Oklahoma City Thunder's offseason maneuvers was framed around the activity of team executive Sam Presti. In fact, while the Thunder were discussed, the show—rather than using game highlights to emphasize the team's new and departed players—employed stock footage of Presti watching games from the stands and walking down stadium hallways (figure 2.2). Similarly, during a less laudatory discussion of the Houston Rockets' offseason, stock footage rolled of then-Rockets executive Morey sitting in courtside seats. Notably, Morey was never identified or mentioned in this discussion. Instead, viewers were meant to visually recognize Morey and connect him to the conversation. This centering of sport's administrators connects back, then, to the previous chapter, for just as managerial sports films elevate largely fictional administrators and their largely fictional administrative tasks, managerial sports talk glorifies real-world administrators and their real-world administrative tasks.

While managerial sports talk's lionization of executives may not lead to many suggestions that viewers directly follow these individuals into financial investments, this idolization nonetheless can be said to have a pedagogical function in shaping "investor-citizens." To that point, in analyzing the spread of financial logics across society, Haiven notes the increasing pervasiveness of financial role models:

> We are treated to a barrage of popular culture that lionizes the entrepreneurial investor. It is not only popular, franchised series like *Dragons' Den* or *The Apprentice* that celebrate ruthless, single-minded, fangs-bared avarice, nor the bemusing drug-addled, sex-crazed anti-heroes of the *Wolf of Wall Street* and his pack; it is also the canny antique-hunter, the shrewd house-flipper, the driven restaurateur, or the single-minded start-up genius of "reality" TV. All are different vantage points on a financialized Vitruvian Man willing to risk and leverage everything, and mobilize every ounce of ingenuity, daring, "social capital" and talent, towards realizing their privatized ambitions.[36]

The administrative idols of managerial sports talk can also be added to this list. As the discourse around Simmons indicates, an executive like Morey can

FIGURE 2.2: Footage of Oklahoma City Thunder executive Sam Presti backdrops a discussion of the Thunder's offseason during an episode of ESPN's *The Jump*.

quickly become a role model and, in particular, a role model for navigating a financialized society. As a case in point, one could further unpack Hudrick's effusive statement that Morey "is one of the most creative executives we've ever seen." As John Patrick Leary argues, "creative" has become a significant part of "the vocabulary of contemporary capitalism, able to link imagination, aesthetic practice, and religious faith in the pursuit of private gain," elaborating that the word can evocatively refer "to the work of forging new modes of production, new markets, and new products" while also retaining "a touch of artistry: the ingenuity, vision, and intuition to make things anew."[37] With that context in mind, Hudrick's effusive declaration can be understood as more than just general praise for Morey, as it also comes to represent a celebration of Morey's particular approach to a financialized world, suggesting, in Leary's terms, that idiosyncrasy can be transformed into an "economic asset."[38] Thus, for individuals looking to thrive in an investment-driven "portfolio society," there is an apparent lesson in this praise of Morey—suggesting economic success comes by way of originality. One can view, then, managerial sports talk not just as further ensconcing investment as the dominant metaphor for understanding the world but also offering investor exemplars to help audiences grapple with that transformation.

Sport as a "Market" in Motion

Dovetailing with investment language, managerial sports talk is also littered with references to "markets" and "marketplaces." Perhaps most prominently, there are "free agency markets" and "trade markets" across the major North American sports leagues, both of which are sometimes referred to either as "the open market," or even more briefly, "the market." In the NBA, too, there is a much-discussed "buyout market" that revolves around acquiring players who are "bought out" of their contracts. There are also smaller "markets" for specific "assets," including players, positions, and draft picks. For example, the contract status of Dallas Cowboys quarterback Dak Prescott was an ongoing topic across many sports talk programs for several years. In these conversations, "market" terminology was deployed in multiple senses. For one, commentators speculated on what would happen if Prescott entered the "free agency market" or the "open market." On *First Take,* for instance, analyst Marcellus Wiley rhetorically asked, "If Dak Prescott were to hit the free agent market, do you think a team would pay him the top-top of the market at the quarterback position?" Answering his own question, Wiley emphatically responded, "I do not." Commentators also discussed the more specific "market" for Prescott. On FS1's *Speak for Yourself* (2016–), for example, guest analyst Eric Mangini suggested Prescott's "market [would] go up" if he played well before entering free agency, while host Jason Whitlock posited that Prescott's lack of arm strength and accuracy was "hurting his market." Finally, such conversations often touched on the position-specific "quarterback market." On a different episode of *First Take,* for instance, analysts Domonique Foxworth and Max Kellerman debated whether Prescott's next contract would "set the market" for other quarterbacks and, in the process, discussed whether the quarterback market might be expanding too rapidly. Kellerman, offering a skeptical view, opined, "The market is irrationally exuberant in terms of quarterbacks—they are overvalued assets."

In considering how the "market" terminology further implants financial logics into sports talk—logics that add onto the already-mentioned logic of investment—it is particularly significant that these "markets" are constantly described as being on the move, as in Kellerman's "irrationally exuberant" comment. That is to say, like financial markets, sports "markets" are also said to vary in volume and to trend in particular directions. A sport's "free agency market," for instance, might grow increasingly "busy"—or even "overheated"—if there are lots of contracts signed. In contrast, a player's "market" might become "quiet" or "dry out" if interest in acquiring them dissipates. As an example of this language of market movement, the discourse surrounding Ben Simmons following the Philadelphia 76ers' elimination from the 2021 NBA Playoffs is again illustrative. As commentators discussed whether Simmons would be traded, conversations often returned to the state of Simmons's "market" and how that market would trend over the course of the coming months. On ESPN's *The Jump*, analyst Richard Jefferson expressed his fears that the "market" for Simmons would trend sharply down in the wake of his poor playoff performances. He mentioned, for instance, the efforts of Morey to publicly express confidence in Simmons and, in the process, prevent a "fire sale." As Jefferson elaborated, Morey's public statements (much like those, one might suggest, of a Treasury Secretary or chair of the Federal Reserve) were meant "to stop the market from crashing." Other commentators also suggested Simmons's "market" might have reached a low point but expressed optimism it would rebound. For example, on his eponymous sports talk show (2018–) within Spotify's *Ringer* podcast network, commentator Ryen Russillo offered his opinion that there remained a "market" for Simmons and that this market would strengthen over time, with more and more teams becoming interested in Simmons in the coming months. "There is a market for [Simmons], and the market will grow," Russillo stated. "It will be stronger." Similarly, on Spotify's *The Bill Simmons Podcast* (2015–), guest commentator Joe House opined that Simmons was hardly a "diminishing asset." He continued, "The NBA market is a dynamic market. It's not a fixed market—it changes on a weekly basis, it changes on nearly a daily basis." With that in mind, House urged Morey to "sit tight and see how the league develops" with the expectation that "buyers" for Simmons would eventually emerge.

Such talk of market movement, though, is hardly limited to discussions of the NBA. Ahead of the annual NFL draft, for instance, commentators frequently invoke the idea of a shifting market. As Oates notes in his examination of NFL draft media, for example, NFL draft coverage often returns to "talk of a prospect's rising or falling 'stock'"—the widely used term "draft stock" indicating how desired a player is at any given moment.[39] As a case in point, in the months before the 2021 NFL Draft, the "market" for quarterback Justin Fields was a frequent topic of conversation, with a particular area of interest being the way his "draft stock" may have cooled after the conclusion of the college season. Indeed, several talk shows ran segments with chyrons like, "Surprised Justin Fields' draft stock has fallen?" (*Speak for Yourself*), "Up and Down Draft Stock: Justin Fields" (CBS Sports HQ), and "Where should Justin Fields' stock be right now?" (*First Take*) (figure 2.3). As such chyrons indicate, discussions literally equated Fields's future with the stock market, carefully observing whether demand for Fields might be trending up

FIGURE 2.3: *Undisputed* (FS1) hosts Shannon Sharpe and Skip Bayless debate the status of Justin Fields's "draft stock."

or trending down. On *First Take,* for instance, Stephen A. Smith suggested Fields's "stock has not elevated—it's dissipated, albeit to a small degree, in some people's eyes." He continued, "It's . . . going in the wrong direction."

In analyzing how this language of market movement points to a financial logic, the idea of a financialized temporality is again relevant. As mentioned in the previous section, financialization has often been said to reorganize time by collapsing the future and the present, as exemplified by the increasing importance of financial devices like futures contracts. This, however, is not the only way financialization has been argued to alter time. As Fabian Muniesa and Liliana Doganova suggest, financialization is also said to reflect the way that the financial industry is relentlessly "focused on the present, and associated with the terminology of speed, acceleration, instant trading, short-termism, or 'quarterly capitalism.'"[40] To that point, in their analyses of CNBC, both Heresco and Cormany emphasize how the finance industry's emphasis on short-termism and speed becomes a prevailing logic within the channel's programming. Heresco notes, for example, how CNBC continually promotes its coverage as being "real-time."[41] These frequent references to liveness, he argues, connect to the temporal logics of finance capital by signaling the unceasing nature of financial markets—communicating that significant financial events are constantly in motion and that being even seconds behind the latest developments could mean losing out on potential profits (or avoiding possible losses). Heresco notes, too, that the CNBC coverage is both visually and aurally dense, as the screen is constantly loaded with information-rich graphics and the soundscape cluttered with music, sound effects, and other ambient noise. This density, he argues, dovetails with the emphasis on liveness—further fostering the sense of a fast-paced, interconnected world that demands constant attention if one is to find financial success. Cormany, too, highlights both CNBC's liveness and its dense "collages" of visual and aural elements.[42] In turn, she also links the "urgency" fostered by these textual cues to the shaping of a financialized subject "invested in second-by-second movement."[43] She summarizes, "Operating at this pace is required of viewers who aspire to keep up with—and therefore succeed within—an ever-moving market."[44]

Managerial sports talk is absent second-to-second coverage of the actual stock market, of course. Nonetheless, as the rhetorical emphasis on market movement suggests, sports talk shares with CNBC a similar relationship to time. Like CNBC, managerial sports talk is often infused with a strong sense of immediacy. As mentioned, sports talk programs obsess over perceived "market" fluctuations—closely tracking, for instance, how a prospect's "draft stock" might change from day to day or, around events like pro days and scouting combines, even hour to hour or minute to minute. Managerial sports talk's rhetorical choices are only the tip of the iceberg, though, in signaling this immediacy. Sports talk television, for example, is often accompanied by graphics that signal the constant, interconnected motion of the sporting world. Most notably, crawling tickers, like ESPN's "BottomLine" graphics, often fill the lower-most portion of the screen, constantly scrolling through sports scores and news. These sorts of graphics immediately recall the stock tickers that are omnipresent on financial news channels like CNBC and Fox Business. Heresco notes the temporal importance of these stock tickers, arguing that CNBC's stock crawl is "not just a news device, but also serves as a metronome of the market—a way to keep the market rhythm and indicate a global co-presence."[45] One could make much the same argument of the sports tickers that accompany most sports talk programming. No matter what programming is being showcased on sports television, the crawling tickers set a constant pace for sports television—signaling that the programming at hand is immersed within a much wider sporting world where games, transactions, and other events are constantly happening.

This sense of urgency is not isolated to the scrolling tickers, either. Managerial sports talk is often programmed around calendar-based events like trade deadlines (dates by which trades must be completed) and the starts of free agency periods (when free agents are first able to negotiate with new

FIGURE 2.4: ESPN's Adrian Wojnarowski and Zach Lowe discuss the NBA trade deadline as a countdown clock looms behind them.

teams). When these events draw near, sports talk programming works to emphasize the immediacy of these timelines. As a case in point, in advance of the NBA's 2019 trade deadline, ESPN broadcast a half-hour special featuring Wojnarowski and fellow NBA journalist Zach Lowe. As the two reporters discussed both potential trades and already-completed trades, a ticking clock loomed on a giant screen behind them, counting down the seconds until the league would cut off trading activity—much like, it might be noted, CNBC programming has long highlighted the closing bell of the New York Stock Exchange (figure 2.4). Notably, too, the special drew extra attention to its liveness, with a red box containing the word "live" frequently popping into the telecast. Sports radio and television, of course, are closely associated with liveness, with game coverage, in particular, dependent on the sense that audiences are watching events happening at the same time as they unfold in actuality. As Michael Real comments, "For sports fans, liveness matters," and, to that point, Real mentions the significant discrepancies in Olympics television ratings between events aired live and those aired on delay.[46] Sports talk, however, is generally less associated with liveness. Indeed, part of the appeal of many sports talk programs is that they can be consumed on viewers' own schedules, as evidenced by the emergence of sports-related podcasts. As this trade deadline special indicates, though, managerial sports talk occasionally embraces the connotations of liveness.

As mentioned above, both Cormany and Heresco call attention to the great emphasis CNBC places on its liveness, with Heresco noting "references to being 'live' and 'real-time' permeate CNBC's discourses and representations of the market."[47] Drawing on television scholars who have explored television's use of liveness, like Jane Feuer, Cormany and Heresco suggest that televisual liveness carries specific associations, including the sense of audience co-presence with the broadcaster and the possibility of interruption. Undoubtedly, programming like Lowe and Wojnarowski's trade deadline special is meant to take advantage of these associations, with many viewers carrying the expectation that news of a trade could be broken at any moment. There is, though, a broader significance to this liveness in the context of financialization. As Heresco and Cormany both write, the emphasis on liveness signals that viewers are located in the here and now, or as Cormany describes it, "part of the action."[48] Accordingly, then, the suggestion is that viewers cannot afford to follow the market on delay, for as Heresco notes, "getting financial news late means any opportunity to take advantage of current events is lost."[49] The references to liveness within managerial sports can be understood similarly—urgently reiterating the need for audiences to be immersed in the moment. While most sports talk audiences do not need to worry about losing money if they hear news of a breaking trade a few minutes or a few hours late (unless, of course, they have a bet or fantasy team to fret over), the programming nonetheless uses the cues to liveness to stoke that same vigilance—suggesting that the world of sport also requires constant attention.

Another televisual element that contributes to the immediacy of managerial sports talk television and financial media is the ubiquity of screens. Examining CNBC, Heresco comments, "It is difficult not to notice the plethora of screens that appear in the televisual frame: the hosts have laptops and smartphones, there is a big-screen serving as the backdrop for several programs, market flashes and updates often take place near multiple screens, and the act of investing is presented as depending on ubiquitous access to a screen of one sort or another."[50] The same might be said of managerial sports talk television. Sports talk sets are, like the sets of CNBC, laced with screens. To that point, in 2014, ESPN unveiled a new $125 million facility to host several of its studio shows. As part of the unveiling, ESPN touted the vast number of screens in the building, promoting, for instance, the fact that the *SportsCenter* set contained 114 monitors, including a "multidimensional display wall comprised of 56 monitors."[51] It is not just that a plethora of screens backdrops managerial sports talk, but also, like financial media, that the commentators bring their own mobile devices into the

84   CHAPTER TWO

frame. As mentioned in the introduction, this tendency is most typified by breaking news reporters like Schefter and Wojnarowski. Particularly around events like trade deadlines, these reporters frequently glance at and use their phones—tapping away silently while other commentators continue to talk. That reporters like Schefter are frequently more engaged with their phones than their co-hosts signals they are following—and perhaps shaping—the latest transactional news. As sports media reporter Bryan Curtis observes, this is a relatively recent trend. He comments, "Once upon a time, the sight of Adam Schefter madly punching the keys of his [mobile device] was one of the strangest things you could see on a sports studio show."[52] As Curtis argues, though, this sight has now become common, if not expected, for influential reporters like Schefter and Wojnarowski.

In analyzing CNBC, Heresco suggests the ubiquity of screens "contributes to an emphasis on the real-time and the global," as the screens come to represent "worldwide telepresence at instantaneous speed."[53] The ubiquity of screens in sports talk programming can be read similarly. As *SportsCenter*'s hosts provide details on the latest sporting news, monitors in the background show various sporting events. The implicit message is that *SportsCenter* sits atop a broader world of sports defined by continual action. When Schefter visibly interacts with his phone, meanwhile, he indicates that he has immediate access to events happening across the NFL. This pairs with the recurring emphasis on liveness. That is to say, in communicating that he is locked into happenings across the league, Schefter signals that important events are constantly in motion—suggesting not just that he has access to these events but that he *needs* access to these events. If he discarded his phone, in other words, he would be perilously out of the loop. Again and again, Heresco argues, CNBC "helps represent a world in which the knowledge of the farthest reaches of the world and the smallest fractions of a second are both accessible and financially necessary."[54] As the above examples indicate, managerial sports talk often works similarly—repeatedly implying that the world of sport, like investment and banking, is defined by a rapid pace in which one must continually track second-by-second movement. In more and more parts of everyday life, to look away is to fall behind.

Sport as "Risk and Reward"

Fitting with the idea of sport being a world of speculative investment— where assets are closely managed, and market fluctuations are ceaselessly monitored—sports talk is also replete with the language of "risk and reward." Transactions, for instance, are often described as either being "dangerous" or "safe." They may require, then, performing a "cost-benefit analysis" in which executives might weigh, for example, the "hidden cost" in offering a player a new contract or the "opportunity cost" in passing on a possible trade. The language of "risk and reward" is particularly pervasive in player evaluations, especially in programming that surrounds entry drafts. For example, Oates observes NFL draft coverage, in assigning value to college prospects, often labels certain prospects as "risky."[55] Building on Oates's observations, it can also be noted that draft evaluations are frequently discussed in terms of "volatility," "unpredictability," and "unknowns," as prospective players might be referred to as "unknown quantities" or "complete unknowns." Teams, then, attempt to figure out how "unknowns" will, in the parlance of draft experts, "translate" to the professional level. Relatedly, too, the language of betting is pervasive within managerial sports talk, as front office executives are frequently described as "taking gambles," buying "lottery tickets," and "hedging bets"—all in the hopes of achieving significant "payoffs."

As Martin and other scholars have argued, risk management is a central component of the financialization of everyday life. Martin, for instance, argues that financialization "insinuates an orientation toward accounting and risk management into all domains of life."[56] Dovetailing with the increasing role of investment in individuals' everyday lives, scholars like Martin point, for example, to households having to constantly evaluate the risks involved in taking on debts to pay for education, housing, medical services, and other needs. This increasing importance of risk management in everyday life is, in turn, frequently linked to neoliberalism and a broader "risk shift" that has seen risks previously borne by states and institutions passed on to individuals.[57] Notably, while individuals' absorption of risk means they must work to minimize their exposure to financial loss—among other calamities—this risk is not always framed as something to be minimized. Instead, financialization has also often meant treating risk as an opportunity—with uncertainty being something individuals might capitalize upon to "secure their future wealth and well-being."[58] With this context in mind, it might be suggested that—as in the case of investment and market movement—managerial sports talk not only borrows the financially oriented language of risk but also embraces this financialized *approach* to risk. More specifically, it might be suggested that sports talk fosters a financialized logic in which, as Paul Langley comments amid the rise of everyday investment, an individual "embraces financial market risk, deploys various calculative measures of risk/reward . . . and manages risk through portfolio diversification."[59]

Beginning the analysis with the first part of Langley's statement—that financialized individuals are meant to embrace risk—Langley adds helpful context in noting that earlier money management models based on thrift and insurance primarily aimed to minimize risk. However, the move toward investment products like mutual funds in recent decades has come with a new orientation toward risk, viewing it as something that can help maximize returns. This logic—in which a healthy appetite for risk is essential to financial success—is often present in managerial sports talk. When players, for instance, are evaluated in terms of risk and uncertainty, there is typically some sort of judgment attached. In some cases, commentators will disavow risk. Players, for example, might be determined to be too risky—their performances or personalities deemed, perhaps, too "erratic," "inconsistent," or "unpredictable." Executives, then, will be praised as gravitating toward "proven commodities" without these risks. However, risk is not always something to be avoided within managerial sports talk. Rather, executives are often praised for executing "high-risk, high-reward" moves—embracing the same volatility eschewed by others. Relatedly, executives might be praised for "betting everything" or "going all in"—trading away, for instance, a number of their future "assets" in return for a player with a high "upside." One term that arises particularly frequently is "aggression," with that word having come to signify risk-taking behavior. For instance, during the NFL's 2021 offseason, a frequent topic of conversation was a trade between the Detroit Lions and the Los Angeles Rams. In exchange for quarterback Jared Goff and several high draft picks, the Lions sent quarterback Matthew Stafford to the Rams. As commentators noted, this trade represented just the latest instance of the Rams' longer-term strategy of taking significant risks in trading away future draft picks. Although some analysts denounced this strategy as short-sighted, this "aggressiveness" represented a wise choice for other commentators. On *The Herd with Colin Cowherd* (ESPN/Fox Sports, 2004–), co-host Joy Taylor declared, "I love how the Rams do business—I love that they are aggressive." Similarly, on *PFT Live* (NBC Sports, 2015–), co-host Chris Simms said of the Rams, "I love them because they are aggressive as hell—they really are," before praising the team for constantly asking, "how are we going to make a move to win the Super Bowl"—even if it might occasionally put them in a "tough spot." He continued, "I love that aspect about them."

Poker references like "going all in" are not unusual within sports talk. In poker, risk taking is necessary if a player is going to win. Still, that risk must also be carefully managed, with a player constantly assessing the pitfalls and the potential rewards of any given move. In sports talk, too, risk is an opportunity, but also one that must be appropriately evaluated. Any "aggressiveness," in other words, must be a calculated aggressiveness. This pertains, then, to Langley's second point about the investor subject's need to shrewdly perform risk/reward calculations—welcoming risk into their life to secure their future, but also responsibly managing that risk. As an example of sports talk's emphasis on carefully calculating risk, one can look to any number of television studio shows in which executives are praised for maneuvers that reduce uncertainty, whether that might mean trading for extra draft picks or renegotiating a contract on more favorable terms, and conversely lambasted for exposing themselves to unnecessary risk, whether that might mean signing an injury-prone player or trading for an inconsistent performer. The ongoing discourse around Cowboys quarterback Dak Prescott is indicative. On FS1's *Speak for Yourself,* Emmanuel Acho, Bucky Brooks, and Marcellus Wiley debated the contract Prescott eventually signed with the Cowboys in advance of the league's free agency period. In Langley's terms, the conversation repeatedly circled back to "calculative measures of risk/reward"—assessments, in other words, of the prudence of the risks involved in the contract negotiation. Acho, beginning the conversation, criticized the "fiscal responsibility" of the Cowboys and team owner/general manager Jerry Jones, taking them to task for negotiating against themselves and extending Prescott's contract before he hit the "open market." Responding, Wiley defended the Cowboys and Jones, stating it was too big of a "risk"—an "unnecessary risk," he elaborated—for the team to let Prescott enter free agency, perhaps leaving them with an "unknown" prospect at the position. Acho, in turn, countered against the claim that this would be an "unnecessary risk." He stated, "The Cowboys were not going to take a risk—they were going to take a calculated cost." He emphasized again, "It would not have been a risk—it would have been a calculated cost." References to "calculations" across managerial sports talk also point to the increasing place of quantitative metrics within the managerial discourse—a phenomenon to be covered in more depth in the next chapter.

As Langley suggests, a primary way that investor subjects are expected to address risk responsibly is by investing in a diverse "portfolio" of assets—the basic idea being that risk can be rationally managed by spreading it across a range of different asset types. Again, this logic is ensconced within sports talk. Executives are often praised, for example, for accumulating a bevy of different "resources"—collecting assortments of young players, veterans, draft picks, and so forth. Alternatively, while they might be praised for a certain level of "aggression," they might also be condemned for extending that aggression too far and "putting all their eggs in one basket"—a saying often used as shorthand for a non-diversified portfolio—in signing a player to a large contract that limits their "flexibility," or trading away an excessive number of their "assets." To that last point, if the discourse around the Rams' trade for Matthew Stafford indicated the potential value in being "aggressive" in taking risks, the discourse around an earlier NFL transaction, a 2019 trade between the Houston Texans and the Miami Dolphins, emphasized the potential pitfalls of aggressive maneuvering and, in particular, the danger in concentrating one's risk in just one "asset." In that trade, the Dolphins sent offensive lineman Laremy Tunsil to the Houston Texans in exchange for several high draft picks. On CBS Sports's *Pick Six* podcast (2017–), co-host Sean Wagner-McGough took issue with the Texans' decision making, arguing that the team was "flushing their future down the drain." Mentioning the poor outcomes of previous trades in which teams had given up multiple high picks in exchange for a single player, he opined, "The lesson here is that it rarely works out," later adding, "It's just the worst type of process." His co-host, Will Brinson, vehemently agreed. "You cannot give up these kinds of picks—not for one player," he stated. "It's out of control." Similarly, on the NFL Network's *NFL Total Access* (2003–), reporter Jim Trotter suggested the decision of Texans acting general manager Bill O'Brien to trade so many draft picks for Tunsil reeked of "desperation." He contrasted O'Brien's maneuvers with those of Seattle Seahawks executive Jon Schneider, whom Trotter suggested was smartly spreading money around to several key players and building up "ammunition" in acquiring additional draft picks. Rapoport, also featuring on the show, used similarly positive martial language in noting that the Dolphins, in trading away Tunsil, were building up "an incredible amount of artillery." Meanwhile, on the NBC Sports podcast *Chris Simms Unbuttoned* (2019–), even Simms—who emphatically praised the Rams' aggressiveness in trading for Stafford—criticized the Texans, agreeing with his co-host Ahmed Fareed's contention that the Texans had "really compromised their future."

We arrive, then, at a final tally of the financial logics of managerial sports talk. Laced throughout managerial sports talk is a sense that the world of sport can best be understood as a site of investment—a site, in other words, in which financial resources are speculatively acquired and managed, all in the hope of eventual gains. Aligning with this worldview is a complementary logic that understands the world of sport as a market constantly in motion, where the values of sport's financial resources are continually in flux and, accordingly, demand constant attention. Finally, managerial sports talk positions sport as a site of risk and, even more specifically, as a site where risk must be embraced but also carefully calculated and balanced. With all these attributes in mind, managerial sports talk clearly represents another site where one can see "the expansion and infiltration of the themes, ideas, tropes, measurements, metaphors and influence" of finance "into spheres seemingly in no way related to the core operations of the financial economy."[60] Within the world of sports talk, to adopt a managerial lens on sport—focusing on sport's bureaucrats and their administrative work and, in the process, viewing the world of sport through the perspectives of these administrators—is, in short, to also adopt a financial lens on sport.

Given the primacy of sports media in American culture, this importation of financial logics into the popular sports talk genre is hardly insignificant. The pervasiveness of these logics not only points to just how far the creep of financial "themes, ideas, tropes," and such has spread but also begins to demonstrate how exactly these financial values and rationalities have propagated beyond the realm of finance. One can quickly see, for instance, how sports talk, as a form of popular entertainment, makes financial rationalities fun and exciting—transforming a principle like risk management into a visually rich, fast-paced subject of conversation. However, to go beyond these broad observations, it is necessary to continue grappling with what it means for financial logics to have taken hold within this particular site and, in turn, to probe further what this specific convergence—the close entanglement, in other words, of financialization and managerial sports media—can indicate about the ideological consequences of sports media's managerial fixation.

A Recurring Dream

In the previous chapter, I suggested that narrative sports films have recently updated the genre's traditional formulas by valorizing administrators and turning the "Athletic American Dream" into a "Managerial American Dream." As the above examples indicate, managerial sports films like *Moneyball* (2011) and *Draft Day* (2014) are hardly the only sports media texts to foreground administrators and managerial work. Within the confines of managerial sports talk, administrators are stars, and their daily administrative tasks are the subject of impassioned arguments. Significantly, though, managerial sports talk does not just extend the sports film's tendency to elevate administrators but also, in the process, extends its racialized, gendered project of reasserting the masculinity and agency of white men. As mentioned in the prior chapter, the "Managerial American Dream" has continued—with new wrinkles—the sports film's traditional project of remasculinizing straight white men in the face of perceived threats to their status, suggesting that front-office work offers them access to a newly fulfilling version of white-collar masculinity. In much the same way, managerial sports talk positions administrative work as a site where white men, in particular, can assert authority. In this case, though, it is the financial logics outlined above that fuel this project, as these logics both connect administrative work to

90   CHAPTER TWO

broader reconfigurations in hegemonic masculinity and foster a racialized approach to sport positioning athletes as manipulatable assets.

The argument that managerial sports talk works to reinforce white hegemonic masculinity might appear rather unintuitive at first, given the conventional gender dynamics of sports media, thereby recalling the analysis offered in the previous chapter. As detailed in that chapter, the sports film—much like other forms of sports media—has typically equated normative masculinity with a hyperphysicality embodied by the genre's athlete protagonists. Managerial sports films, on the other hand, have run counter to this history in featuring protagonists more at home in a conference room than on a field. In a similar vein, one might observe how the centering of executives within managerial sports talk has entailed a comparable pivot away from the physicality of the playing surface and, accordingly, a decentering of traditional traits like "violence" and "bodily strength." Indeed, sports talk's discussions of executives deemphasize physical attributes not only in terms of their subject matter—highlighting the administrative work of salary cap management, for example—but also in terms of how these discussions are presented, particularly on television. One might draw attention, for instance, to the many television graphics that feature executives. In these sorts of graphics, there are none of the action shots more commonly associated with sports photography that highlight the body in motion. Instead, these executive-laden visuals primarily turn to static poses or simple headshots. Take, for example, a simple graphic that ESPN's *NFL Live* used to complement a discussion of Washington Commanders executive Martin Mayhew. As in so many other similar graphics, this graphic featured a photo of a standing, stationary Mayhew completely devoid of any suggestion of movement. Relatedly, one can recall the B-roll that accompanied *The Jump*'s extended discussion of NBA executives Sam Presti and Daryl Morey in which the executives are shown stolidly watching games from the stands—a significant departure from the action-oriented B-roll typically used in sports television. The appearance of executives in these sorts of visuals is worth highlighting, too. As in managerial sports films, executives on sports television are almost always shown in business attire that hides the contours of their bodies—a stark contrast, of course, to the hypervisibility of the athletic body so common within sports television.

All that said, it again needs to be emphasized that hegemonic masculinity constantly shifts in response to cultural and societal change. To that point, the last chapter highlighted how hegemonic masculinity has adjusted to the growth of the "administrative sector" and white-collar work. Here, it can be added that hegemonic masculinity has also adapted to changes related to the growing importance of finance. More specifically, it has reconfigured around the same sorts of financial logics increasingly demanded elsewhere in society. Films that have depicted the financial industry are perhaps the clearest evidence of this reconfiguration. Kate MacLean argues that Hollywood films traditionally cast financiers—and their financial rationalities—as villainous, as exemplified by *It's a Wonderful Life* (1946) "chastising the cold calculations" of banker Henry Potter.[61] As financialization took hold, though, these depictions began to shift. MacLean observes, for instance, the ambivalence around characters like investor Gordon Gekko in *Wall Street* (1987). Characters like Gekko, MacLean writes, may have been treated with some skepticism, but they were also presented with a certain degree of awe, if not glamor. Indeed, in an ethnographic examination of the hedge fund industry, Megan Tobias Neely describes how in the 1980s "bold and aggressive" financiers like Gekko became not just "media icons" but also cultural "ideals."[62] As MacLean and Neely further explain, the gradual elevation of these figures has much to say about the shifting contours of hegemonic masculinity, with a character like Gekko even standing in as a new "archetype of masculinity."[63] To that point, MacLean details how normative masculinity has long been associated with risk taking. However, what has been conceived of risk—and how it should be controlled—has changed with time, and with characters like Gekko, one sees a martial sense of risk—risking one's life in battle, for instance—de-emphasized in popular culture in favor of a financial one. In many of these financial films, then, financiers become "the inheritors of the hegemonic masculinity associated with heroism and warfare."[64]

As sports talk has increasingly centered on financial logics, then, it has both reflected and driven these broader shifts in hegemonic masculinity. The executives of managerial sports talk may be depicted without physical glory, but like the "Financial Alpha Males" of the financial film, they are positioned as impressively attuned to the market's rhythms and primed to act accordingly. Indeed, as the sections above documented, within managerial sports talk, sports management is *defined* by these qualities. Thus, executives may not be risking their bodies on the field of play, but they are nonetheless framed in line with the "trope of the 'warrior' as the person who not only takes risks, but can control danger"—taking and controlling those risks, of course, from the front office.[65] On that note, one might observe that there is another relevant convergence here between managerial sports talk and financial media. In examining CNBC's place within financialization, Heresco notes the preponderance of sporting references within the channel's programming. He quotes, for instance, commentators discussing whether to "play" a stock or stay "on the sidelines."[66] As Heresco also mentions, the opening titles of the

CNBC program *Mad Money* even feature host Jim Cramer exhorting viewers, "You need to get in the game!" In a separate analysis of *Mad Money,* Gonen Dori-Hacohen and Timothy White also highlight this commingling of sport and finance, observing that Cramer frequently incorporates references to sports into his program.[67] As Heresco notes, the intersection of sport and finance does more than just work to make finance appear fun and entertaining. Rather, it also works to further connect finance to qualities like "aggression and competition."[68] Significantly, then, as Dori-Hacohen and White argue, the juxtaposition of sport and finance serves "to reinforce each field's masculinity and essence (winning)," helping to further cast *Mad Money* as a masculine realm that "contributes to, and resonates with, the larger masculine financial world."[69] In considering the financial logics of managerial sports talk, one might flip this equation around—positing that the links to a financialized worldview heavy on opportunism and risk taking further buttress managerial sports talk's associations with hegemonic masculinity even as its discourse frequently casts qualities like strength, violence, and such as incidental.

In examining the gender dynamics of managerial sports talk, it is also important to note that financial masculinity has itself changed over the past few decades, particularly in response to the financial crisis of 2007–2008. More specifically, books like *Flash Boys* and films like *Margin Call* (2011) have suggested that financial sprawl has become so complex—and so potentially disastrous—that it requires newly technical approaches. Indeed, *Margin Call* makes one of its Wall Street protagonists a rocket scientist–turned banker with a Ph.D. from MIT. Again, then, risk's entwinement with hegemonic masculinity evolves, with technical risk management newly ascendant relative to the "bulldozer mentality" seen in the earlier depictions of the "Financial Alpha Male."[70] To that same point, James Brassett and Frederic Heine suggest that "financial masculinity" has increasingly intersected with what scholars have termed "geek masculinity."[71] As mentioned in the introduction, culture has increasingly emphasized an "alternate" form of masculinity revolving around the figure of the geek. Discussing the contours of this geek masculinity, Anastasia Salter and Bridget Blodgett explain:

> It is still seen as being oppositional to femininity, but instead of physical strength and weakness the distinction is based upon intellectual ability. The geek hypermasculine ideal is found in Batman, not Superman: while physical prowess is still lauded and demonstrated, intellectual achievement, technical mastery, and other skills are perhaps even more important.[72]

Salter and Blodgett suggest this increasingly ubiquitous geek masculinity, rather than undercutting hegemonic masculinity by, for instance, destabilizing gender binaries or subverting gender-based hierarchies, instead represents an "evolution of hegemonic masculinity"—reformulating it, in other words, also to include qualities associated with geekdom that have traditionally been figured as "un-masculine," like technical expertise.[73] This sort of "evolution" is on clear display in a film like *Margin Call,* as a "hypertechnical expertise" based around intelligence and educational credentials displaces prior forms of financial mastery.[74]

While there are traces of this waxing financial/geek masculinity in the managerial sports film—witness, for instance, the rising fortunes of the Yale-educated, mathematically inclined character of Peter Brand in *Moneyball*—this new ideal becomes particularly pronounced in managerial sports talk. As sports talk programming has increasingly emphasized financial logics, qualities like "intellectual achievement" and "technical mastery" have taken on new prominence, with commentators, for instance, implicitly granted authority based on their intricate knowledge of baroque items like collective bargaining agreements. Indeed, administrative work is often discussed in terms of its complexity, as in a *Lowe Post* podcast (ESPN, 2014–) episode in which Marks described a potential trade of Brooklyn Nets guard Kyrie Irving as "complicated" given the intricacies of the NBA salary cap and then joked about needing to give listeners an extended "lesson" on the base year compensation rule within the NBA's collective bargaining agreement and how he would require a white board and graphs to fully explain the complexity. Moreover, the primary icons of managerial sports talk—executives like Morey—are not just implicitly positioned as the rare individuals able to adapt to this complexity but are also explicitly discussed in terms of their intellectual savvy, with their educational and occupational backgrounds even becoming fodder for conversation. The spotlighting of team executives like Morey establishes, in particular, clear parallels with Heather Mendick et al.'s arguments that popular culture has increasingly centered "geek entrepreneurs" like the fictional inventor-cum-superhero Tony Stark—a centering, they suggest in a similar vein as Salter and Blodgett, that has reconfigured the outlines of hegemonic masculinity.[75] Executives are often framed much like these geek entrepreneurs—praised, for instance, for their "genius" and "disruptive innovation." One recalls, for example, the Philadelphia talk radio host valorizing Morey for his "creative" maneuvering. It is notable, too, how the idealized masculinity laced throughout managerial sports talk perpetuates unequal gender relations. Like most other realms of sports media, managerial sports talk is a space primarily reserved for men, with women often either excluded or positioned as hosts and moderators rather than as analysts.[76] The underlying suggestion throughout managerial sports talk, then, is that the financial, technical expertise admired within managerial sports talk is primarily reserved for men. It is very possible to conclude, then, much as Salter and Blodgett do in analyzing depictions of geekdom, that this discourse reinforces cultural beliefs that subjects like sports finance are unfit for women.

This broader reconfiguration of hegemonic masculinity—with attributes like technical mastery joining, or perhaps supplanting, traditionally normative qualities like physicality—sheds new light on previously mentioned examples. As described above, sports talk television often depicts executives in relatively still positions—still positions not typically associated with the traditional hegemony of sporting masculinity. However, while static, these positions are not necessarily meant to be read as passive. To elaborate, while David Rowe notes sports photography has tended to contrast an active masculinity with a passive femininity, he also adds that the genre "concentrates on the 'motivated' body: it is doing something to itself and to other bodies."[77] Significantly, while executives might be shown in static positions, these are also, in Rowe's terms, "motivated" bodies because they are, in brief, bodies doing something to other bodies. More specifically, they are bodies watching other bodies and, even more notably, closely analyzing those bodies, one might infer, using the technical, financial logics increasingly valued within hegemonic masculinity. Far from existing outside the bounds of hegemonic masculinity, then, these sorts of images might be read as symbolizing a new masculine ideal.

On that note, Margaret Morse observes that sports television has been the rare site where audiences have been encouraged to gaze at the male body. Sports television, though, has long attempted to frame this gaze as normatively masculine—to de-eroticize it, in other words—by positioning it as analytical "scientific inquiry" primarily concerned with assessing performance.[78] Notably, this emphasis on "scientificity" not only works as an immediate act of disavowal but also plays to broader gender norms that, as Ava Rose and James Friedman suggest, have figured masculine spectatorship as "contemplative" and "goal-oriented."[79] Victoria E. Johnson summarizes, then, that the gaze of sports television—for all its sustained attention on the male form—"conforms to and actually reinforces conventional cultural associations of reason, logical inquiry, distance, and objectivity with cisgendered, heteronormative masculine ideals."[80] Managerial sports talk can perhaps be viewed as a new phase of this ideological project. As hegemonic masculinity has increasingly valued intellectual achievement and technical expertise, "scientificity," particularly in the financialized guise discussed throughout this chapter, no longer just *frames* the athletic male body—further buttressing sports television's claims to normative masculinity—but instead begins to *displace* it, as made particularly clear by the increasing inclusion of managerial bodies that exemplify this "scientificity."

Managerial sports talk's gender politics are, in turn, closely related to its racial politics—an entanglement that again echoes the ideological workings of the managerial sports film. As discussed in the previous chapter, managerial sports films have not just idealized a version of masculinity oriented around white-collar work but have also suggested that this white-collar masculinity is primarily reserved for white men and frequently entwined with the control of athletes of color. Quite similarly, managerial sports talk has framed its financial logics as primarily the domain of white men. Significantly, too, managerial sports talk has cast this financialized expertise as rooted in racialized domination—suggesting that managerial skills and knowledge are to be shrewdly deployed *on* athletes of color. Again, managerial sports talk's financialized orientation to the world is central to this project of control, as it is, more precisely, the ubiquitous financial logics that are disproportionally exercised on athletes of color.

As an entry point into the racial politics of managerial sports talk, it can first be noted that many of the financial logics prominent within managerial sports talk have been largely associated with white masculinity and, in the process, worked to legitimize the authority of white men. Neely observes, for instance, that financial risk taking has long been valorized when linked to white men, yet rendered as overly aggressive or "reckless" when linked to Black and Brown men.[81] It is significant, then, that managerial sports talk primarily centers on the financial wisdom of white men. This centering, of course, is at least partially a legacy of the historic exclusion of women and people of color from front-office roles within professional sports. In 2021, for instance, only five people of color held general manager positions within the NFL, while only four people of color held comparable roles in MLB.[82] Perhaps unsurprisingly, then, as managerial sports talk has obsessed over the maneuverings of current front-office executives and relied on the analysis of former front-office executives, it has largely spotlighted white men. However, one might understand this representational imbalance not just as reflecting this history of gendered and racialized exclusion but also perpetuating it by reinforcing, for example, racialized associations related to financialized managerial work, as in the suggestion that technical approaches to controlling risk are the exclusive expertise of white men.

Significant, too, is that managerial sports talk does not just position administrative expertise as the domain of white men but also that it—like the managerial sports film—frames administration as enmeshed in a racialized act of control. In establishing this point, it is helpful to draw on Oates's examination of NFL draft media and, in particular, his observation that draft coverage obsesses over detailed measurements and comparisons of athletes' bodies. According to Oates, this obsessive attention to athletes' bodies becomes an act of "studied dehumanization," for in breaking players down "into component parts," this coverage treats players as little but bodily capital.[83] As the above discussion of managerial sports talk indicates, though, draft coverage is hardly the only realm of sports media to fixate on the granular. As illustrated above, the logics of managerial sports talk, in figuring athletes as speculative investments, entail a comparable obsession over financial minutiae, such as players' contract terms. Indeed, just as draft coverage obsessively tracks players' heights, weights, wingspans, and other physical attributes, managerial sports talk ventures deep into salary figures, contract lengths, and other details like "trade kickers" and "voidable years." In the process, the players themselves can move outside the frame of the conversation. In fact, players will occasionally be referred to purely by their contracts—sometimes darkly so—as when players become simply "cap fillers" or "dead money." With players reduced to their contracts, they quickly become, as economist Paul Dembinski writes in a broader critique of financialization, "nothing more than portfolios of assets."[84]

That the financial logics of managerial sports talk regularly dehumanize athletes speaks to how these logics foster a broader power imbalance. To that point, Oates argues NFL draft coverage, in obsessing over the measurability and comparability of the draft prospects, can be seen "as a kind of ceremony of control, as it exposes the male athletic body to power's view and normalizing judgment."[85] Similarly, in continually positioning players as "nothing more than portfolios of assets," managerial sports talk subjects players to a surveilling gaze that figures them as speculative investments under the control of their teams' administrators. This power imbalance is hardly hidden. As mentioned above, the language of "control" is a staple within managerial sports talk, with commentators explicitly discussing players as being under "control" of their teams for as long as they are under contract. And while discussions may occasionally touch on the "leverage" possessed by players in contract negotiations or trade talks, power in managerial sports talk is explicitly discussed as one-way, with players' fates figured as in the hands of others. In the aforementioned discussions of Ben Simmons, for instance, it was 76ers executive Morey—not Simmons—who was overtly positioned as possessing agency, Morey having been framed as one of the all-important managers of these human "portfolios of assets."

These issues of power manifested by the financial logics are, in turn, inseparable from race. Oates explains, for instance, that while all NFL prospects are subject to the draft's "ceremony of control," a large majority of the draft prospects are African American. As mentioned above, though, the league's organizations are primarily run by white men. Significantly, then, the draft's surveilling gaze can also be understood as an act of racialized containment that places Black athletes "under the imagined control" of these white men.[86] This dynamic is not unique to NFL draft coverage. Across most major North American sports leagues, there are wide racial discrepancies between playing workforces and front offices. Indeed, these discrepancies have perhaps been worsened by the shift toward financially oriented executives. As journalist Joon Lee details in examining the influx of Ivy Leaguers into MLB front offices, this influx has primarily been composed of white men.[87] As managerial sports talk has reduced players to manipulatable assets under the control of front-office executives, it has produced its own racialized "ceremony of control" wherein athletes of color are frequently placed "under the imagined control" of white executives.

In applying Oates's critique of NFL draft coverage toward managerial sports talk, though, one important caveat needs to be highlighted. In his analysis, Oates writes:

> In draft coverage team presidents, general managers, and head coaches receive so little attention, while the athletes who may be drafted receive so much. Rather than seeing team authorities as objectified commodities, or as football's ruling class, draft discourses almost always tell the story through the eyes of this powerful group, inviting readers, viewers, and listeners, to imagine what it would be like to be in their shoes. In an age when blacks are perceived as athletically dominant, especially in macho team sports like football and basketball, the draft, and the looking it enables, serves to reassert the white male power structure by positioning increasingly athletic bodies of color as commodities, and encouraging fans to imagine themselves as potential possessors of these bodies. As commodities, draftees are ideally positioned to be judged, controlled, directed, and admired.[88]

Whereas Oates observes that team executives "receive so little attention" in draft coverage and prospects conversely "receive so much," the above sections have made clear that managerial sports talk frequently makes executives the very center of attention—constantly invoking their names, showing footage of them "in action," and even diving deep into their managerial histories. This overt focus on executives, though, hardly undercuts Oates's argument. Rather, this focus only underscores the centrality of the managerial point of view. That is to say, in repeatedly spotlighting the importance of these executives, managerial sports talk further emphasizes that its programming is meant to be vicariously experienced through these administrators. Accordingly, managerial sports talk only further reinforces a power structure that positions athletes of color "as open to power's inspection"—repeatedly figuring them, in other words, solely as assets "to be judged, controlled, directed, and admired."[89]

What starts to emerge across managerial sports media, then, is a relatively unified ideological project. In the previous chapter, I suggested that the sports film, amid fears/claims of white masculine precarity, has shifted toward management and begun offering a new idealized version of white masculinity centered around administrative work rather than athletic feats. Many of the same features appear within managerial sports talk. Once again, administrators are represented as a privileged class with near-total control over the fates of athletes. Again, too, this project serves to shore up white masculinity, as this valorized administrative work tends to diminish athletes of color in favor of white men serving as executives, and is framed around financial logics that legitimate the authority of these white men. Traces of the regressive "Managerial American Dream" of the managerial sports film can thus be seen to extend beyond the fictional confines of narrative cinema, stretching into the real-world coverage of real-world athletes in sports television, radio, and other audio media. Across these media, management is presented as an alluring summit of sport, becoming a site where one— particularly if they are a white man—can find just as much glory as on the playing field.

Financial Dissent

The prior section has outlined why the prevalence of financial values in managerial sports talk is something to be wary of. These logics foster a dehumanizing view of sport and form the base of retrograde racial and gender politics. Before completing this analysis of managerial sports talk's financial values, then, it is worth considering the hold of these rationalities—to consider, in other words, whether there have been any signs of resistance to the financial lens. As the previous chapter argued, while a similar project of white remasculinization has repeatedly accompanied the sports film's move toward management, this framework has not gone unchallenged, as exemplified by the film *High Flying Bird*. Significantly, *High Flying Bird* not only demonstrates that the ideological project of the managerial sports film is not as complete as it may initially appear but also illuminates how that sub-genre might be subverted from within. We can similarly wonder whether there are any cracks in managerial sports talk's financial rationalities—cracks that might, in turn, illustrate what it might look like to challenge these rationalities and all that comes with them.

It might first be noted that managerial sports talk—like the broader genre of sports talk—does not necessarily produce the most coherent discourse. Commentators are apt, for instance, to change their opinions from show to show, or even from segment to segment or from point to point. One of the most popular broadcasters—quoted above in multiple instances—is Stephen A. Smith, reportedly ESPN's highest-paid commentator.[90] As writer David Roth comments, Smith is well-known for his meandering, circuitous analysis. Roth comments, "The low thrill of watching Smith comes mostly from the way he will begin a sentence without any real sense of how he's going to finish it and then add switchbacks of blustering stagey distress and various tire-screeching caveats as needed until he figures out how to wrap things up."[91] Smith, though, is hardly alone in this tendency, as sports talk is full of what Roth describes as "clock-killing," "circular" commentary. The fact that much of sports talk is structured around debate also means that it tends toward a muddled discourse. Any given discussion topic on many sports talk programs must feature two diverging opinions. Thus, on a debate show like Smith's *First Take,* any praise of an executive's "aggressive," "all-in" maneuver is apt to be countered by commentary advocating for a more conservative, risk-averse approach that runs counter to the financial logics typically associated with financialization. All this is to say, then, that while this chapter has sought to identify tendencies within managerial sports talk, the very nature of sports talk means that these tendencies are just that—tendencies. The chaotic nature of sports talk discourse means that the financial rationalities of managerial sports talk are inevitably messy.

Contributing, too, to the messiness of this discourse is that the financial logics of managerial sports talk are not just occasionally incoherent or even contradictory but also prone to intermittent opposition. Over the past few years, for instance, discussions of administrative maneuvers within the NBA and NFL have occasionally touched on the increasing leverage held by the leagues' top players to dictate where they will play and under what circumstances—a phenomenon frequently referred to as "player empowerment." In these conversations, administrators and their financial impulses are often decentered, with attention instead turning to the actions and desires of the league's star players. Much of the 2019 NBA free agency discussion, for instance, focused both on which team star player Kawhi Leonard would choose to play for and on how Leonard might use his free agency leverage to coax teams into executing transactions that would align with his vision of team building. This periodic shift in focus represents an implicit challenge to the ideological project of managerial sports talk, suggesting that what truly matters in dissecting the league—at least on occasion—is its players and their worldviews.

On occasion, too, challenges to managerial sports talk's logics will become more explicit, with commentators even expressing outright skepticism of managerial sports talk's financial values. At times, broadcasters will note a discomfort with the dehumanizing effects of the financial lens. Amid the discussion of Ben Simmons's future, for instance, *First Things First* co-host Nick Wright argued that the 76ers should wait to trade Simmons, declaring, "You don't sell an asset at its low point." However, he then added, "I don't mean to be dehumanizing in talking about this guy as an asset, but you know what I mean." Occasionally, too, commentators will condemn the racial politics that underlie the financial logics and the broader managerial fixation. For example, on an episode of Spotify's *Ringer NBA Show,* Wosny Lambre shifted a discussion of turnover within the Boston Celtics' front office to a larger criticism of sports talk's interest in executives and roster construction. "I'm somebody who is annoyed by GM talk," Lambre began. He elaborated, "It started a few years ago where you could just see a shift—the transaction-praising and, 'Oh my god, he got a trade exception! Did you see he got another second-round pick? Oh my goodness!' It just became ridiculous." Significantly, for Lambre, the elevation of executives and their maneuvers—and he mentions, to this point, the frequent labeling of former Celtics executive Danny Ainge as a "savant" and "genius"—is entwined with the racial issues mentioned in the previous section, with "white guys talking about white guys in a game full of Black dudes who do the actual special shit." He continued:

> We play to win the games, right? Not collect assets and, oh my god, the war chest. Do you know how many times I heard the fucking Celtics' asset portfolio described as a war chest? . . . This idea that these GM dudes are the most important, the smartest in the room, and they're playing the chessboard—it's fucking stupid. As an industry, we need to give more credit to the dudes that are doing it out on the floor. The constant praising of transactions and the cottage industry that has grown up, that's sprung up out of it annoys me. . . . In a league that's Black as hell and the best, most electrifying people, the most special people are predominantly white? Maybe that's what makes me feel weird about it.

In Lambre's comments, the implicit subtext within many of the "player empowerment" discussions comes to the foreground, with Lambre making clear that managerial sports talk's elevation of mostly white front-office executives comes at the expense of the league's majority-Black playing workforce.

However, one must be careful not to overstate the frequency or prominence of this opposition to managerial sports talk and its financial values. While sports talk may produce a muddled, contradictory discourse in which commentators occasionally cast a wary, critical eye on financial rationalities, those financial logics are nonetheless powerfully ensconced. For instance, even as "player empowerment" has become an increasingly discussed concept in coverage of the NBA and NFL, conversations surrounding those leagues have continued to emphasize managerial figures and managerial activities and, in the process, to draw on the financial logics outlined above. Moreover, even on those occasions when the actions and desires of players like Leonard have moved to the forefront of managerial sports talk, those financial logics have held firm, if slightly reframed through the lens of the player—discussing, for instance, how the player should manage their risk in choosing his next team or signing his next contract. Speaking, too, to Leary's contention that, amid the increasing use of "empowerment" as corporate jargon, "empowerment often functions quite differently than 'power,'" working "individually and not collectively," discussions of any leverage or control a player might have over their teams tend to neglect larger structural issues.[92] A conversation about an NFL player's contract dispute, for instance, is more likely to focus on the player's individual demands than on any power imbalances in the sport. Perhaps, though, the most unmistakable evidence of the strong hold of managerial sports talk's financial logics is that even commentators with reservations about these discursive tendencies seem unable to avoid them. For example, immediately after revealing his discomfort discussing Ben Simmons as a dehumanized "asset," Wright moved back into that financial mode in again urging the 76ers to hold off on trading Simmons. "You will be getting sixty cents on the dollar for him," Wright declared. Meanwhile, as an above example illustrates, weeks after denouncing "GM talk" and its racist subtext, a discussion of Simmons's future had Lambre putting himself in the imaginary position of a team executive and discussing contract terms and potential trades, in the process labeling Simmons a "depressed asset." Such turns suggest that managerial sports talk's logics have become so ingrained that avoiding them within this space is extremely difficult.

Nevertheless, the fact that managerial sports talk is often scrambled in its output and that commentators have shown a willingness to think beyond its pervasive financial logics indicates that this is not a totalizing discourse. Moreover, these critiques point us toward a version of sports talk that goes beyond management and the accompanying financial lens. In this alternative version, we can glimpse again the sort of complex gaze toward sport exemplified by *High Flying Bird* in the previous chapter—a view of sport that asks questions about how sport is entangled in the broader economic, cultural, and societal structures around it and how those entanglements are inseparable from questions of power.

3

Datavisuality
The Quantified Aesthetic of Managerial Sports Television

As suggested in the introduction, it is difficult to discuss the phenomena of managerialism and financialization without touching upon the connected phenomenon of quantification. In their treatise on managerialism, for instance, Robert Locke and J. C. Spender argue the managerialist drive to ever-greater efficiency has fostered a growing "obsession with numbers," with managers seeking to quantify as many aspects of their businesses as possible.[1] Meanwhile, in discussing the financialization of daily life, scholars like Randy Martin have noted that financial logics like risk management have gone hand in hand with a calculative rationality that attempts to translate the world into manageable quantitative data. Unsurprisingly, then, at the same time as it has newly elevated management and financial logics, the sports world has also witnessed a recent drive toward quantification.

To be more precise, the sporting landscape has been progressively influenced in recent years by "sports analytics." While "analytics" has become a buzzword with a slippery definition that varies widely depending on whom you ask, this project will largely hue toward the definition offered by Benjamin Alamar and Vijay Mehrotra. Sports analytics, they write, encompasses "the management of structured historical data, the application of predictive analytic models that utilize that data, and the use of information systems to inform decision-makers and enable them to help their organizations in gaining a competitive advantage on the field of play."[2] As this definition makes clear, sports analytics can most usefully be thought of as a process. More specifically, it can be thought of as a process that prioritizes the systematic gathering of data—often quantitative—and using that data throughout an organization's decision making, impacting everything from roster building to in-game

FIGURE 3.1: Graphic displaying a baseball player's season statistics, including OPS and OPS+. (*Sunday Night Baseball,* ESPN)

strategizing. With sports analytics ascendant, to be a front-office executive increasingly means employing data-driven approaches to team building.

As I emphasize in this chapter, sports television has come to reflect the changing nature of sports management—a shift exhibited in even the most banal programming. On July 10, 2022, the New York Yankees faced off against the Boston Red Sox at Fenway Park in Boston. A Sunday night game, it aired on national television as part of ESPN's *Sunday Night Baseball* (1990–). Not long after ESPN's telecast began—during the bottom of the first inning—Boston's designated hitter, J. D. Martinez, came to the plate to face off against New York starting pitcher Jameson Taillon. As Martinez came to the plate, a graphic containing a wide array of statistics flashed across the bottom of the screen (figure 3.1). A few moments later, Taillon threw a ball just outside the strike zone. Immediately after, a graphic appeared to show precisely where the ball had been thrown and at what velocity (figure 3.2).

For many sports fans, the use of such data-rich graphics, whether in major events like the World Series or in less consequential games like this midseason Yankees versus Red Sox matchup, has probably become incredibly familiar—perhaps now even drawing little notice. After all, these sorts of data-driven graphics have rapidly become ubiquitous. However, the likely ordinariness of these examples belies the fact that the recent incorporation of graphics like these represents a significant change in sports broadcasting. As I document

FIGURE 3.2: Graphic displaying a baseball's location and velocity. (*Sunday Night Baseball,* ESPN)

in this chapter, sports television has become home both to ever-increasing quantities of quantitative data and ever more complex quantitative data—a dual-pronged phenomenon I term "datavisuality." In examining datavisuality, I not only define the parameters of the phenomenon but also explain its emergence, rooting it in a confluence of factors that include the sports industry's increasing fixation with advanced statistical measures, new technological developments within the sports television industry, and attempts by sports broadcasters both to keep pace with the sports industry and to separate themselves from a growing field of competitors. Moreover, I offer a critique of datavisuality, arguing that this new mode of data-driven broadcasting potentially reifies several worrying phenomena that have accompanied the ongoing datafication of sport and society, including a growing faith in quantification and the ascendance of shallow big-data mythology, while also further ensconcing the instrumentalizing approach to sport highlighted in the previous chapters.

Defining Datavisuality

Starting with the increasing use of informational graphics in the mid-1990s and accelerating during the subsequent decades, sports television has recently seen drastic changes in its look and presentation. To be more precise, sports television has increasingly privileged quantitative data across its various forms, thereby leading to a new mode of data-driven broadcasting. An ongoing process more than a static shift, datavisuality has entailed not only ever-increasing amounts of quantitative data but also ever more intricate quantitative data. Much as John Caldwell details in describing American television's increasing emphasis on visual style in the 1980s and 1990s, a transformation he terms "televisuality," the phenomenon of datavisuality entails a noticeable "shift in the conceptual and ideological paradigms" that govern sports television.[3] While quantitative data has long been part of sports, it has traditionally been a relatively minor part of sports television. Datavisuality, though, brings numerical data to the foreground.

As in the case of televisuality, datavisuality has "many variant guises."[4] Not only do the specific manifestations of datavisuality vary, but as examples throughout this section will illustrate, datavisuality also affects far more than live game telecasts. Indeed, its influence can be found everywhere from national news shows like *SportsCenter* (ESPN, 1979–) to shoulder programming like the pregame and postgame shows that fill the schedules of the many regional sports networks (RSNs) across the country. And although the focus of this chapter is primarily centered on the particularities of American television, it can also be noted that datavisuality is hardly confined to the United States. In fact, companies outside the United States have taken the lead in developing many of the technologies that are facilitating datavisuality. Moreover, many of the first adopters of these technologies have also been located outside the United States.

Because datavisuality operates in many guises, no one example can fully capture the ongoing process of datafication in which sports television is enmeshed. Nonetheless, a few representative examples illustrate the current extent of datavisuality. First, it might be helpful to see how datavisuality is playing out in even the most ordinary sports television programming. To that end, the *Sunday Night Baseball* example from above is instructive. The primary attribute of datavisuality is the foregrounding of quantitative data. In figure 3.1, then, it is significant that so many numerical figures are being displayed. Not only is the viewer given information about the game's progress—by way of the score box that provides both the score and situational information, including the inning and ball-strike count—but they are also given a wealth of quantitative data about the player's performance. While the use of quantitative sports data in sports media has a long history—statistical analyses of baseball, for example, were appearing in print publications as early as the 1850s—the incorporation of so many statistics into sports television is a recent development.[5] As Dustin Hahn, Matthew S. VanDyke, and R. Glenn

106   CHAPTER THREE

Cummins document in a study of National Football League (NFL) game telecasts, there has been a "significant rise" in the number of statistical references over the last several years, noting that "the number of statistics presented in an NFL broadcast has doubled since the early 2000s."[6] Similarly, while graphics are hardly new to sports television—even early baseball telecasts, for example, used superimpositions to occasionally overlay text and photos—their use has multiplied rapidly in recent years.[7] To that point, through the 1980s, sports television viewers—even during major events—were provided with just brief glimpses of text containing only the most basic information about the game in progress. Indeed, now-familiar features like the score box only debuted in the mid-1990s.[8] For viewers to now be routinely given such a wealth of statistics in visual form thus represents a sea change in broadcasting.

The sheer quantity of information is not the only piece of import in figure 3.1. Attention must also be paid to what sorts of data are being highlighted. To that end, it can be observed that most of the player performance metrics on display in this shot are simple counting statistics that are familiar even to non-sports fans. A home run, for instance, is both easy to measure and easy to work into everyday metaphors. What stands out, then, is the inclusion of the statistics OPS (short for "on-base plus slugging"), which adds together a player's on-base percentage and slugging percentage, and OPS+, which normalizes OPS across the league. OPS and OPS+ are not only less-familiar statistics than the others, but also more complex statistics than a basic counting statistic like home runs or a simple rate statistic like batting average, with OPS+, for instance, attempting to adjust for how player performance can vary across different ballparks. Such complexity was by design, as OPS and OPS+, as well as many other new baseball metrics that have emerged over the past several decades, developed out of sustained attempts by the sport's community to reevaluate the usefulness of traditional statistics, including home runs and batting average, and to look for potential alternatives—alternatives that would not shy away from elaborate calculations.[9]

Figure 3.1, then, shows how datavisuality has entailed both increasing amounts of statistical information and increasingly intricate statistical information. That is to say, viewers are receiving not only *more* quantitative data but also *more complex* quantitative data meant to help them better evaluate player and team performance. However, the statistical information in figure 3.1 represents perhaps the simplest manifestation of datavisuality: the basic presentation of numbers. Complexity is evident, but that complexity comes by way of a dense display of numbers, as well as the use of more-sophisticated metrics. Figure 3.2, though, demonstrates how the process of datafication has expanded well beyond the simple display of numerical data. To understand

FIGURE 3.3: Graphic displaying a golf ball's speed, apex height, and curve. (*Golf on NBC,* NBC)

why this graphic represents new terrain, one must know how it was generated. In brief, every MLB stadium is now outfitted with tracking systems that can continuously log the locations both of the players and of the ball, thereby allowing networks to incorporate a wide variety of data that was once beyond easy measure. In this case, ESPN relies on those tracking systems to display where the ball crossed the plate and at what velocity, all overlaid on top of an approximated strike zone. ESPN first began using these "K-Zone" graphics intermittently in 2011, but in 2015 committed to using them for every single pitch in every game it broadcast and, more recently, to adding new "K-Zone 3D" features that allow the network to display the exact trajectory of a ball over the plate.[10]

And baseball is far from the only sport for which the implementation of tracking systems has led to new broadcast features. Indeed, across coverage of most major sports, sports broadcasters have increasingly unveiled new metrics and visuals that rely on real-time positioning information—a transition that fully moves sports broadcasting into the realm of big data. Soccer broadcasters, for instance, can display the distance traveled by players over the course of a game, while golf broadcasters can display the ball's location while it is in flight alongside measures like ball speed and apex height (figure 3.3). Several broadcasters have even begun drawing on wearable technologies to integrate biometric data, like athletes' heartrates, into telecasts.[11]

FIGURE 3.4: Graphic displaying a baseball player's season statistics, including WAR. (*First Take*, ESPN)

The above illustrations from a routine live game telecast broadly represent the ongoing datafication of sports television, but as mentioned above, sports television is much more than live event coverage. Rather, sports television encompasses everything from national news shows to local debate shows. Significantly, increasingly intricate statistics and data visualizations have begun appearing across this entire spectrum of programming. To draw on another banal example, one can look at an appearance by Yankees outfielder Aaron Judge on the ESPN studio show *First Take* (2007–). Throughout Judge's appearance, his most recent season statistics remained at the bottom of the screen (figure 3.4). Notably, one of the statistics on display was WAR (Wins Above Replacement), which, like OPS and OPS+, is a relatively complex statistic that has only recently come into vogue.

While the above examples may represent the more typical guises of datavisuality, perhaps the most conspicuous displays of datavisuality have come in less traditional venues. In recent years, much industry attention has been directed toward offering television audiences newly "personalized" viewing experiences.[12] Although many of these efforts have focused on engaging viewers across secondary screen devices—as in, for instance, the introduction of complementary mobile apps—several broadcasters have also rolled out experiments focused not on incorporating these "second screens" but rather on creating primary screen alternatives.[13] Significantly, these alternative telecasts have become sites for some of the purest expressions of datavisuality. Fox, for instance, has experimented with offering traditional coverage of an MLB playoff game on its flagship broadcast network while simultaneously using its cable channel FS1 to air a secondary telecast devoted to statistical analysis and, accordingly, heavy on complex statistics like wOBA (weighted On-Base Average). ESPN has embraced these sorts of data-driven alternative telecasts with even more enthusiasm. In a similar vein as Fox's experiment, for instance, the company has been using its secondary cable channel ESPN2 to offer what it has termed "alternative viewing experiences" of select MLB games. Described as being "driven largely by on-screen graphics, data, and information" from the league's tracking systems, these "Statcast" telecasts have been data-rich presentations (figures 3.5a-b).[14]

Baseball, though, has not been the only sport to receive such treatment from ESPN. For example, in recent years, the company has also experimented with alternative basketball telecasts featuring additional informational graphics and live data overlays developed in tandem with sports data company Second Spectrum (figure 3.6).

Since 2014, too, ESPN has been covering its major college football properties, including the sport's championship game, by employing what it terms a "Megacast." While a traditional telecast of these games has aired on ESPN, the company's other outlets, including both its secondary cable channels and its streaming platforms, have been filled with alternative telecasts, each with a slightly different focus. Significantly, a regular feature of the Megacast coverage has been a data-dense streaming feed that ESPN has titled the "DataCenter" (figure 3.7).

If Fox and ESPN's alternative baseball telecasts showcase datavisuality's tendency toward ever more complex quantitative data, as seen in the emphasis on intricate statistics, then the Megacast coverage draws particular attention to datavisuality's push toward ever-growing quantities of quantitative data. Indeed, so many metrics are squeezed into the DataCenter frame that it can be challenging to read them, even on giant televisions. But if these alternative telecasts show off different aspects of the twin inclinations of datavisuality—quantity and complexity—they are united by an underlying sense that the process of datafication is proceeding so forcefully that it is not always easy to contain within the space of a primary telecast. Thus, one final tendency of datavisuality might be overflow, with quantitative data primed to spill into new, relatively uncharted spaces.

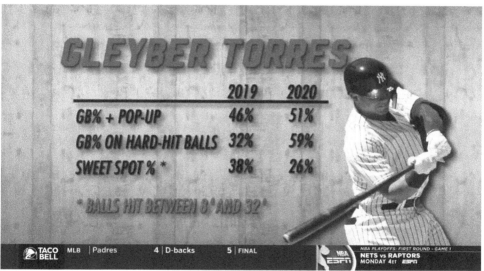

FIGURES 3.5A-B: Graphics displayed during an alternative "data-driven" baseball telecast. (*Sunday Night Baseball* "Statcast," ESPN2)

FIGURE 3.6: Graphic displayed during an alternative "data-driven" basketball telecast. (*NBA on ESPN* "Full Court Press," ESPN3)

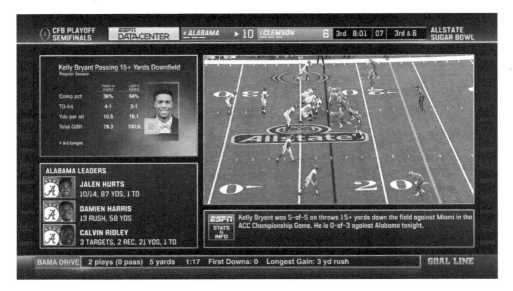

FIGURE 3.7: Several text-based graphics displayed alongside live game footage during an alternative "data-driven" college football telecast. (*ESPN College Football* "Megacast DataCenter," ESPN3)

The Rise of Datavisuality

The Ascendancy of Sports Analytics

In beginning to address how datavisuality has taken hold so firmly and quickly, it can first be noted that it is very much an industrial phenomenon. The following sections, then, will explore the televisual technologies and corporate decision-making processes that have precipitated the rise of datavisuality. Underlying all the new technology and industrial maneuvering, though, is an assumption that audiences increasingly want quantitative data to be a part of sports television. Thus, technological shifts and industrial practices are necessary, but not sufficient, explanations for datavisuality. A parallel idea emerges in Caldwell's work on televisuality. As Caldwell explains, if technological and industrial developments enabled the creation of televisuality, it was "landmark" programs like *Miami Vice* (NBC, 1984–1990) that offered the "ideational resource" required to effect such a change.[15] In other words, such programming "provided the conceptual framework—that is, the audience expectation and the cultural capital—needed to effect a shift in the televisual discourse."[16] In the case of datavisuality, the necessary "conceptual framework" has emerged from the rising place of advanced statistical analysis within both front offices and popular culture.

Before proceeding into the details regarding the ascendance of sports analytics, it must be clarified that the use of quantitative data in sports is not exactly a new development. Instead, sport has long been numerically driven, with sociologist Allen Guttmann even influentially declaring quantification one of the "distinguishing characteristics of modern sports."[17] Scholars like Christopher Phillips and Brad and Rob Millington have highlighted, for instance, the long history of quantification in baseball, noting how over the course of the nineteenth century the sport, much like other institutions during this period, bore the traces of a growing societal interest in collecting numerical data—a development most clearly exemplified by the codification of the box score in the mid-1800s.[18] Figures within the sports industry acknowledge the long history of quantification, too, observing that front-office executives have long used analytical reasoning informed by quantitative data.[19] But even though front offices have long relied on statistics to make their decisions, the recent fascination with sports analytics has nonetheless represented a substantial change in perspective. Not only has the analysis of quantitative data become more critical to the process of roster building, but the gathering and implementation of such data have also become rigorously systemized. To that point, Millington and Millington, while acknowledging the long history of sport's quantification, suggest sport is in the process of a "newfound statistical turn."[20]

The sports industry's transition toward the heightened rigor and complexity of analytics is often traced back to the events recounted in Michael Lewis's 2003 book *Moneyball*—a work that continues to hold an enormous place in sports analytics mythology. As documented in previous chapters, *Moneyball* dramatizes how Billy Beane, the Oakland Athletics general manager, put together a roster of baseball misfits and castaways that had been "undervalued" by other teams—a unique strategy necessitated by Oakland's relatively small budget. According to Lewis's account, Beane and his assistants placed a significant emphasis on statistics as they scoured the league for players that had been overlooked—but not the sorts of statistics that had typically been valued within the sport's front offices, like hits and runs batted in (RBIs). Instead, Oakland bucked conventional wisdom and relied on other quantitative measures that seemed to more closely align with on-field success—including relatively complex metrics. As Lewis explains, the novel attention to these metrics played a significant role in guiding Oakland toward the proverbial diamonds in the rough and, in turn, unexpected success.

However, the apparent novelty of Oakland's data-driven strategy must be further contextualized. For example, while Oakland may have been ahead of other front offices in turning to advanced metrics, interest in such metrics was hardly unprecedented within the sport's broader community. To the point above about quantification long having a significant role within modern sport, Alan Schwarz notes there have been many generations of baseball fans who have attempted to refine statistical analysis of the sport. He writes, for instance, about the scores of dedicated fans who experimented with crunching baseball statistics on early generations of mainframe computers and who tackled ambitious projects like the research-intensive *Baseball Encyclopedia,* a massive reference volume first published in 1969.[21] To that point, the emergence of aforementioned statistics like OPS came as part of a particularly concentrated "explosion" of analytical work in the 1970s and 1980s spearheaded by writer Bill James, whose annual, statistically dense guides to the sport gradually grew more and more popular during this period—even if, as Schwarz mentions, front offices were, at this point, resistant to these sorts of approaches.[22]

One can zoom out even further in adding layers of contextualization to the *Moneyball* narrative. As Phillips observes, for instance, the aforementioned "explosion" of statistical analysis of baseball in the latter half of the twentieth century is itself grounded in broader developments, for that explo-

114   CHAPTER THREE

sion was enmeshed in the wider "success of the various mathematical sciences of modeling and prediction."[23] Relatedly, throughout *Moneyball*, Lewis continually draws parallels between the team's roster moves and financiers' searches for market inefficiencies. As these comparisons suggest, the events of *Moneyball* signaled front offices becoming entangled in the fetishization of quantification that had already been accelerating among the managerial caste for decades. Locke and Spender, for instance, detail the many attempts to "turn management into a positivist science" over the course of the twentieth century, highlighting, for example, the growth of mathematical finance within business schools and the subsequent influence of that field within the corporate world.[24] Meanwhile, scholars in other areas have documented how the managerialist drive toward quantitative measures has transformed realms as varied as education and policing.[25] The introduction of newly intricate mathematical models into teams' front offices, then, can be viewed as another front in an ongoing datalogical turn covering much of society.

Given this broader context, it is not surprising that in the years after Lewis wrote *Moneyball*, the use of advanced statistical analysis became increasingly commonplace in baseball front offices. Beane, for example, was once considered an oddity within the sport, but his approach has since become the norm, and he is now one of the most recognized executives in sports. The path of Keith Woolner, who is perhaps best known for developing the complex statistic Value Over Replacement Player (VORP), is instructive in how this normalization has unfolded. A 1990 graduate of MIT, Woolner subsequently worked in Silicon Valley as a software developer.[26] In his free time, though, he wrote articles for *Baseball Prospectus*—a niche publication focused on statistical analysis of the sport. As *Baseball Prospectus* co-founder Rany Jazayerli recollected, writers like him and Woolner grew accustomed to working in relative obscurity. "Not only was statistical analysis something that wasn't sort of mainstream, but it was almost mocked. It was really degraded both by baseball teams and also by the media," Jazayerli recalled years later.[27] However, not long after *Moneyball* was released in 2003, both mainstream media and baseball teams began taking notice of the type of work done by *Baseball Prospectus*. In 2007 Woolner was able to turn his analytical skills into a position in Cleveland's front office—the type of hiring that exemplifies the growth of analytics. Woolner comments, "In the early days of [*Baseball Prospectus*], we were very much the outsiders. By the time I joined Cleveland, I came into an organization that was data-driven and had buy-in toward analytics."[28]

For several reasons, baseball was the ground zero of the "analytics revolution"—the sport, in other words, that has had the most vibrant history of statistical experimentation, as exemplified by the development of metrics like OPS, and the one that first saw professional teams embrace such experimentation (if belatedly). The most significant reason for this fact is that baseball is, in Lewis's words, "an individual sport masquerading as a team one."[29] That is to say, a baseball game can largely be boiled down to a series of discrete matchups between batters and pitchers. This means, then, that it is relatively easy to quantify each player's contribution to a victory (or a loss). But even though baseball most easily lent itself to measurement, the fascination with analytics has hardly confined itself solely to that sport. As Lewis would write several years after publishing *Moneyball*, "The virus that infected professional baseball in the 1990s, the use of statistics to value players and strategies, has found its way into every major sport."[30] Across Major League Soccer (MLS), the NBA, the NFL, the NHL, the NWSL, and the WNBA, organizations now regularly hire analytics experts in front-office positions. Predictably, the MBA-trained executives mentioned in previous chapters, such as Sam Hinkie and Daryl Morey, have been at the forefront of these movements. Morey, for example, received his own Lewis profile that documented Morey's attempts to go beyond traditional basketball statistics and into more complex calculations of efficiencies. Indeed, Morey's quest for quantitative efficiency has even produced its own colloquialism: "Moreyball."

Notably, as each of the major sports leagues have gradually embraced analytics, they have all also become host to big-data methodology, for, as Andrew Baerg suggests, analytics "[slips] easily into Big Data."[31] For example, MLB, the NBA, and numerous soccer teams use optical tracking technology able to track both players and balls continuously. Meanwhile, the NFL and the NHL have implemented tracking systems based on RFID chips embedded in playing objects and players' shoulder pads. Numerous teams have also been aggressively pursuing biometric monitoring programs. "The idea," Millington and Millington suggest, "is evidently to 'datafy everything.'"[32]

Across the major sports leagues, then, there has been a significant change in thinking. Traditional managerial tasks—detailed film study, scouting trips to observe college prospects, and so forth—remain important, but they are now accompanied by an increasing emphasis on quantitative analysis relying on vast new collections of data. In the course of the shift, a different type of front-office executive has been increasingly valorized: an efficiency-minded executive as comfortable with complex data models as they are with anecdotal scouting reports gathered from a far-flung scouting network. As Lewis reflected in 2011, "The geeks have definitely been let off the leash."[33] The question remains, though, as to how this rapid transformation has affected sports media.

116   CHAPTER THREE

Technological Developments

The previous section detailed how the sports industry—much like many other industries—has become increasingly smitten with quantification. This change, then, undergirds much of the imagined audience demand and cultural capital—"the ideational resource"—required for the emergence of datavisuality. However, datavisuality does not spring directly from the growing popularity of sports analytics. Rather, it is very much a television phenomenon and, as such, also requires explanations that address the workings of the sports television industry. Beginning that work, this section will focus, in particular, on the development of new televisual technologies that have facilitated the rise of datavisuality. In emphasizing the significant role of these technologies in fostering data-driven coverage, this section again underscores the parallels between the emergence of datavisuality and the emergence of televisuality. As Caldwell notes, tools like film-to-video transfer machines played a crucial role in creating televisuality by providing "the 'technical competence' needed for a change in the television industry."[34] Similarly, new televisual technologies have played a significant role in datavisuality by creating "an array of conditions, and a context" that have allowed sports television to keep up with the sports industry's growing fixation with quantitative data—whether that might mean the development of graphics systems able to constantly display numerical metrics or the creation of even more advanced tools able to render real-time tracking data.[35]

On a basic level, datavisuality has been fostered by the progression of display technologies, particularly in terms of resolution. Over the 1990s and 2000s, high-definition television sets became more and more common. These new sets provided increased resolution—and, as Amanda Lotz argues, "a radical adjustment in the visual experience of television"—by more than doubling the number of pixels on-screen.[36] This increase in resolution has given broadcasters more screen real estate to fill and, thus, allowed for denser and more intricate graphics. Sports television has not been the only realm of television where broadcasters have taken advantage of increased resolutions by incorporating more complex visual elements. Speaking again to the intersection of sports media and finance media, Aaron Heresco notes, for instance, how CNBC programming has become "densely populated" with graphics displaying a wide range of financial information such as stock price and commodity movements.[37]

The rise of datavisuality, though, is not solely rooted in the expansion of the television image. For the last few decades, even as resolutions increased, sports graphics could broadly be divided between the two basic categories of interstitial graphics, such as the bumpers that precede game action or studio show segments, and informational graphics, like the familiar score boxes that remain on-screen during game telecasts. In recent years, though, broadcasters have increasingly turned toward a new type of graphic: the "virtual graphic." In brief, it is now possible for broadcasters to insert digitally rendered visual elements anywhere and everywhere. During an NFL pregame show, for example, a dancing robot, or, more subtly, a virtual banner displaying team logos, might appear next to an anchor desk.

Significantly, too, these sorts of virtual graphics—also referred to in the television industry as "augmented reality"—have become commonplace during live game telecasts. Some of these virtual graphics operate much like traditional informational graphics in displaying information that otherwise would have been placed in a static box. It has become a regular sight, for example, to see NFL broadcasters placing data-filled graphics directly on or above the playing field (figure 3.8). Other virtual graphics, though, are more thoroughly integrated into game action. An early and prominent example would be the yellow first-down line that has become a regular part of college and professional football broadcasts over the last two decades (figure 3.9). Virtual graphics are not just limited to football, though, as major technology providers like ChyronHego, SMT, and Vizrt have developed systems that allow nearly any sport to feature a bevy of virtual graphics. Soccer telecasts, for example, now routinely feature enhancements like on-field graphics displaying player formations and offside lines, while swimming telecasts regularly overlay the pool lanes with information about swimmers' speeds and positioning while also adding moving lines indicating record paces.

In the 1990s, graphics became a regular part of the sports television experience thanks to the introduction of score boxes and the increasing usage of lower third and full-frame graphics. At any given moment in a game telecast, graphics were now sure to be present—a significant change from just a decade before, when graphics were primarily limited to occasional flashes of text that might indicate the score or the name of an announcer. However, the emergence of virtual graphics represents another significant moment in the history of sports television. With graphics no longer confined to certain areas of the screen or structured by breaks in play, entire games become subject to graphic "enhancement." In this way, the lines between sports video games and sports television become increasingly blurry. To that point, Abe Stein argues that sports television and sports video games have a "dialogic" relationship. He elaborates, "Sports videogames undoubtedly refer to the televisual, while television borrows from and refers back to the popular genre of game," thus creating "a feedback loop of reference."[38]

118   CHAPTER THREE

FIGURE 3.8: Virtual graphic placed above a playing surface. (*Sunday Night Football,* NBC)

FIGURE 3.9: Football telecast featuring several virtual graphics; in this shot, one displays text information regarding down and distance, while others mark the locations of the line of scrimmage, the first down line, and the approximate field goal range. (*NFL on CBS,* CBS)

Indeed, drawing on interviews with game designers and television producers, Stein observes that this "borrowing" is often explicit and intentional. "The producers of videogames borrow and remediate the televisual," he writes, "while producers of sports broadcasts keep an eye on sports videogames, looking for opportunities to reinvigorate their medium with a game-like aesthetic."[39] Virtual graphics make this "reinvigoration" particularly clear, as many virtual graphics, such as the K-Zone example mentioned above, replicate visuals first pioneered in sports simulation games.[40]

The increasing ubiquity of graphics during sports telecasts has had significant ramifications for production technology providers. As their executives suggest, broadcasters are increasingly looking for innovative technologies to set them apart from their competitors.[41] Press releases from broadcasters bear this statement out. Fox, for example, has promoted its golf coverage as making use of a "high-tech arsenal" that continues the network's "leadership role in the use of production technology"—an arsenal very much heavy on virtual graphics.[42] Similarly, ESPN has touted its use of new virtual graphics technologies in its soccer coverage.[43] Virtual graphics, then, have not just affected the look of sports broadcasts but also how the sports broadcasting industry operates. Now charged with setting broadcasters apart, technology providers have raced to develop a rash of new virtual capabilities. The golf "arsenal" promoted by Fox, for example, included virtual graphics that trace colorful ball trails as well as floating signs displaying the distance to course features like bunkers and water hazards. The soccer technology that ESPN has touted, meanwhile, includes virtual graphics that allow the network to highlight team tactics and single out notable players. In both cases, the playing surface becomes covered in graphics. Data now knows no boundaries.

Undergirding this significant change—in which the entirety of a game broadcast becomes subject to data overlays—has been another change just as substantial: a massive influx of data. External data providers like Opta and Sportradar collect and disseminate much of the information that eventually winds its way into sports telecasts. Traditionally, these data firms would provide broadcasters with basic statistics and notes that could be highlighted during a broadcast. However, advances in technology mean that external data providers can pass on more and more information and, accordingly, these providers are now offering broadcasters both increasing quantities of data and increasingly complex data. Opta, for instance, has advertised its abilities to provide broadcasters with data feeds containing live stats for players and teams, text commentaries, positional information, season-to-date cumulative stats, historical data sets, and more.[44] Moreover, these data providers have also waded into the types of intricate statistics associated with analytics. Opta, for example, has advertised to soccer broadcasters "advanced level feeds" that feature complex metrics like expected goals (xG) and expected assists (xA).[45]

Production technology and data providers have also moved aggressively into real-time tracking. For instance, "high-tech" golf graphics like those touted by Fox generally require optical or radar technology to constantly measure a ball's flight. Similarly, ESPN's advertised soccer graphics rely on optical systems that continually track players' positions throughout the game. Other companies, meanwhile, are working with RFID chips and GPS units, among other tracking technologies. As Brian Perkins, an executive at MLB Network, argued at a recent industry event, broadcasters are just "scratching the surface" in drawing on these tracking technologies, suggesting that "so much more data is being collected" than broadcasters have yet been able to use.[46]

In summary, then, the sports television industry has recently witnessed significant technological developments, including the introduction of virtual graphics and the influx of massive amounts of information, that have increasingly allowed quantitative data to be anywhere and everywhere during sports television programming. While this explains the "technical competence" that lies behind many of the guises of datavisuality, some related questions remain, particularly in terms of the demand that has underlaid the embrace of these new technological developments. Technology and data providers, after all, do not operate in isolation. Instead, they work in accordance with the desires of the broadcasters who eventually make use of their offerings. To get a fuller sense of the emergence of datavisuality and, in particular, the industrial demand for a quantified aesthetic thus requires a closer look at the decision-making processes of a broadcaster.

A Broadcaster's Perspective

In examining the industrial rationales that have laid behind the turn to datavisuality, the rest of this section will analyze perhaps the most notable broadcaster within the American sports television landscape: ESPN. As will be explained below, ESPN has been at the forefront of data-driven broadcasting. Indeed, it is no coincidence that several of the examples of datavisuality cited above have come from ESPN programming. As a window into ESPN's move toward a quantified aesthetic, this section will specifically focus on the company's growing embrace of sports analytics—an embrace that has signaled, in particular, the company's increasing comfort with featuring more complex statistical analysis across its many properties.

As ESPN employees I talked to in 2015 emphasized, the company's recent involvement with sports analytics has represented the culmination of a long history with sports data. ESPN launched in 1979. For most of its early history, the company—like other sports television broadcasters, not to mention newspapers and radio stations—relied on external data providers for much of its sports data. As the company grew, though, it had an ever-increasing demand for data—needing to provide information not only to its mainstay programs like *SportsCenter* but also to new platforms like the ESPNet online service and ESPN2, a secondary cable outlet that premiered in 1993. In light of this growing need, in 1994, ESPN purchased 80 percent of SportsTicker, a sports-wire news service that had previously been owned by Dow Jones & Company.[47] Based out of New Jersey, the company provided "scores, statistics, news, and features" to a wide range of clients, including radio and television broadcasters, newspapers, wire services, and professional sports teams. Bringing such a company into ESPN's corporate control thus removed the need to outsource all its data needs. As Richard Glover, an ESPN vice president, said at the time of purchase, "We had audio, video, and graphics, but we didn't have a text-based data service."[48]

For twelve years, SportsTicker served as ESPN's primary source of data. In addition, SportsTicker continued to work with the many clients it had served both before ESPN's purchase and after, including major companies like Fox, Microsoft, and Yahoo.[49] Complementing SportsTicker, meanwhile, were two separate groups within ESPN that also worked with sports data, including the Production Research department, which directly assisted game and studio broadcasts, and the BottomLine department, which oversaw the scrolling tickers that appeared on the bottom of the company's television networks. In 2006, though, the company decided to consolidate its information services and, in the process, leave the syndication business to instead focus entirely on serving its own needs. To that end, ESPN sold SportsTicker to PA Sport, a European sports information provider.[50] In its place, the company created a new Stats and Analysis department tasked with supplying information across ESPN's many platforms. That division was then placed alongside the Production Research department and the BottomLine department under a new umbrella organization dubbed the Stats and Information Group (SIG)—an all-encompassing group meant to serve, in the words of current SIG employee Clark, as "a total sports consciousness—knowing everything that's going on around the sports world, having every stat, every score, from every minor league soccer game in Venezuela, all the way to the NFL."[51]

According to Roger, formerly a director with the Stats and Analysis department and later a SIG executive, a primary reason that ESPN had been looking to form its own information gathering division was that it was eager for the freedom to fully pursue its own initiatives and to "get out on the cutting edge"—not something it could necessarily do when it also had to fulfill the needs of other corporate clients.[52] As Roger explains, the growth of sports analytics was partially fueling this desire for data independence—starting at the top of the company. According to both Roger and Alan, also a SIG executive, John Walsh, a powerful ESPN leader who served as the chairman of the company's editorial board, had become a strong proponent of sports analytics and was eager to see the company produce its own analytics content.[53] Walsh, too, was hardly the only ESPN employee looking to embrace analytics. Alan, for example, describes how many staff members within the Production Research department had long sought to go "way deeper" than basic statistics. He adds that certain analysts and anchors were also eager to discuss advanced statistics.[54] In 2010, then, SIG began laying the groundwork for a new unit devoted entirely toward sports analytics. In the years after, that unit's efforts gradually started to appear across the company's properties, as evidenced in the increasing use of win probabilities and discussions of new metrics like Total Quarterback Rating (QBR) and the Football Power Index (FPI).

There have also been other visible signs that analytics has gradually become a more significant part of ESPN's efforts. Alan, for example, highlights the aforementioned addition of metrics like OPS to baseball telecasts. "People who came up in the TV industry, you just did batting average, homers, and RBIs—and that's just what you did."[55] Incorporating newer, advanced metrics, then, represented a significant change of thinking. Meanwhile, Roger mentions ESPN's close involvement with the MIT Sloan Sports Analytics Conference.[56] As detailed in the preface, the Sloan Conference has become a significant gathering for academics, industry figures, and media members interested in sports analytics. And, thanks to the growing role of analytics across the sports landscape, the event has become, as Paul Flannery suggests, "one of the signature events on the sports calendar."[57] While it took several years for the Sloan Conference to make its presence felt across the sports industry, ESPN was involved with the event from the very beginning. Moreover, as the conference grew in scale, so did ESPN's involvement. By 2010 ESPN had become the conference's "presenting sponsor," and, to this day, its employees are ubiquitous at the event. Indeed, ESPN has even broadcast a daily NBA talk show, *The Jump* (2016–2021), from the conference.

As its increasing interest in sports data and, eventually, analytics content indicates, ESPN's approach to sport has become more data-driven over time. However, what has yet to be established are the underlying reasons for this growing interest. Speaking to the contention above that the growth of analytics has provided the "conceptual resources" for datavisuality, the answers broadly lie in the wider spread of advanced statistical approaches across the sports landscape. As ESPN figures emphasize, it is the company's responsibility to adjust to this new data-driven world so that they can adequately cover the sports industry—a pressing concern if ESPN is going to continue to bill itself as the leader in sports media, a brand reputation that the company cherishes and is expressed in the ubiquitous company tagline "The Worldwide Leader in Sports."[58]

Talking about an increased demand within the company for analytics content, Nick, formerly a leader within the analytics unit, mentions advanced metrics are "becoming more and more a part of sports" and then explains that the company's logic became, "Because we are 'the worldwide leader in sports,' we are ESPN, we have to be on board with that, we have to understand that trend."[59] Clark makes similar claims. "There's a movement in sports towards analytics-based decision making and analysis," he says. ESPN, then, is "trying to stay ahead of the curve."[60] Roger is even more specific about why it is essential for ESPN not to be "caught behind." After discussing the rise of analytics within the sports industry, he argues that if the company is going to be treated as an "organization that's legitimate," it has "to be looking through the same prism" as the wider industry. He comments:

> If the teams are quantifying performance, the teams are projecting outcomes or performance—around their athletes, or their games, or their strategies—we have to do that. So we need to hire people who are capable of doing that, we need to acquire the right kind of data, we need to build the right kind of tools, and work with the right third-party vendors that are leaders in this space—to do those things, too. Otherwise, we're going to be left behind.[61]

As the ESPN employees explain the importance of keeping pace with the industry's move toward analytics, they all bring up a related argument: the need to stay in front of the company's many rivals. Roger, for instance, brings up the fact that both leagues and teams have become much more aggressive about covering themselves with their own online, radio, and television outlets. For Roger, data-driven coverage represents a way to keep pace with these new "in-house" media outlets. He comments, "We have to be able to tell the most unique and differentiating stories, and if we're not using analytics to tell those stories, we're going to be left behind."[62] Other ESPN employees I talked to in 2015 also used the same language of "differentiation" employed by Roger—emphasizing how the analytics content helps set ESPN apart from other outlets within the crowded sports media landscape.[63]

Both of these stated justifications for ESPN's growing embrace of analytics—being able to mirror developments in the sports industry at large and helping to set the company apart from a raft of competitors—rely on a critical assumption: that ESPN audiences are interested in analytics. Although the sports industry may be increasingly oriented around data-driven approaches, fan interest in these approaches is not necessarily a given. According to each of the ESPN employees I interviewed, though, sports fans are growing more engaged with data-driven content. Indeed, several of them suggest a subset of fans are already intensely interested in analytics. Clark, for example, comments, "There's this niche of fans who is really interested in analytics," and argues that, thanks to its recent efforts, ESPN is now "serving that niche."[64] However, ESPN employees are also reluctant to describe data-driven content as purely niche content. Instead, as might be expected, they repeatedly emphasize the ability of analytics to appeal to mass audiences. Nick, for instance, states that many sports fans have a developing, natural curiosity about analytics given the wider industry swing. "They read the same news articles—they understand, they see that teams are hiring all these analytical people." He continues, "There's a segment that really wants to understand that. Like, what's going on there? Why is that useful? Why is my team hiring this guy who was a professor of electrical engineering?"[65] Similarly, Alan suggests that fans have gradually become more attuned to advanced statistical analysis as analytics has pervaded more and more segments of the sporting landscape. He comments, "People are more comfortable with that kind of information—it's in video games, on the back of baseball cards." He argues, then, that fans are familiar with advanced metrics "even if they don't understand all the math and the concepts behind it."[66]

Another potential driver of fan interest in data-driven coverage may be the growth of fantasy sports. To that point, Hahn, VanDyke, and Cummins argue for a link between the rising popularity of fantasy sports and the decision by broadcasters to "depend more on quantitative information in their storytelling."[67] Another potential part of the equation is the increasing visibility of sports gambling, particularly in the wake of its legalization in a growing number of states. As Hahn, VanDyke, and Cummins suggest, viewers with "financial investments" in games may have "greater interest in relevant statistics related to athletes and team."[68] Indeed, sports analytics and gambling have a close relationship, with sophisticated mathematical models lying at the heart of many advanced sports betting operations.[69] Evidence of this tight relationship is easy to find, ranging from gambling panels at the Sloan Conference to personnel moves. For example, in 2018, prominent professional sports bettor Haralabos Voulgaris moved into the front office of the Dallas Mavericks, becoming their "Director of Quantitative Research and Development."[70] The intimacy between ESPN's analytics efforts and sports gambling is hinted at in statements by executive Connor Schell. Discussing the company's growing coverage of sports betting, he comments, "We know there are sports fans who are interested in that type of content. . . . We're going to serve those fans with information and analytics."[71] And speaking to that intention, some of the strongest examples of datavisuality come from ESPN's sports betting coverage. The studio show *Daily Wager* (2019–), for instance, is typically blanketed in numbers (figure 3.10), many of which draw on ESPN's analytics work.

More generally, though, a common refrain among the ESPN employees I talked to is that statistical analysis assists storytelling—both creating new narratives and adding fresh layers to existing ones. According to this argument, all fans can find themselves engaged by analytics—not just the diehard fans who might debate the merits of OPS versus wOBA. To that point, Greg, one of the first members of the analytics unit, stresses that while ESPN may draw on the same sorts of tools and techniques as professional teams, they use those tools and techniques differently—attempting to build "stories" that will resonate with as many fans as possible. "If I was working for a team, I might do something totally different and worry about salary cap and optimization," he says. "In our case, it starts from fan questions." Alan, meanwhile, says, "I think what we're talking about, generally, are things that should appeal to a very wide audience of fans. . . . The hard math, leave that to us. Just, what's the story?" He mentions, for example, using advanced metrics to drive debates about the best teams and players in college football—conversations, he argues, in which almost any college football fan can become invested. Notably, these types of data-driven debates have a long history. For example, in his history of baseball scoring and scouting, Phillips mentions how print publications covering baseball in the nineteenth century turned to statistical analysis to generate "fodder for discussions about year-end laurels." As Phillips observes, "Then, as now, lists ranking top players were popular because they created controversies and increased sales."[72] Such uses for statistical analysis in mind, Alan draws comparisons between the company's analytics unit and the many ex-players that ESPN employs as analysts. Both, he argues, provide unique perspectives that fuel more extensive conversations.[73] Clark agrees, commenting that the analytics unit is like "one more facet to the jewel that is ESPN," while Roger shares a parallel metaphor of advanced metrics being "just tools in a toolbox" that the company can use when necessary.[74]

126   CHAPTER THREE

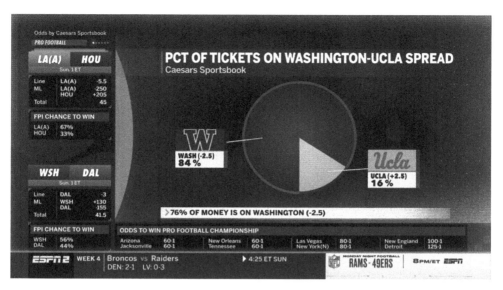

FIGURE 3.10: Graphics displayed during ESPN's sports betting programming. (*Daily Wager*, ESPN2)

Reached several years after our initial discussion of ESPN's interest in sports analytics, Alan reinforces the idea that the company's recent embrace of advanced statistical analysis has been neither accidental nor representative of a short-term experiment. He notes, for instance, that the analytics unit has continued to expand its efforts—creating more advanced metrics for more sports, with a particular attention devoted to women's sports. He mentions, too, greater use of tracking data and cites additional examples of analytics efforts being worked into the company's television programming, including in major properties like *Monday Night Football* (ABC/ESPN, 1970–) and NFL draft coverage. "Not surprisingly," he comments, the company's adoption of advanced statistical analysis "is greater every year as analytics become a more accepted part of sports."[75] For the foreseeable future, a quantitative lens seems likely to remain ascendant at ESPN. What the next section asks, then, is what such a lens means not just for the look and feel of sports television, but also for how we interpret the use of quantitative data both in sport and wider society.

Critiquing Datavisuality

In the wake of *Moneyball*, the gradual ascendance of sports analytics across the sporting landscape has often been framed much as it was in the book—as something of a march of progress. As Phillips observes, *Moneyball* made "for a good story, a modern-day parable about the power of data and rationality to overcome superstition and guesswork," and outlines of that triumphant narrative linger many years later.[76] As Phillips also observes, though, this sort of evolutionary framing—pitting the outdated subjectivity of traditional sporting knowledge exemplified by scouts against the newfound objectivity of analytics exemplified by mathematically inclined data analysts—is overly simplistic. "Parables, like myths, are important cultural markers," he writes. "But they are not necessarily accurate portrayals of how things work."[77] To that end, he closely examines the history of baseball scoring and scouting to demonstrate, for instance, how scouts have long offered their own claims of quantified objectivity.

In concluding his study, Phillips argues that critical interrogations of the sports analytics narrative are necessary for, as he writes, sport "has become synonymous with the promises of data analytics and the power of replacing traditional forms of expertise with new, data-driven ones" and, accordingly, examining these sorts of promises within sport offers "a way to recast our understanding of the meaning of data in the modern world."[78] This points to the similar necessity of analyzing the ideological and epistemological tenets of datavisuality. As the above sections have detailed, sports television has become increasingly datafied—becoming home to greater quantities of quantitative data and more-complex quantitative data. Accordingly, sports television is deeply enmeshed—like sport, more generally—in the broader datafication of society. Indeed, sports television may be one of the most visible indicators of this datafication. With that in mind, the rest of this section will subject datavisuality to critique—asking what assumptions and claims lay beneath this new mode of data-driven broadcasting and, in turn, what these ideas might be able to tell us not only about modern sport but also about the wider ascendancy of data analytics across society.

"Faith in Numbers"

Datavisuality is partially defined by a growing flood of statistical measures into sports broadcasting, so much so that certain programming strains the limits of how many numbers can be placed on-screen at any one time. Moreover, datavisuality has entailed the use of increasingly complex metrics based on intricate formulas and elaborate tracking systems. Both tendencies of datavisuality—quantity and complexity—revolve around a pervasive desire to more thoroughly capture and communicate player and team performance using numerical metrics. As such, datavisuality continues—and intensifies—

the project of quantification that has long been at the heart of modern sport, thus making it part and parcel of sport's recent "statistical turn."

The intensifying quantification of datavisuality speaks to several of the ideological trends identified in previous chapters. For instance, as mentioned in the last chapter, one hallmark of sports media's managerial fixation is the growing dominance of financial logics, as exemplified by the now-familiar treatment of players as financial "assets." Among other effects, these commodifying logics have placed athletes at a remove, in the process deemphasizing their humanity. The quantification of datavisuality potentially works toward similar ends. Ted Porter posits, "Quantification is a technology of distance" in that quantitative metrics can be easily transported and understood across varying contexts.[79] That distancing, though, not only makes statistics convenient as a communication strategy but also raises questions about what happens when it is humans who are subject to that distancing. Helen Kennedy and Rosemary Lucy Hill argue that this remove can be dehumanizing, writing, "The numbers and calculations produced through data-gathering distance these same numbers from the human subjects to which they refer and, in turn, distance viewers and consumers of these numbers from an awareness of and sensitivity to those human subjects without whom the numbers would not exist."[80] Applied to sport, this line of argument suggests that statistical analysis may have the effect of pushing athletes further into the background of the competitions in which they compete. To that point, Baerg, in writing about the spread of sports analytics, draws on Bruno Latour, who "suggests that inscription technologies like numbers . . . push the objects out after extracting data from it such that extracted data becomes 'all that counts.' " Baerg asks, then, "Will organization decision makers become devoted to data that selectively reveals and denies and push the object as athlete out? Will athletes understand themselves primarily as data producers rather than as more fully orbed and complete subjects?"[81] As datavisuality becomes the norm, the average sports television viewer becomes implicated in such questions. Will they, in other words, understand athletes primarily as data producers rather than as individuals with agency?

The escalating quantification of datavisuality raises questions about how viewers understand sport, more generally. As David Beer writes, "metrics and statistical insights" have not only reshaped how sports decision makers operate and, accordingly, how games are played but also how sports are consumed and discussed by fans.[82] On a similar note, Benjamin Burroughs details the growth of "statistical fandom" around the sport of baseball, arguing that statistics have come to serve as "a lens through which audiences now consume and interact" with the sport.[83] For Beer, this shift in how fans understand sport has broader ramifications. A sociologist interested in metrics, more broadly, Beer turns his analysis to sport because of its "potential to enable a granular analysis of the measurement and calculation of life, people and experience."[84] And, to that end, Beer ties the quantitative impulse in sport to what Philip Mirowski labels "everyday neoliberalism"—a term meant to capture neoliberalism's deep entrenchment in daily life. According to Beer, sport becomes an example of how "systems of measurement and competition become a routine part of everyday attitudes, imaginaries and practices."[85] Datavisuality can be included in this phenomenon, helping metrics like WHIP, DVOA, and xG become a regular part of many fans' media experiences and, as such, their everyday lives. Following Beer, then, it might also be suggested datavisuality's influence stretches beyond sport, playing a role in the "politics of data circulations and the place of numbers in contemporary social life."[86] Datavisuality may, for instance, help foster a more generalized "faith in numbers" that eventually stretches into realms like education and health care.[87]

It must be recognized, too, that even though broadcasters' move toward datavisuality has followed broader shifts in sports and sports fandom, this data-driven form of telecasting nonetheless represents a series of deliberate choices toward quantification. It is also worth considering, then, what choices are *not* being made by broadcasters. To that point, Yago Colás argues that sports analytics, in "prioritizing what can be measured, as well as efficiency and economic value, serves as a kind of limiting horizon containing whatever other desires might be stirred, and values embodied by a given player."[88] For Colás, the ascendancy of analytics means that relatively amorphous pleasures—like a basketball player's surprising ability to "overcome seemingly insurmountable obstacles"—"are relegated to the realm of illusions that must give way to reality, which is to say, quantitative appraisals of efficiency."[89]

Notably, too, both media members and fans have articulated similar ideas as the ones emphasized by Colás—rejecting, in other words, the data-driven lens of "statistical fandom" in favor of a more ineffable engagement with sport. Nationally syndicated commentator Dan Patrick, for instance, has repeatedly lamented the effect of sports analytics—commenting, for example, that data-driven decision making has made sports "robotic" and less "aesthetically pleasing"—while the production personnel at the RSN SportsNet New York (SNY) have garnered national media attention for publicly flouting statistical analysis in favor of an "experimental," film-inspired approach to baseball coverage, as in the use of superimpositions to explore a coach's interiority or in the use of split screen shots of batters and pitchers to approximate the tense confrontations of a western.[90] "There's a lot of numbers and analytics out there these days," SNY producer Gregg Picker comments, "but we've always believed the reason people watch sports is to be moved by great athletic endeavors or the passion of the fans."[91] His colleague, SNY director John DeMarsico, similarly proclaims that "advanced analytics or odds and probabilities" are not his "cup of tea." He elaborates in arguing, "This is the entertainment business . . . [broadcasters] should be taking more chances and showing the spectacle of the game."[92] Many fans, too, have suggested that a quantitative lens can be a tedious lens, as in a widely circulated meme that contrasts a gloomy "advanced stats nerd" with a more gleeful casual fan—a framing that suggests there is more pleasure in the informal enjoyment of skill and determination than in the intricate analysis associated with analytics.

This critical discourse in mind, one might imagine what sports television would look like if, somewhat in the vein of the SNY telecasts, it attempted to further emphasize the "aesthetic delights" celebrated by Colás and others.[93] What might it look like, for example, to have sports television deliberately seek to emphasize the athletic "grace" praised by theorist Hans Ulrich Gumbrecht, in which an athlete's bodily movements seem to separate from their consciousness, such that their performance appears to become uncoupled from intention?[94] What new televisual techniques might be deployed to understand this uncoupling? Can this phenomenon, which borders on the ephemeral, even be captured? Such questions speak to a form of sports television pointing in a different direction than datavisuality's elevation of measured efficiency.

Bigger Data, Better Data?

Sports organizations are not just increasingly invested in quantification but are also now drawing on complex technologies, including optical tracking systems and biometric sensors, to aggregate and process increasingly large amounts of data. Millington and Millington comment, "Unstructured data, motion tracking, 'data scientists': this is sport in the Age of Big Data."[95] Broadcasters, too, have entered this new "age," even using some of the very same tracking and biometric monitoring systems employed by leagues and teams.

As sports organizations have increasingly drawn on big data tools and methodologies, scholars have critiqued aspects of this trend. Millington and Millington, for instance, link sport's move into the realm of big data with issues like privacy, noting that organizations are gathering ever-more information not just about athletes but also about fans.[96] Baerg has also waded into

Managerial Sports Television   131

questions related to surveillance, arguing that the rise of big data is creating troubling divides between organizations and athletes, as organizations often not only have more access to athlete data than the athletes themselves but also greater ability to analyze that data.[97] Brett Hutchins, meanwhile, questions the growing divide between organizations able to implement big data approaches.[98] Women's and semiprofessional sports, for example, often lack the same resources to gather extensive data sets and, therefore, may be unable to draw attention from data-hungry fans. As a result, he writes, these sports might also struggle to attract corporate sponsors looking to capitalize on fan data.

While the ascendency of datavisuality touches on these sorts of issues—fans consuming alternative data-driven telecasts on streaming platforms may, for instance, find themselves surveilled by way of trackers that gather data on their browser configurations and IP addresses—a more specific concern presented by datavisuality involves how sports television frames big data practices. As danah boyd and Kate Crawford write, the rise of big data is a phenomenon that entails not just new technologies and new means of analysis but also a distinct mythology suggesting "large data sets offer a higher form of intelligence and knowledge that can generate insights that were previously impossible, with the aura of truth, objectivity, and accuracy."[99] Of course, such a belief is problematic. As boyd and Crawford argue, numbers do not speak for themselves—even if some big data proponents may suggest that they do.

A banal example from an MLB Network studio show highlights how datavisuality risks reinforcing flawed big data mythology. During an episode of *MLB Tonight* (2009–) that aired soon after the league introduced its new tracking systems, the show's three commentators found themselves discussing pitcher Koji Uehara, in the process arguing that spin rate—a new metric drawing on these tracking systems—could serve as a helpful tool in complementing the sport's traditional emphasis on pitch velocity. Impressed by the technologies that had enabled this new measurement—and the flashy graphic used to display it—one of the commentators, longtime Rockies general manager Dan O'Dowd, enthusiastically declared, "It allows you to look inside a player's ability so much deeper . . . it should allow you to make so much better evaluations of your players." He continued, "You can't measure that with the naked eye. . . . This allows you to measure it down to an exact science." The keywords here—"deeper," "better"—are very much in line with the mythology that boyd and Crawford describe. The implicit idea is that this technologically complex metric outstrips human comprehension. Indeed, as Baerg comments, such convictions—particularly those casting doubt on the human eye—are endemic within the sports analytics discourse, with new

132   CHAPTER THREE

metrics often "said to reveal things that cannot be seen" and new technologies frequently associated with a "push for greater and greater revelation of that which is currently hidden."[100]

What is needed in place of these sorts of grand claims of novelty is additional complexity—complexity that speaks to big data's history, its constructedness, and its inability to deliver an objective "truth." As Crawford, Kate Miltner, and Mary L. Gray argue, "Rather than invest in big data as an all-knowing prognosticator or a shortcut to ground truth, we need to recognize and make plain its complexities and dimensionality as an emerging theory of knowledge."[101] This need is particularly acute in relation to datavisuality because sports television represents one of the rare locations within the media landscape where big data has become a regular point of conversation. Sports television, then, offers a significant opportunity to better inform viewers about what a massive dataset looks like and how it is being used, in the process giving viewers a sense of the complexities and complications of big data methodology. This, then, could offer viewers an improved understanding of how big data might be used in the wider world beyond sports.

As of yet, though, sports television has not fully seized the opportunity to illuminate the "dimensionality" of sport's big data practices. Baseball viewers, for example, might be offered information about a player's speed to a ball and how that speed ranks in comparison to other players—thus imparting some knowledge about the league's tracking technologies and how those technologies can be used to evaluate players—but they are generally offered relatively little insight into how this type of data is gathered and how it might be used by teams in their decision-making processes. In the case of the *MLB Tonight* example, for instance, this introductory discussion of spin rate might have further emphasized how exactly Uehara's spin rate was calculated or the longer history behind the metric, for as Phillips notes, MLB's tracking systems build on previous data operations—a trajectory that suggests, he adds, "the rhetoric of revolutions or sharp breaks with past baseball data-gathering efforts should be moderated."[102] Of course, such historical and methodological context will not instantly erode the perniciousness of big data mythology. Moreover, as the ESPN employees I interviewed emphasize, there can be challenges in trying to interest casual fans in the nuances behind any given metric, as in Alan's comments about the need to avoid "hard math." Still, it is worth advocating for as much context as possible, as additional information would allow glimpses—rare moments of transparency—into a major industry's big data practices. As big data continues to play an increasingly significant role in everyday life, such clarity—even if limited—could have immense value in qualifying the broader claims made for big data.

Data on Display

Part of what makes datavisuality a unique phenomenon is not just that it brings numerical metrics and big data into the foreground of television programming but also that it works to represent all this data visually. In so doing, datavisuality invites questions about the broader ramifications of the way "data are mobilized graphically."[103] As several scholars have noted, data visualizations are an increasingly prevalent mode of representation and, as such, demand scrutiny. Kennedy and Hill write, for instance, that "data visualizations are not neutral windows onto data" and, as such, argue "data cannot be uncoupled from their visual representation."[104] Meanwhile, Jonathan Gray et al. suggest data visualizations "come with particular 'ways of seeing,'" elaborating that they "reflect and articulate their own particular modes of rationality, epistemology, politics, culture, and experience."[105] Digging into those particularities, Johanna Drucker has expressed several reservations about data visualizations, arguing that visualizations are always loaded with unspoken premises. In her words, "Graphical tools are a kind of intellectual Trojan horse, a vehicle through which assumptions about what constitutes information swarm with potent force."[106]

What are these assumptions? First, there is the problem of the "data" used to construct visualizations. Drucker argues that designers tend to proceed forward with the idea that they are working with preexisting "data" offering a transparent window into the world, assuming that the statistical information they are depicting unproblematically represents "a priori conditions."[107] Drucker's second related argument is that visualizations tend not just to be based on this flawed conception of "data" but also that they conceal such faulty assumptions. She explains, "The rendering of statistical information into graphical form gives it a simplicity and legibility that hides every aspect of the original interpretative framework on which the statistical data were constructed." Elaborating, she adds that graphics "do not present themselves as categories of interpretation, riven with ambiguity and uncertainty."[108] In a similar vein, Kennedy et al. argue that certain graphical conventions, like clean layouts, create an "aura of clarity and simplicity" that "obscures the complexity of data and their visualization."[109] Such obscuring, then, works to imbue data with "a sense of objectivity."[110]

Such critiques help illuminate the significance of the visuality of datavisuality. Take, for instance, the "completion probability" graphics occasionally used in NFL telecasts. These graphics, produced via the league's tracking systems, display a metric meant to capture the likelihood of a ball having been caught based on factors like the distance the ball traveled in the air and

FIGURE 3.11: Graphic displaying "completion probability" statistic. (*NFL on CBS*, CBS)

the distance between the receiver and their defenders (figure 3.11). These completion probability graphics do not just take for granted that the various measurements are accurate, but also presuppose that the measurements matter—that "completion probability" indicates something of significance and, as such, is worth passing along to audiences. Whether the measurement is actually correct and valuable is unclear, but the graphic aims to remove uncertainty. Relying on the types of visual conventions that Kennedy et al. identify, like the use of simple geometric shapes, the graphic tries to be as "neat" as possible, thereby communicating that the data themselves are also neat. As Drucker might suggest, the graphics "contain no graphical trace of the multiple decision points and processes of reduction, abstraction, standardization, or other procedures" that went into their creation.[111] Such simplification, then, works to give the graphics an aura of objectivity, helping them appear trustworthy and valuable. This is perhaps a particularly troubling outcome in the case of graphics, like the completion probability ones, derived from tracking systems. In rendering these systems objective and valuable, graphics potentially further the problematic big data mythology mentioned in the previous section.

It is also worth considering how visualization, like quantification, more generally, can have potentially dehumanizing effects. Drucker observes that the most commonly used forms of visualization, like the bar graph, have historical roots that are too frequently forgotten.[112] Such forms, she points out, have links to centuries-old notions of bureaucracy, management, and objectification that structure their presentation. The flow chart, for example, arises out of bureaucratic structures and, accordingly, "The directional force of power relations and movement of goods through a production system often have a conspicuous absence of human agents, as if processes were an inevitable and natural fact."[113] A similar critique comes from Lauren Klein. Klein cites Drucker's "Trojan horse" metaphor as she examines Thomas Jefferson's papers and the graphs within. Klein notices how Jefferson's visualizations went hand in hand with "subjugation and control—that is, the reduction of persons to objects, and stories to names."[114]

Applying these critiques to datavisuality, it is not uncommon for sports television to draw on the same forms of visualization that these scholars examine in their scholarship, like line graphs and bar graphs. Of course, though, the argument stretches beyond the continued use of these specific visuals. The greater significance is that the visualizations that are part of datavisuality—whether they are simple bar graphs or three-dimensional marvels that represent the latest in virtual graphics technology—risk continuing the project of configuring power relations in uneven ways and, in the process, removing human agency. Take, for instance, the increasing use of "shot charts" in the coverage of basketball—charts that use simple, top-down renderings of a basketball court to display where a player or team has been making and missing their shots (figures 3.6 and 3.12). To borrow from Drucker, such charts have "a conspicuous absence of human agents," having transformed players' efforts into dots or Xs and Os. This sort of visual representation risks treating athletes primarily as data producers, with their outputs more significant than either the process or the person.

While the visualizations of datavisuality risk reifying the worrisome trends, like the spread of big data mythology, scholars have also pointed to ways visualizations might work toward other ends. Drucker, for instance, raises the possibility of employing graphical features that, rather than bearing "the hallmarks of positivist, quantitative, and/or statistical approaches to knowledge," instead "express fundamental principles of interpretation: uncertainty, parallax, contradiction, partial knowledge."[115] While it may be challenging to incorporate all these features into the broadcast mode, it is also worth asking what it may look like to integrate these principles into sports television. What would it look like, for instance, for completion probability graphics to acknowledge uncertainty in their calculations? Kennedy and Hill, meanwhile, emphasize that data visualizations are inevitably experienced emotionally, making it possible, they argue, "to feel numbers, metrics, data

FIGURE 3.12: Graphic displaying a basketball "shot chart." (*SportsCenter*, ESPN2)

and statistics," rather than only perceiving them cognitively.[116] Accordingly, they suggest that visualizations, rather than only furthering the dehumanization that can accompany quantification, may also be able to "[diminish] the distance that quantification is said to produce," thereby allowing consumers to "imagine and empathise with the plight of the human subjects represented within [a] visualisation."[117] One might, then, consider the affective possibilities of datavisuality, asking, for instance, whether a visualization might be able to evoke empathy in highlighting the precariousness of an athletic career. While it is unlikely that such visualizations would ever become the norm on sports television, these sorts of alternative possibilities do suggest the "particular 'ways of seeing'" that accompany visualizations do not necessarily have to reinscribe, for instance, the hyperrationality at the heart of so much data-driven programming and that visualizations' lack of "neutrality" can work in a range of directions.

Wielding Data

The above sections have touched on how datavisuality frames the relationship between individuals and the new technologies and methodologies at the heart of data-driven sports decision making, suggesting, for instance, that datavisuality may reinforce the pernicious big data mythology elevating algorithmic outputs above human knowledge. Also significant in this framing is who is positioned to wield these new technologies and methodologies. Datavisuality, of course, does not mark the first time new technologies have been incorporated into television programming, and human-computer interactions have become standard across a variety of genres, ranging from game shows to news and weather broadcasts. Speaking to this long history, as well as the stakes involved, Lisa Parks argues that the incorporation of technology into television comes loaded with "hegemonic assumptions."[118] As a key example, she points to the rise of network quiz shows in the late 1990s and early 2000s, with *Who Wants to Be a Millionaire* (ABC, 1999–2002) serving as the most prominent example. Scrutinizing *Millionaire,* Parks observes that the show—which prominently featured a quasi-computer interface—overwhelmingly featured white men, thus positioning them as the primary users of the show's technology. In the process, Parks argues, the show tended "to reinforce white, middle-class masculine control over new media."[119]

Datavisuality has worked similarly, almost exclusively positioning white men as the wielders of new technologies and methods. For example, Fox's alternative baseball analytics telecast featured a desk of several white men at the control of the new metrics and visualizations prioritized by the broadcast. ESPN's data-driven alternative telecasts, too, have repeatedly positioned white men at the center of advanced statistical analysis. Moreover, alternative telecasts have not been the only examples of this tendency. The many former front-office executives employed by sports television networks are often those positioned to comment on data-driven broadcast features, as evidenced by former GM Dan O'Dowd discussing spin rate. As mentioned in previous chapters, these managerial figures are typically white men. Datavisuality, then, echoes 1990s-era network television in reinforcing "white, middle-class masculine control over new media."

This skewed representation, of course, speaks to the broader ideological project of managerial sports media detailed throughout this project, wherein managerial sports media has served to remasculinize white men. To that point, datavisuality is another clear indicator of sports media's recent elevation of the "geek masculinity" highlighted in previous chapters and the incorporation of elements of this geek masculinity into hegemonic masculinity. Within data-driven telecasts, traits like "intellectual achievement" and "technical mastery" become front and center. Although the ascendancy of these sorts of attributes has not been entirely uncontested—witness, for instance, a prominent 2015 incident that saw basketball player-turned-broadcaster Charles Barkley decrying the rise of analytics and referring to data-driven NBA executives like Morey as "idiots" who "never played the game"—the integration of advanced metrics

138   CHAPTER THREE

into sports broadcasts has, at this point, become increasingly normalized and, in the process, served to further position technocratic administrators as central figures in the sporting landscape.[120] In turn, the skewed representation has suggested that technocratic competence is primarily reserved for white men. With that in mind, the increasingly quantified realm of sports television can be viewed, like the media discussed in previous chapters, as working to "resecure a normative and dominant place for straight white men in American culture and society in the present and into the future."[121]

The close entwinement of race, gender, and analytics has not gone unnoticed within sports media. ESPN analyst Jalen Rose, for instance, has suggested the rise of analytics has provided a convenient rationale to exclude retired Black players from positions of power, with playing experience increasingly devalued in favor of academic expertise (whether real or nominal).[122] In these critiques, one sees echoes of David J. Leonard's argument that discussions of intelligence within the world of sport are often racially coded—with white athletes frequently celebrated for "cunning, smarts, and athletic intelligence" and Black athletes alternatively positioned as achieving success through "physical rather than mental prowess"—and, moreover, that this racist framing shapes who is deemed capable of taking leadership positions within sport.[123] Hardly commented on, though, has been sports television's role in reproducing this sort of framing around analytics. As data-driven telecasts continue to position white men as analytics experts—in total control of new technologies and new metrics—what Rose refers to as the "cultural overtones" of analytics only become further ensconced.[124]

Managerial Sports Television   139

4

White-Collar Play

Managerial Sports Games and the Modeling of Neoliberal Capitalism

As has been thoroughly documented throughout this project, a wide range of sports media texts—from films to podcasts to studio television shows—have recently demonstrated a deep and sustained interest in the duties and responsibilities of front-office executives. However, perhaps no realm of the sports media landscape has shown more explicit evidence of a managerial fixation than the world of digital sports games. Some of the most popular sports video game franchises, including the perennially best-selling *FIFA, Madden,* and *NBA 2K* series, feature intricate managerial modes that ask players to handle a wide array of administrative tasks ranging from draft scouting to salary cap management. Indeed, there exists a popular niche of sports simulations, exemplified by the *Football Manager* and *Out of the Park Baseball* franchises, that makes this sort of administrative work its primary focus, in the process largely deemphasizing the sort of action gameplay more commonly associated with sports video games. Notable, too, has been the rising popularity of fantasy sports leagues that task players with managing virtual rosters of athletes.

Given how strongly digital sports games have embraced management, they are a particularly appropriate candidate with which to further inquire into the appeal of managerial sports texts and, in the process, revisit some of the scholarly consensus that has begun to emerge around managerial sports media. Significantly, several scholars have already begun addressing digital sports games' interest in administrative responsibilities. In their work, an initial take on these games' managerial fixation emerges. Recalling the types of critiques offered in previous chapters, these scholars have posited that managerial sports games are deeply imbricated in issues of power, as exemplified by the use of quantitative player rating systems that position athletes as arrays of numbers. As the scholars suggest, then, these games reinscribe troubling inequalities and signal yet another advance of neoliberalism, with athletes figured as interchangeable resources to be optimized in a marketplace environment.

Seeking to complement this initial line of analysis, in this chapter I consider how players might make sense of the "neoliberal fantasies" offered by managerial sports games by further situating these games within everyday life amid neoliberal capitalism. As I argue, managerial sports games, in attempting to model the imperatives of both contemporary sport and contemporary work, make explicit the rationalities that undergird neoliberal capitalism as well as how those rationalities have rippled across ever more spheres of social life. Indeed, as simulations, managerial sports games offer players unique opportunities to experiment with those rationalities and their effects—probing, for instance, how sport has transformed in the wake of financialization. As I suggest, too, this modeling of the imperatives of contemporary sport and contemporary work speaks to how these games operate as "affective systems" that can meaningfully resonate amid the rhythms and sensations of neoliberal capitalism—allowing players to renegotiate, for instance, the precarious conditions of their everyday work lives.[1] I suggest, then, that while managerial sports games frame the world through neoliberal values, they may also serve as key sites for critical reflection on the spread of those values into everyday life.

Background

The Managerial Sports Game

Before delving into the nascent scholarship around managerial sports games, some additional context would be beneficial to more clearly define the genre and historicize its fit within the broader gaming landscape. Managerial sports games will be categorized here as digital sports games that ask players to construct virtual rosters of athletes—a definition that includes a wide variety of texts ranging from dedicated "management simulation" games like *Football Manager, Franchise Hockey Manager, Motorsport Manager,* and *Out of the Park Baseball,* which are primarily concerned with closely replicating the many details associated with running professional sports organizations, to popular multiplatform video game franchises like *FIFA* and *Madden,* which include managerial gameplay modes among a suite of other gameplay options, to fantasy sports websites and applications, most of which lack the intricacies of more complex games like *Football Manager* and *Madden* yet feature similar gameplay features, like the ability to virtually acquire and trade athletes.

Although managerial sports games have had particularly visible success in recent years, their current popularity is but the latest chapter in a much longer history.[2] In fact, several scholars note their origins can perhaps be traced all the way back to tabletop baseball games first introduced in the nineteenth century, like the 1866 game *Parlor Base-Ball* that simulated the sport by having players use a spring-loaded bat to hit a rolled coin.[3] More commonly, though, contemporary managerial sports games are linked to the card-and-dice simulations that emerged in the mid-twentieth century—games like *All-Star Baseball, American Professional Baseball Association (APBA), Statis-Pro,* and *Strat-O-Matic*. As Adam Criblez emphasizes, these tabletop simulation games grew increasingly popular over the course of the 1960s and 1970s, receiving mainstream media coverage and building dedicated fanbases. Indeed, Criblez points out the surging popularity of games like *APBA* and *Strat-O-Matic* during this period inspired spin-off hobby magazines and countless "second wave" competitors.[4]

Important, too, in historicizing the ubiquity of contemporary games is the converging trajectory of fantasy sports, for at the same time as tabletop simulations were growing their passionate fanbases in the '60s and '70s, a growing number of sports fans—many of them devotees of tabletop simulations—were experimenting with ways of vicariously assembling rosters of real-world athletes and competing based on these athletes' performances in actual games rather than in simulations. In 1960, for example, sociologist William Gamson devised an early version of a fantasy baseball league in which participants would draft teams and then compare their players' performances based on several statistics that were widely available in newspapers.[5] One of the participants, film historian Robert Sklar, would pass on knowledge of Gamson's fantasy competition to an undergraduate student, Daniel Okrent. Okrent would then go on to create his own version of a fantasy baseball league in 1979 that further intensified, in Sklar's phrasing, the goal of making a participant a "virtual GM."[6] Okrent's league, for example, added the ability to trade players and expanded the number of statistical categories. Media coverage of Okrent's league—named Rotisserie League Baseball—would, in turn, help launch fantasy sports "into the public spotlight" and inspire the creation of ever more fantasy leagues.[7] A decade later, thousands of sports fans were participating in fantasy leagues and the hobby was becoming rapidly commercialized.[8]

Over the course of the 1980s and 1990s, both simulation games and fantasy sports transitioned from being primarily analog activities to largely digital ones. In the case of simulations, Criblez notes tabletop game sales began to wane as sports fans increasingly turned to digital simulations appearing on video game consoles and personal computers.[9] These early digital simulations—which included both adaptations of familiar tabletop titles, such as *APBA Baseball* and *Strat-O-Matic Computer Baseball,* as well as new entrants to the field, like *Diamond Mind Baseball*—were soon followed by the earliest editions of the simulation franchises that continue to dominate today. For example, the initial iteration of the *Madden* series debuted in 1988, while the first version of *Football Manager*—then titled *Championship Manager*—was released in 1992. In the case of fantasy sports, meanwhile, the hobby was rapidly transformed by its move to the internet in the 1990s. ESPN, for instance, began offering an internet-based fantasy service in 1995 and was soon after followed by other companies like CBS Sports and Yahoo.[10] Notably, these new internet-based fantasy services were able to automatically compile player statistics and score results—rather than requiring participants to manually process newspaper box scores—and thus made fantasy leagues much easier to administer and follow. This increasing "ease" of participation—as well as the continuing expansion of access to internet services—proved key in the rapid growth of fantasy sports over the course of the following decades.[11]

As the significant role of digitization in this brief history makes clear, the present ubiquity of managerial sports games hardly emerged out of a vacuum. Unsurprisingly, then, there are also other factors that help explain this ubiquity. As mentioned in the introduction, for example, scholars have linked the growth of fantasy sports with the introduction of free agency systems in the 1970s, with Adam J. Ploeg arguing, for example, that Rotisserie League Baseball's focus on the performances of individual players was symptomatic of the increasing roster turnover within Major League Baseball (MLB).[12] Brody J. Ruihley, Andrew C. Billings, and Nicholas R. Buzzelli, meanwhile, suggest growing interest in fantasy sports was fostered by changes in the television industry, with the expansion of cable and satellite services allowing fans to more easily watch—and follow—teams outside their local markets.[13] They also suggest that participation in fantasy sports has more recently been assisted by the proliferation of mobile devices, as fans now have additional ways to track their fantasy teams—including while simultaneously watching games on other screens.[14]

Significant, too, in providing context for the current spread of managerial sports games is the "exploding" interest in intricate statistical analysis discussed in the previous chapter. It is something of conventional wisdom, for instance, that the public's increasing awareness of advanced statistical analysis by way of texts such as *Moneyball* has also contributed to the grow-

144   CHAPTER FOUR

ing appeal of fantasy sports.[15] With that said, the link between "statistical fandom" and managerial sports games is not a simple one-way relationship, nor just a recent one. Criblez mentions, for instance, how tabletop simulations helped provide early fuel for the growing interest in advanced statistical analysis in the mid-twentieth century. Notably, as game developers honed their card-and-dice baseball simulations, they approached their creations through the lens of statistics—seeking to render the sport of baseball into ever more realistic series of probabilities. This statistical view of the sport, in turn, helped shape baseball fandom—and, indeed, the eventual growth of analytics. Criblez notes, for example, that influential analytics figures like Bill James and Billy Beane were enthusiasts of tabletop simulations like *Ball Park Baseball* and *Strat-O-Matic* and that their pursuits of statistical analysis were partially rooted in early experiences with these simulation games.[16]

Moreover, this mutually reinforcing relationship between statistical analysis and managerial sports games continued in the wake of digitization. In his history of baseball scouting and scoring, for example, Christopher Phillips discusses how the development of the early computer simulation *Diamond Mind Baseball* went hand in hand with the baseball community's broader efforts to further quantify the sport. As Phillips details, the game's creator, Tom Tippett—like the developers of card-and-dice simulation games—wanted to model the sport with as much precision as possible. Tippett, though, hoped to use the possibilities of computerization to simulate the sport with "much finer-grained detail" than what was possible in tabletop simulations.[17] To that end, Tippett incorporated data from "Project Scoresheet"—a volunteer-based effort that had recently been launched by James in an attempt to collect and log play-by-play game events so as to "turn the messy, chaotic, and often unpredictable events of a baseball game" into standardized data.[18]

It is also worth repeating here that the growing fascination with advanced statistical analysis within sport in the mid-twentieth century was itself enmeshed in a broader societal interest in quantification—a fact further borne out by the development of managerial sports games. Sam Walker suggests, for instance, that it is impossible to separate Gamson's early fantasy league from a quantitative turn in the social sciences that defined Gamson's professional life in academia. "Gamson's generation of social scientists," Walker observes, "was the first to be drilled in statistics, psychometrics, and econometrics."[19] Walker argues, then, that Gamson's fantasy league provided Gamson and his fellow academic participants "an informal way to flex their new analytical muscles" in optimizing their teams.[20]

To properly contextualize contemporary managerial sports games, too, requires a recognition that although they are usually grouped either by themselves or alongside other sports games, they share deep affinities with other popular game genres. Like many strategy games, such as those in the *Age of Empires* or *Civilization* series, managerial sports games often offer their players an omnipotent perspective beyond the scope of any one real-world figure, combining the coach, general manager, and owner roles into one all-powerful front office worker with complete and total knowledge of a team's doings. And like business simulation games, such as the titles within the *Rollercoaster Tycoon* series, managerial sports games often allow their players to delve deeply into financial matters—obsessing over contractual details and closely monitoring ever-fluctuating budgets. Even the most basic fantasy football apps can leave their players anxiously pondering how to maximize limited acquisition budgets and outwit their competitors in cutthroat auctions where every dollar counts. Unsurprisingly, then, these sorts of generic overlaps are reflected in the history of managerial sports games. For instance, Avalon Hill, one of the major publishers of tabletop sports simulations—and one of the first publishers to begin developing digital sports simulations—got its start with military strategy games before also branching into sports simulations.[21] Suffice it to say, then, that managerial sports games do not stand alone in the gaming landscape—a fact that will eventually help us understand their features better.

"Neoliberal Fantasies"

As mentioned above, something of a consensus has started to emerge within the growing amount of scholarship critically analyzing managerial sports games. Again and again, scholars have suggested managerial sports games—whether simulation video games or fantasy games—promote neoliberal values. Meredith M. Bagley, for instance, writes "fantasy sport play coaches a type of citizen/subject well suited and quiescent to neoliberal capitalism and its modes of living," while Kellen Hoxworth argues fantasy football "offers participants the opportunity to inhabit a neoliberal fantasy of agency, enterprise, empowerment, and market competition."[22] Similarly, in a broader analysis of video games, media theorist Patrick Jagoda refers to *Football Manager* as a particularly clear example of how video games "shape everyday experience through neoliberal principles."[23]

As a starting point in reviewing the substance of this burgeoning line of analysis, it might be helpful to first provide a brief primer on neoliberalism and the role of media texts in shaping neoliberal subjectivity. As mentioned in the introduction, neoliberalism generally refers to an elevation of market ideology and a parallel demand that, amid attacks on the welfare state and labor unions, individuals take responsibility for their own fates. Because one of the primary tenets of neoliberalism is dismantling state support and, in turn, empowering "active citizens," scholars have suggested neoliberal governance becomes a matter of "governing at a distance"—that is to say, dispersing rule throughout society.[24] As Nikolas Rose writes, neoliberalism asks "whether it is possible . . . to govern through the regulated and accountable choices of autonomous agents—citizens, consumers, parents, employees, managers, investors."[25] As such, scholars have also suggested the study of neoliberal governance requires a focus that extends beyond the state, with Laurie Ouellette and James Hay contending, for instance, that one must "look beyond the formal institutions of official government to also emphasize the proliferation and diffusion of the everyday techniques through which individuals and populations are expected to reflect upon, work on and organize their lives and themselves as an implicit condition of their citizenship."[26] For many scholars, media texts have represented key sites for the circulation of such "techniques." Rose, for instance, describes how "the mass media" operates as one of many "technologies that install and support the civilizing project by shaping and governing the capacities, competencies and wills of subjects, yet are outside the formal control of public powers."[27] Media scholars, then, have sought to build on such work to explain how exactly media texts have provided this "support."

As the quotes at the start of this section indicate, managerial sports games have been repeatedly identified as one such site where this dispersed neoliberal governance comes into play, with scholars arguing these games explicitly operate by logics that, in Hoxworth's phrasing, habituate players to "neoliberal modes of thinking."[28] Several of these critiques, for instance, speak to managerial sports games' historical entwinement in a statistical approach toward sport—arguing that these games, in line with neoliberalism's emphasis on a self-optimizing calculative rationality, emphasize the "quantitative over the qualitative, measurement over interpretation, effectiveness over empathy."[29] Andrew Baerg's work offers a case in point. For Baerg, of particular significance has been the way managerial games classify virtual bodies, particularly by way of quantitative classification systems. As he notes, both sports video games specifically concerned with management simulation—as in *Football Manager*—and those that further emphasize action gameplay—as in *FIFA* and *Madden*—rely heavily on player rating systems. That is to say, all these games translate athletes' abilities into numeric ratings. In *FIFA*, for example, one player might be rated as 70 out of 100 on their "dribbling" ability, while another might be rated as 85 out of 100. In *Football Manager*, meanwhile, one player might be rated as 10 out of 20 on

Managerial Sports Games   147

the "bravery" category, while another might be rated as 5 out of 20. These ratings, then, become a significant part of gameplay. If, to continue the *FIFA* example, a virtual athlete has a poor "dribbling" rating, they will be more likely to lose the ball over the course of a game.

In line with the critiques of managerial sports media offered in the previous chapters, Baerg argues that the ability to render athletes as calculable is inevitably a matter of power. On one level, this is power exercised by game developers. They can control what constitutes an athlete and their ability, as well as how users might interact with virtual athletes. On another level, though, this is power exercised by a game's players, as "the quantification of the athletic body through the system positions gamers to exert power through an instrumental rationality."[30] In other words, numeric rating systems transform athletes into resources to be overseen and managed by players for their own competitive purposes. This transformation of athletes into resources, Baerg continues, removes any sense that athletes are individuals with distinct thoughts and desires. For instance, in the case of *FIFA,* Baerg describes how players "exist in its rating system as data aggregations to be manipulated rather than as subjects with agency."[31]

Baerg argues, in turn, that sports video games' emphasis on quantitative optimization has ramifications beyond their virtual spaces, contending that these games naturalize "broader neoliberal discourses of scientifically and actuarially inflected risk management."[32] That is to say, sports video games may encourage players to impose an artificial grid of rationality on other terrains that are similarly messy, whether that be education, policing, or any number of other realms of life. Similarly, he posits that the notion of control offered by fantasy sports—one that is "directly related to managing others"—"may have the effect of moving participants to perceive other decisions that need to be made through this neoliberal, risk-oriented perspective."[33] Concluding this line of analysis, Baerg suggests managerial sports games "may have much more far-reaching social and cultural effects than we might imagine."[34]

As scholars like Baerg have emphasized how managerial sports games advance a neoliberal orientation toward sport and, potentially, the world beyond—rendering everyday life a realm of quantitative risk management based around individualistic competition—they have also repeatedly drawn attention to how these logics have been racialized, with Hoxworth commenting, for instance, that fantasy football "binds together neoliberal subjectivities and racial formations."[35] The work of Thomas Oates is indicative of this type of analysis. Recalling his critiques of NFL draft media discussed in the second chapter, Oates argues football video games and fantasy football are very much defined by their neoliberal "presentation of athletes as commodities to be consumed selectively and self-consciously by sports fans."[36] The *Madden* franchise, for example, "offers up fantasies where the skills of a tycoon merge with control over elite athletes," while fantasy football games explicitly use the "contemporary marketplace" as the predominant metaphor for imagining athletes.[37] Like Baerg, then, Oates finds sports games positioning athletes as resources for fans to control—a process that necessarily erases those athletes' agency. Significantly, though, Oates notes how the positioning of athletes as commodities within managerial football games has the effect of having fans evaluate and type a labor force composed mainly of Black men. As such, Oates argues managerial sports games like *Madden* "serve to contain Black masculinity," thus placing them alongside other managerial texts, like the NFL draft telecast, that also measure and rank Black bodies.[38]

A related thread in the existing work on managerial sports games is the frequent suggestion that their neoliberal lenses toward sport are also gendered ones. Baerg, for instance, notes that the quantitative orientation of sports video games is enmeshed in "traditionally masculine discursive frames" around statistics and scientificity.[39] Oates, meanwhile, draws on Baerg in highlighting links between football gaming and "geek masculinity"—observing that fantasy football and football video games invite players to associate statistical mastery with normative masculinity.[40] Oates, too, highlights how the financialized logics of managerial sports games—positioning athletes as commodities to be shrewdly optimized—touch on "deep, historic connections that establish capitalist competition as a masculine proving ground."[41] Furthermore, Oates and Bagley both call attention to promotions for managerial sports games, arguing that advertisements repeatedly position managerial gaming, in Oates's words, as "clearly masculinized entertainment."[42] Bagley notes, for instance, how fantasy sports service providers like ESPN have run commercials equating neoliberal expertise vis-à-vis fantasy football with normative masculinity, while Oates argues fantasy football advertisements have negotiated the evolving relationship between geek masculinity and hegemonic masculinity by reinforcing the connections between fantasy football's quantitative, financialized gameplay and the traditional sporting masculinity exemplified by NFL athletes.[43]

There exists, then, a notable amount of consistency among the increasing number of scholars who have begun critically examining managerial sports games. Repeatedly, these scholars have argued that managerial sports games promote racialized, gendered neoliberal logics in which athletes are primarily figured as resources to be optimized. Notably, this is a line of analysis that closely aligns with the arguments offered in previous chapters. Again, the suggestion is that in foregrounding administrative work, managerial sports media reify—or even exacerbate—preexisting power imbalances while simultaneously naturalizing an instrumentalized view of the world. Managerial sports games, then, provide yet more evidence of the strong hold of the "Managerial American Dream" across the sports media landscape. With that said, the rest of this chapter will suggest there are more layers to add to the existing analysis of managerial sports games. While the aforementioned scholarship does much to capture the foundational logics of managerial sports games, there is room to further examine how exactly players might interact with these "neoliberal fantasies" by considering, in particular, how these games' modeling of sport and work might speak to players' own everyday experiences with neoliberalism.

Modeling Sport

As mentioned in the discussion of the existing work on managerial sports games, much of this analysis has centered on how these games have modeled sport—the recurring argument being that these games have figured sport as a hyperrational space driven by commodity logics. It is worth lingering, though, on how players might make sense of this particular interpretation of sport—considering, in particular, what happens as players come to recognize the neoliberal principles that undergird these simulations.

As a starting point in teasing out this thread, it is helpful to further consider how these texts operate as games. Notably, a number of game scholars have argued that analyzing digital games requires attention to their distinctions from other media forms, as in Ian Bogost's argument that video games employ "procedural rhetoric" tied to their computational mechanics, or Alexander Galloway's suggestion that video games are "action-based" in that they depend on material interactions between gamers and machines.[44] Another case in point is Ted Friedman's examination of simulation and strategy games, particularly the *Civilization* and *SimCity* series. In this work, Friedman suggests that games are distinct from other media forms in that players encounter texts repeatedly—engaging them until they are mastered and, in the process, their logics fully understood. He explains, "Unlike a book or film that is engaged only once or twice, a computer game is played over and over until every subtlety is exposed, every hidden choice obvious to the savvy player."[45] As Friedman notes, games often come loaded with "questionable ideological premises," as in *Civilization*'s glorification of colonization or *SimCity*'s attempt to render the world neatly calculable.[46] And, as Friedman further explains, critics have seized upon these ideological assumptions, fearing that "technology may mask the constructed-ness

150   CHAPTER FOUR

of any simulation"—an obfuscation that, in the worst-case scenario, helps instill a game's problematic assumptions in its players.[47] However, Friedman argues that because games are played repeatedly until their logic is fully understood, they "reveal their own constructedness to a much greater extent than more traditional texts"—thus making their assumptions explicit.[48] If, for example, one plays *SimCity* with any sort of frequency, it will become quite clear that the game punishes players for raising taxes, in the process signaling an underlying premise that low tax rates spur economic growth and high tax rates lead to economic calamity.[49] Indeed, the player will have to identify these assumptions if they want to do well in the game. However, as Friedman writes, this is not necessarily a gateway to indoctrination. Instead, this is an opportunity for heightened understanding, for as games become demystified, players are implicitly invited to question how games model the world. Friedman summarizes, "The distinct dynamics of computer gaming give the player the chance to transcend" the ideological premises of games.[50]

One can carry these observations toward managerial sports games. To repeat, these games render sport through an explicitly neoliberal lens. As Friedman's work reminds us, though, these sorts of premises are not hidden from gamers. To return to *Football Manager*, a novice player may begin a new game with their favorite team. If they are a big fan of that team, they might default to playing their favorite athletes and signing them to lucrative long-term deals—drawing, perhaps, on their outside knowledge of the players and, in the process, rewarding them for their loyalty to the team or for being particularly kind to fans. However, the game will not reward this humane approach; to win and, in turn, avoid being fired, players must instead learn to fit athletes into formations and contracts that align with the numerical ratings assigned by the game's designers. Similarly, many fantasy football veterans will be familiar with the first-time player who, ignoring statistics and their league's scoring system, drafts their favorite players and quickly plummets to the bottom of the standings. Again, if players want to succeed, they must instead learn to select athletes based on quantitative data.

As Friedman argues, this process of learning a game's logic and deciding how to react to it makes a game's assumptions transparent. Inevitably, then, the ideological premises embedded in managerial sports games—that the sporting world is neatly calculable, for instance—come to the fore. Moreover, upon recognizing these premises, players are not necessarily led to believe this is the way that sport should be understood. Rather, following Friedman's lead, one might suggest that players are only led to believe this is the way these specific games simulate sport. It is left to players, then, to judge how sensible—or flawed—these models of the sporting world may be. While many players will undoubtedly accept their neoliberal premises as reasonable—see, for example, the eager fan discourse that surrounds the annual reveal of *Madden* player ratings—other players may reject these assumptions, perhaps decrying them as overly simplistic or even callous. As Jagoda argues in a broader examination of the neoliberal tendencies of video games, if games tend to promote neoliberal principles, "they also point, through their own artifactual construction and artificial conflict, to the constructedness of that worldview."[51]

And, on that note, it should be acknowledged that some players do seem to delight in rejecting the neoliberal lens encouraged by managerial sports games by playing against the grain in a variety of ways. Fantasy sports leagues, of course, are apt to feature players who even after absorbing the game's hyperrational logics continue to pursue other approaches by, for example, prioritizing athletes from their favorite teams. Meanwhile, there is a sub-genre of *Football Manager* playthroughs in which players excitedly turn their intimate knowledge of the game's reward systems back in on itself in experimenting with how to get fired from their virtual management roles as quickly as possible by, for instance, intentionally antagonizing the simu-lated boards of directors that oversee their teams. If the fantasy player who stubbornly prioritizes their favorite players and teams reveals the pleasures of bringing to the managerial sports game a loyalty or local connection that might otherwise be absent, then the gleefully disastrous *Football Manager* player evidences the joy in creatively undercutting the game's competitive framework that prioritizes wins and financial optimization above all else. The *Football Manager* playthroughs, in particular, suggest a comparison with Bo Ruberg's analysis of video game failure as a form of "queer play."[52] Noting that video games "come to life not when their developers declare them complete but in the moment that players make contact with their control interfaces and step into their worlds," Ruberg emphasizes that not all video game players necessarily play to win and, to that end, highlights the potential of failure as a way to resist "normative expectations."[53] As *Football Manager* players excit-edly giggle as they try to anger their virtual bosses by explicitly refusing to increase revenues or work within a budget, one sees the "counterhegemonic potential" of playing to lose, with players elatedly luxuriating in the overt resistance to the game's neoliberal logics.[54]

Notably, though, managerial sports games might not just invite reflection on their own underlying logics but also the related logics of the wider sporting world in which they are immersed. To that point, one angle that has thus far remained largely in the background of critical analysis of managerial sports games is how these games' instrumentalized conception of sport is enmeshed in broader changes in the sporting landscape. Bearing the traces of neoliberal capitalism—financial deregulation, globalization, and so forth—the sports industry has undergone massive changes over the past few decades as vast sums of money have flowed into a wide variety of sporting organizations and, accordingly, as they have also become entwined in broader phenomena like managerialism and financialization. This has meant, among many other effects, an embrace of the financial logics and data-driven decision making mentioned in previous chapters—outlines of which are also seen in the neoliberal lens of managerial sports games, as in the figuring of athletes as quantifiable financial assets.

While some of sport's transformations amid the flows and rationales of neoliberal capitalism have likely become readily apparent to many sports fans, as in the purchase of sports teams by multinational investment groups, the numerous sprawling effects of these transformations are often less visible. Significantly, though, few texts may be as well positioned to capture these changes as managerial sports games. In his writings on simulation games, Friedman eventually builds to a larger point about the genre. Drawing on theorists of postmodernity like David Harvey and Fredric Jameson, Friedman explains that contemporary capitalism has often eluded straightforward depiction. Elaborating, he states that this most recent economic stage has entailed an interconnectedness that has been difficult to adapt to traditional methods of representing the world. Economic fluxes and changes, for example, are abstractions that are hard to represent within the confines of a two-dimensional map. However, Friedman argues that simulation games are particularly ideal vehicles for taking on the challenge of depicting these complexities. He claims, for instance, that games like *Civilization II* and *SimCity* consist of both "maps-in-time" and "charts-in-time" able to capture the interconnectedness of postmodern systems, "demonstrating the repercussions and interrelatedness of many different social decisions."[55] That in mind, he suggests simulation games are well-positioned to help individuals understand their place within contemporary capitalism.

Friedman's work in mind, one can similarly examine the potential of managerial sports games to illuminate the workings of contemporary sport. In *Football Manager* and *Out of the Park Baseball,* for instance, players are tasked with scrupulously managing their club's budgets by way of complex financial screens that include information both on expenses like player and staff salaries and on income streams like game receipts, media rights, and merchandising (figures 4.1a-b). Immersed in these fluctuating, byzantine tables and charts, players are faced with some of the principal logics that shape modern sport, as in the suggestion organizations should strive to maxi-

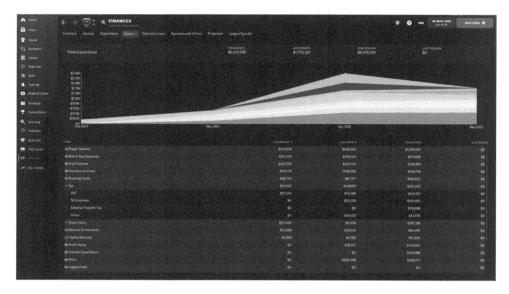

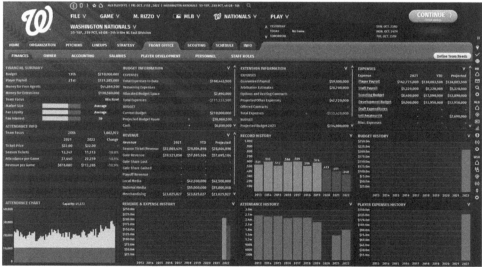

FIGURES 4.1A-B: Financial screens in the managerial sports games *Football Manager* and *Out of the Park Baseball*.

mize as many revenue streams as possible, lest plateauing or falling revenue affect team performance (and, in turn, declining team performance affect revenue, and so on). Again, too, these are principles that players absorb as they play the game to mastery, and so, again, these are principles that become transparent. As such, players are once more invited to judge these premises and, once more, it is possible that some players will respond by questioning whether the effects of neoliberal capitalism have benefited sport or, instead, have skewed it for the worse.

Indeed, it speaks to these sorts of possibilities that another subgenre of *Football Manager* playthroughs features players probing the game's modeling of contemporary sport by, for instance, simulating the effects of infusing lower-division teams with massive amounts of capital or attempting to manage teams loaded with massive amounts of debt. Although managerial sports games like *Football Manager* are themselves hardly critical of contemporary sport—and, indeed, one might conclude that the primary effect of these games to acclimatize players to capitalist transformations—one nonetheless sees in these videos an exemplification of Jagoda's contention that "immersive and interactive game worlds can enable players to experiment with the reality of both the neoliberal subject and a world that is perpetually in flux."[56] As the gamers in these playthroughs work through their experimental scenarios, they use *Football Manager* to not just playfully tease out the rules and processes of the game but also explore what these rules and processes might indicate about the broader workings of modern sport amid neoliberal capitalism—examining, for instance, the sprawling reverberations of enormous media contracts.

Notably, too, some *Football Manager* players create or install game modifications (mods) that touch on the financial underpinnings of sport, as in a number of mods that create fictional countries whose soccer setups are inextricably intertwined with these countries' imagined economies. Occasionally, these sorts of mods serve as something of implicit critiques of the capitalist imperatives of contemporary sport. Several mods, for instance, punish or remove teams that (in the real world) had attempted to launch a "European Super League" meant to restrict the distribution of media rights fees to a small group of powerful teams, while a handful of other mods add a promotion and relegation system to soccer in the United States, thereby allowing the potential of more teams to compete in Major League Soccer (MLS), which—unlike most other upper-tier soccer competitions across the world—has a fixed membership list meant to inflate franchise valuations. Moreover, modders have taken aim at *Football Manager*'s restriction to men's soccer by adding women's teams to the game, in the process calling attention to the undervaluing of women's sport by both the game's developers and the broader sporting apparatus. Game scholar Anne-Marie Schleiner has referred to game mods as "ludic mutations," commenting that they can serve as a "resistant power grab" in which players work against the "subjectification" that games impose on players via their rules and systems.[57] With a number of the mods mentioned above, *Football Manager* players might be said to be, in Schleiner's terms, "seizing back some of that which was lost to the game" by using these mods to reimagine the structures and systems of contemporary sport.[58]

Importantly, Jagoda cautions against too easily celebrating "playful experimentation"—a reminder that is perhaps all the more applicable when discussing games like *Football Manager* that are, in Jagoda's phrasing, "overtly capitalist management simulators."[59] To that point, even as some *Football Manager* players gleefully disregard the game's requests to be prudent with player wages or modify the game to penalize breakaway "Super League" teams, they still largely adhere to the game's instrumental logics and remain locked into the objectifying orientation toward sport that Oates terms "vicarious management."[60] Moreover, as Jagoda notes in discussing "nonnormative ways of engaging games," these alternative approaches tend to remain limited in their prevalence. "For all the creativity and artistry of many such approaches to games," he observes, "such modifications, design practices, and alternative play modes do not represent the fundamental way that games are created, marketed, and played by the majority of players in our time."[61] Testifying to that point, what one might loosely term "critical" mods to *Football Manager* are dramatically outnumbered by ones that tweak player uniforms.

Relevant here, too, is Garry Crawford's argument that while a game like *Football Manager* may allow players new ways of engaging with sport in the wake of fan alienation caused by the "rapid influx of capital and control from transnational big business," this is also but "an elusive and imagined" engagement that is ensnared in these very same capitalist transformations.[62] To that point, while a *Football Manager* player might imagine themselves destroying the finances of a wealthy, state-owned club or, as Jonathan Ervine describes, benevolently intervening on behalf of a team that has become subject to the "mercy of a rich entrepreneur who may be more interested in balance sheets than the history and culture" of that club, the vehicle for these experiments—the game—is itself a product that represents another front in the ongoing "hypercommodification" of sport.[63] "In an industry where fans' influence and control is becoming less apparent," Crawford summarizes, "capitalism profits by selling consumers a sense of control, influence, and support."[64]

Nonetheless, acknowledging "nonnormative" approaches to managerial sports games adds another dimension to work on the genre's relationship to modern sport—indicating that their neoliberal approaches to sport are not totalizing and, moreover, that these games can serve as particularly clear illustrations of sport's ongoing entwinement in the logics and imperatives of neoliberal capitalism. As implied in previous chapters, it is something of a signature of managerial sports texts that they simultaneously illuminate and obscure the workings of contemporary sport—inevitably calling attention, for instance, to many ascendant managerialist principles, like the stress on measurement and efficiency, but also frequently obfuscating, for example, the exact relationship between management and ownership. While managerial sports games are full of their own obfuscations—see, for instance, the way many of these games also blur the lines between management and ownership—it is also true that these games can make particularly explicit many of sport's "structures of interconnection" that have often escaped representation and examination.

Modeling Work

The previous section has attempted to locate managerial sports games within everyday life in neoliberal capitalism by stressing, in particular, how these games simulate contemporary sport. Notably, though, this is not the only act of simulation taking place within managerial sports games. As this section will emphasize, these games also represent an ongoing attempt to model the aesthetics and rhythms of contemporary digital work. Indeed, the resemblance between these games and much of the digital labor now required by the "information economy"/"knowledge economy"/"postindustrial economy" can be striking. While the sports video game modes most frequently held in the popular imagination are those concerned with simulating action via the familiar aesthetics of televised sports, managerial gameplay has long deemphasized the televisual mode.[65] For example, fantasy sports websites are, in essence, glorified tables that very much recall spreadsheet software programs like Microsoft Excel. To play, users manipulate table cells as if they were preparing a budget for an upcoming accounting project. Simulations like *Football Manager* and *Out of the Park Baseball* take this resemblance even further. Users do not just manage data tables but also receive messages in windows meant to recall email clients like Microsoft Outlook (figures 4.2a-b). Indeed, these email screens are central interfaces; to play a game like *Football Manager* or *Out of the Park Baseball* is to repeatedly read and respond to emails. As much, then, as managerial sports games are *sports*

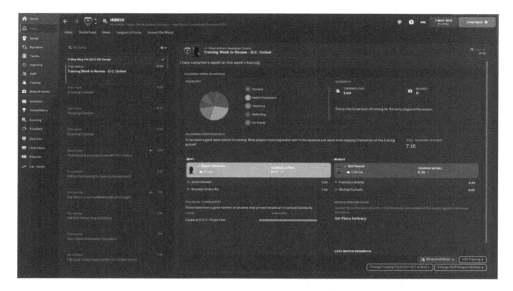

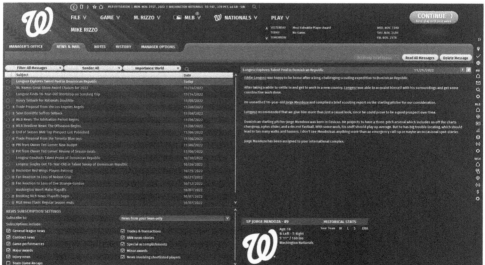

FIGURES 4.2A-B: Inbox interfaces in *Football Manager* and *Out of the Park Baseball*.

simulations, they are also *digital work simulations.* Accordingly, this section seeks to situate these games within everyday life in neoliberal capitalism by focusing on how they speak to contemporary digital work.

The atypical administrative affordances of managerial sports games in mind, perhaps a natural place to start this line of analysis is with a fundamental question that, despite its simplicity, has been largely unaddressed: What exactly makes the work-like nature of these games appealing? What, in other words, draws players to games that are, in many cases, themed versions of productivity software? The way games can blur the lines between work and play has long interested scholars, as in work comparing arcade gameplay and assembly-line labor.[66] However, a first resource here might be the budding line of game scholarship that has questioned, in particular, the stability of the work/play dichotomy within contemporary video games. Nick Yee, for instance, has documented how the work performed in many recent video games, particularly MMORPGs (Massively Multiplayer Online Role-Playing Games), is "increasingly similar to actual work in business corporations."[67] Players in *World of Warcraft* guilds, for example, can find themselves in "tedious management roles" that involve tasks like recruiting and interviewing new members, scheduling meetings, and mediating disputes.[68] Looking across the gaming landscape, Yee summarizes, "Video games are blurring the boundaries between work and play very rapidly."[69] Other scholars have made similar claims about MMORPGs. For example, Andras Lukacs, David G. Embrick, and Talmadge Wright also turn their attention to *World of Warcraft* and conclude, "Modern virtual realms are simultaneously play and work environments: to make the distinction between the two is counterproductive."[70] Scott Rettberg, meanwhile, details how *World of Warcraft* players take on any number of administrative responsibilities, whether that might mean achieving sales goals or cajoling underlings to work harder.[71] He, like the other scholars, summarizes, "Though playing the game is itself a form of escapism from the demands of life in the real world, it is somewhat paradoxically a kind of escapism into a second professional life, a world of work."[72]

In this scholarship around MMORPGs, the notion of "escapism" emerges as something of a puzzle, with Rettberg suggesting it is a "paradox" that gamers would desire to escape from daily life into "a world of work"—a mysterious incongruity that recalls the question asked above: What is it that draws players into the virtual work of managerial sports games? Addressing these sorts of inquiries, Andrew Kuo, Richard J. Lutz, and Jacob L. Hiler draw on interviews with *World of Warcraft* players to suggest that many individuals turn to games as a way of alleviating feelings of "helplessness and frustration" in everyday life, using games to regain a sense of control.[73] That control should dominate in these interviews is perhaps not surprising. Control, after all, has long been a central idea in discussions surrounding games and play, as in Mihaly Csikszentmihalyi's description of "flow" as a person being in "control of his actions and of the environment."[74] Nonetheless, Kuo, Lutz, and Hiler's interviews are striking in the way they render a strong juxtaposition between gaming and nongaming activities. For example, they interview a doctor who remarks that medical work entails countless variables and unknowable outcomes—a potentially overwhelming situation that threatens his sense of agency. However, within *World of Warcraft,* there is less ambiguity, and the doctor can reaffirm his confidence in his decision making. He summarizes, "It's about being in control versus not being in control."[75] Similarly, a college student recounts how the results of tests and assignments can elude his careful preparation. That is to say, even for all of his studying, he may still do poorly on an exam. As in the doctor's case, ambiguity threatens his sense of control. Within *World of Warcraft,* on the other hand, the scholars note that "there is an immediacy to his actions and intentions that results in positive changes and consequences." As the student says of the game, "I'm definitely more in control."[76] The scholars go on to suggest these types of responses are hardly surprising. Games are knowable environments where coherent logic prevails and where players have the chance to clearly influence the world around them. Players, then, have the opportunity to reassert themselves and feel newly empowered.

Kuo, Lutz, and Hiler's article suggests a strong relationship between escapism and a sense of agency. In the wake of that insight, though, what remains unclear is how exactly managerial sports games and, in particular, their unusually austere affordances might generate such a sensation. A particularly useful comparison, then, is the subgenre of "social" simulation games like those in *The Sims* series, as these games ask players to entertain themselves with mundane tasks like job hunting and meal preparation—scenarios that roughly parallel managerial sports games' interest in inbox management and spreadsheet optimization. With that in mind, it is helpful to turn to a piece by Sara M. Iversen in which she interviews players of *The Sims 2* and *The Sims 3,* all the while looking to better understand the paradox that finds players seeking "relief from the chores of work and family" by turning to games "that, to a great degree, simulate activities similar to those from which the players seek a respite."[77] According to Iversen, the *Sims* games, for all their mundanity, contain several appealing "utopic" elements, of which the sensation of agency is perhaps the most significant. Like Kuo, Lutz, and Hiler, Iversen finds that control is central to the gameplay experience, with players contrasting the control offered by *The Sims* with the lack of agency in other realms of their lived experiences. Significantly, though, Iversen observes that the games' "realistic" features serve an important function in allowing players to connect to these "utopic" elements by offering players a relatable way to enter these game worlds. This is notable because it is only once players are situated within the world that they can access utopic elements like the sense of control. She argues, then, that these realistic elements "can be seen as a bridge to fantasy, dreaming of and imagining better worlds."[78]

All this scholarship in mind, one can begin theorizing the resonance of managerial sports games. Although escapism may be idiosyncratic, with every digital game player looking for their own version of an "escape," many players are apparently searching for a sense of agency. Moreover, if *The Sims* is any indication, it might be suggested that the highly familiar, work-like interfaces of managerial sports games help ground players in the games, thus making it easier for players to achieve that sensation. Indeed, it is easy to imagine this exact dynamic playing out in managerial sports games. Let us return, for example, to *Football Manager*. The game is sold as a fantasy wherein players get to take over the decision making for a soccer club of their choice. The promise of control is central to this fantasy. As in *World of Warcraft*, *Football Manager* is a world where rules and expectations are clear, and decisions are effectual. That is to say, a player can expect a defender with a high "dribbling" rating to dribble well and can also expect a forward with a high "heading" rating to occasionally score goals off headers. Meanwhile, if the player wants to transfer one of these athletes to another team, their decision will play out, and the game will reshape around that choice. To go back to the example of the doctor, this is not a world in which a mystery ailment baffles minds and resists treatment. Instead, it is a world where the rules and expectations are relatively obvious and, to quote the doctor, "you make a change and you see it happen."

To draw on Iversen, the game's unique, work-like affordances may be important in helping players reach these sorts of "utopic" moments. When a player starts a new game of *Football Manager*, they are quickly thrown into its Microsoft Outlook–like interface. Immediately, the player is greeted with many emails dealing with everything from press conferences to staffing decisions to employment terms. While this well-known interface represents all the drudgeries of contemporary digital work, it is also instantly recognizable. Indeed, most office workers—and many others who use information technology as part of their daily lives—will immediately grasp the small details buried in the interface, like the bolded text representing unread messages. Because this interface is instantly recognizable, it is also particularly intuitive. Notably, managerial sports games are information dense. In *Out of the Park*

Baseball, for example, players must track dozens of virtual athletes scattered across several levels of their organization, while in *Football Manager,* players can load databases giving them access to information on hundreds of thousands of athletes. The intimate familiarity of the interface helps makes this density less daunting. The player, then, is freed to focus on assembling their winning team, and in the process, to exert control. As in the case of *The Sims,* then, the "realistic" (mundane) elements of managerial sports games can help players access the "utopic" ones.

This account begins to answer the question of how managerial sports games facilitate escapism, suggesting that within games like *Football Manager* and *Out of the Park Baseball,* players can feel a sense of control—a sense of control that may be absent in the other parts of their lives. Moreover, this account begins to explain how the austere interfaces of managerial sports games can facilitate escapism by offering gamers a recognizable gateway into the games and, as such, making it easier for them, to borrow the phrasing of Kuo, Lutz, and Hiler's student interviewee, to "do what they want in the game."[79] However, this account also feels incomplete. As Gordon Calleja argues, escapism is highly contextual, with ideas of "escape" inevitably intertwining with an individual's lived experiences.[80] There would seem to be added significance, then, to the way managerial sports games uniquely blur work and play via their administrative gameplay.

As repeatedly argued in the scholarship above, many individuals turn to games for a sense of control because they feel an acute lack of agency in other parts of their lives. However, in games like the *World of Warcraft,* that agency is experienced within a mythological environment aesthetically disconnected from the other parts of players' lives. Within managerial sports games, though, many players will find themselves returning to the very same digital environments in which they work. This has significant ramifications for how that in-game control may be experienced. To understand why, one can turn to a piece by Shira Chess on casual games. In the article, Chess focuses on the *Diner Dash* games, which place players in the shoes of Flo, a dissatisfied white-collar worker who quits her office job to instead run a frenetic diner. Recalling the questions that have been asked throughout this section, Chess is intrigued by an apparent paradox at the heart of the *Diner Dash* games. On the one hand, *Diner Dash*'s narrative emphasizes the need to escape from the drudgery of office work. On the other hand, the games figure that escape—the diner in which the player dashes—as a place defined by repetitive, menial tasks.

According to Chess, there are risks to how the games entangle work and play, particularly for the women gamers who form the bulk of the games' audience. For some players, escape may be hard to find. As she writes, "Play-time could simply become work time," and in-game stresses might "re-enact stresses" that the players encounter in their work lives.[81] The *Diner Dash* games, for example, continually call for emotional management, as gamers must work to please their fictional customers. Chess posits, then, "Just as emotional labor takes a toll on many women, so might emotional play."[82] However, Chess reminds readers that games are open texts that invite vary-ing interpretations.[83] As such, it would be too simple to assume all players have negative experiences with *Diner Dash*'s interweaving of work and play. Again, the idea of control becomes significant. Chess writes:

> The *Dash* games offer players something that real-world labor cannot: control. By allowing players to win the game, to please customers, and to see rewards for caregiving, it has the potential of being satisfying in a way that might be meaningful to many women. The individual and personal experiences of each player [have] become a nuanced negotiation of their own system of beliefs and helps to construct a game space that helps to retell their own personal experiences (or, perhaps, even set them right). Where the *Dash* games illustrate problems, they also create (at least tem-porary in-game) solutions.[84]

Echoing the other scholars cited above, Chess posits that control can be elusive in the course of one's daily life. In a game world, though, players can find empowerment. Chess's argument goes deeper, however. Because the *Diner Dash* games interweave work and play, she writes, players can use the game to make sense of their work lives. Players, for example, may struggle with emotional labor during a day of work—failing, perhaps, to properly stroke a manager's ego—but can see similar labor rewarded within the game environment. There are potentially genuine benefits, then, to the way the game interlaces work and play. As Chess writes, this entanglement might be draining for some players, but for others, it may help them make sense of their lived experiences.

One gets a further sense, then, of the potential resonance of managerial sports games. In these games, players can gain a sense of agency grounded in the interfaces of the productivity software that has become ubiquitous across the working world. Thus, players can find agency in the same types of environments where it may otherwise desert them—and, indeed, there are very good reasons to believe workers might be lacking this agency in their everyday work lives, particularly amid the conditions of neoliberal capitalism under which, for instance, labor unions have repeatedly come under attack. Relatedly, in a treatise on the "spiritual violence" of contemporary work, anthropologist David Graeber notes the frequency with which modern work is plagued by "bullshit" that leaves workers feeling both a lack of control and a lack of purpose.[85] Commenting on Graeber's work, Matteo Tiratelli notes, for instance, how workers today have to waste countless hours navigating bureaucratic dysfunction and wading through meaningless administrative processes and procedures.[86] As Graeber summarizes, "Huge swathes of people, in Europe and North America in particular, spend their entire working lives performing tasks they secretly believe do not really need to be performed."[87] Notably, Graeber continues, there are grave "moral and spiritual" consequences to all this "bullshit," as a lack of agency and purpose has left countless workers with "feelings of hopelessness, depression, and self-loathing."[88]

In managerial sports games, many players might find themselves able to renegotiate the bullshit of their working lives—to imagine ways in which they might have more control over their work or that their work might potentially become more meaningful. A project at the office might feel trivial, but at home, a player might run numbers until their *Madden* franchise finds its way to a championship. Again, too, it is worth repeating just how closely managerial sports games mimic the interfaces of digital work. Unlike the casual games that Chess analyzes, which figure the relationship between work and play through exaggerated, pixelated environments that are "safe, colorful, and full of zany characters," managerial sports games figure the relationship between work and play by way of austere tables of data.[89] This resemblance would seem to reinforce the idea that players may turn to these games not necessarily out of longing for a different *form* of work, as perhaps an office worker might also do when they take on the role of a farmer in *Farming Simulator* or a pilot in *Microsoft Flight Simulator,* but rather a different *connection* to their work—a connection that involves greater clarity and agency. Indeed, managerial sports games would seem to bear out Graeber's suggestion that many workers spend their days fantasizing "not of being a World War I flying ace, marrying a prince, or becoming a teenage heartthrob, but of having a better—just utterly, ridiculously better—job."[90] Speaking to such a suggestion, in interviewing a number of *Football Manager* players about the allure of the game, Alfie Brown notes "the appeal of the game is connected to work and the idea of a 'dream job.' " He continues, "These games do more than distract from those 'real' jobs but create a kind of alternative universe in which to experience simulated 'success.'"[91]

Managerial sports games thus offer the potential for a sense of empowerment particularly resonant amid the conditions of the neoliberal workplace—not just allowing players, as many other games do, to experience a sense of control that may be absent in other parts of their lives, but also, by way of their uniquely stark, work-like interfaces, allowing players the chance to reimagine that loss of control. To that point, it is also possible to envision these games spurring critical reflection. Notably, the affordances of managerial sports games come with a particular set of assumptions about the nature of contemporary digital work. For example, the games tend to presume that digital work is frenetic, if not overwhelming. To play *Football Manager*, for instance, is to volunteer for an information deluge, as players are bombarded by virtual emails. A player's attention, then, is constantly pulled in many directions, for as these emails continuously arrive, they ask players to consider everything from what to say in a press conference to what to make of new scouting reports from across the world. Perhaps unsurprisingly, *Football Manager* forums contain occasional posts from players asking how to reduce their inbox clutter. Indeed, like many digital workers, *Football Manager* players seem to be constantly battling to reach inbox zero. The content of these virtual emails entails more assumptions about contemporary work life, such as an underlying precariousness. For example, *Football Manager* players receive occasional emails from their virtual bosses on the team's board—check-ins in which the board might clarify job performance expectations or, if things go poorly, relieve the player of their duties. Thus, *Football Manager* forums are also full of threads with titles like, "Why in the world did I get sacked?"

Returning to Friedman's arguments from the previous section, one can suggest that as players repeatedly return to the game, its assumptions about the harshness of working life amid neoliberal capitalism become explicit. In reference to the above examples, as individuals play the game, they will need to learn quickly that they must swiftly process their avalanche of emails and that their job is anything but permanent. Accordingly, these premises become open to critique. As players come to understand the game's model of contemporary work—in which the pace of work is feverish and job security is uncertain—they will be invited to compare this model to their everyday realities. In so doing, they may judge both the model—and the world—as unsatisfactory.

In suggesting managerial sports games might call attention to the grinding rhythms and imperatives of the neoliberal workplace, there is something of an overlap with Ruberg's concept of "re-gamification." For Ruberg, re-gamification refers to a process in which a game developer "identifies, literalizes, and thereby critiques the game-like structures that are already being used to shape human experience."[92] Particularly notable for an examination of managerial sports games, though, is that Ruberg's discussion of re-gamification eventually shifts to the potential of situating a critical game within the corporate world, with Ruberg asking readers to imagine

> a hypothetical game in which players must work long hours for unfair wages at unfulfilling jobs in order to "succeed" by achieving meager praise from uninterested bosses, progressing through the ranks of euphemistic job titles, and eventually stumbling across the finish line of a late and weary retirement. This would be a grim game, indeed, but its critique through re-gamification would be clear. It would enact an argument that some social system or institution—in this case, the undercompensated desk job—was already a game.[93]

Although managerial sports games are not designed to be overtly critical, they nonetheless embody several aspects of Ruberg's imagined example of corporate re-gamification. In *Football Manager,* players must spend hours wading through emails and data tables to win praise from the fickle boards that oversee their job performance. In line with Ruberg's analysis, it can be suggested that this sort of gameplay might unintentionally make visible the game-like nature of so much work in the twenty-first century—exposing a repetitive process full of unspoken "winners" and "losers"—and thus invite players to further consider their place within this system.

On that note, it is also helpful to return to parallels with the casual game genre. In a piece that arrived not long after Chess's article on the *Diner Dash* series, Aubrey Anable also analyzed the franchise and, in the process, explored several of the same issues as Chess, including the way the games figure the complex relationship between work and play. According to Anable, in blurring the lines between work and play, the *Diner Dash* games "speak to a longing for a different, less fraught, relationship to labor." Elaborating, she writes that the games "create affective situations that call into question the myths and failures of the digital workplace"—stirring, for example, sensations of overwhelm and precariousness.[94] While Anable is careful to point out that casual games are not necessarily "radical or even progressive media forms," she also notes the potential of casual games to help players work through what it means to be in the world.[95] Managerial sports games would appear to share this link. As mentioned, managerial sports games offer a version of digital work that incorporates sensations like overwhelm and precariousness. As Anable writes of *Diner Dash,* the foregrounding of these sensations may inevitably lead to questions regarding the very nature of contemporary work, with players potentially casting a critical eye toward the conditions in which they labor. With that in mind, managerial sports games might not just end up speaking to a longing for empowerment but also a desire for change.

166   CHAPTER FOUR

Like Anable, then, one may not necessarily look to managerial sports games as being "radical" but nonetheless full of potential for helping players to renegotiate and critically reflect on their everyday lives.

To that point, it should be reiterated that the goal of this chapter has not been to challenge or rebut the existing work on managerial sports games, but rather been to add new layers to this work in further examining how managerial texts fit into everyday life amid the rhythms and imperatives of neoliberal capitalism. Accordingly, it needs to be reemphasized that these texts are hardly progressive. Analyzing fantasy football games, for instance, Hoxworth stresses that the "affective rewards" these games offer players through a sense of control cannot be viewed apart from the games' racialized, gendered dynamics. "If the fantasy of fantasy football is one of empowerment," he argues, "then this 'empowerment' arises largely through the dominant relationship of mostly white, male fantasy participants over the predominantly black athletes who constitute their fantasy teams."[96] Moreover, Brown issues a reminder that while a sense of agency within managerial sports games may act as a temporary reprieve from alienation in the workplace, it does not necessarily follow that a "simulated feeling of career satisfaction" will lead to reflection or critique.[97] Indeed, Brown suggests that felt success in a virtual realm of digital work may only serve to further ingrain capitalist ideals—arguing that after playing a game like *Football Manager,* we might "return to work not only having managed to avoid confronting our dissatisfaction but with our sense of commitment to capitalist success very much renewed."[98]

In closing, then, while a consideration of why players turn to managerial sports games and how these games fit into players' everyday lives sheds further light on the relationships between players and these games—helping, in the process, to illuminate "the collective desires, fears, and rhythms of everyday life in our precarious, networked, and procedurally generated world"—the highly instrumental orientation of these games needs to underlie any such analysis.[99] Players may use these games to develop criticisms of the neoliberal sporting order or to renegotiate the precariousness of their working lives, but this is neither a given nor a credit to the games themselves. On that note, in a critique of reparative reading, Patricia Stuelke observes that amid the "violences of racial capitalism, neoliberal empire, and settler colonialism," that the "celebration of survival strategies and coping mechanisms as beautiful seeds of that which might one day, in the future, save the world . . . can sometimes seem to stave off the difficult work of imagining possible worlds that break definitively with this one."[100] With that in mind, the next chapter—the book's conclusion—will emphasize the need not to find "redemptive possibility" within managerial texts, but rather to think beyond them.[101]

Managerial Sports Games   167

Conclusion

The Banality of Managerial Sports Media

In recent years, administrative content has become something like the elevator music of the sports media landscape. Tuning in randomly to a sports cable channel or talk radio station, one is very likely to be subjected to a generic patter of trade terms, contract numbers, and performance metrics—"cap hold" bleeding into "luxury-tax bill" bleeding into "trade exception." Indeed, the banality of managerial content has played a significant role in its spread. Significantly, sport and media have long been enmeshed in a symbiotic relationship, with media companies—reliant on athletes, teams, and leagues for access, content, and revenues—hesitant to offer any material that might be deemed offensive.[1] In this context, administration has made for the perfect media subject, as breathless attention to the granular details of contracts and player efficiency precludes any broader skepticism that might impinge on these financial relationships.

As an illustration of this phenomenon, one might examine the work of the "insider" journalists who regularly lead managerial coverage. Across platforms, these reporters almost exclusively focus on the minute details of managerial moves, in the process generally offering little in the way of critical commentary. Their reporting produces an endless stream of content that is likely appealing to sports media companies not just for its volume but also for its obsequiousness.[2] Another suggestive illustration involves managerial sports films. The majority of these films have been made with the close cooperation of sports leagues, with the leagues' brands, locations, and personnel being exchanged for some degree of oversight.[3] In the case of *Draft Day,* for instance, the NFL was not only reportedly paid a rights fee and given a share of the movie's revenue, but also granted approval rights, with league executives seeing "every daily during filming."[4] Indeed, the league's involvement in the film was so intimate that the league's commissioner Roger Goodell even has an extended cameo. Given the content of these films, it is no surprise sports leagues have been more than happy to participate in their production. Offering insulated portraits of front-office activity that turn roster transactions into subjects of extended monologues, there is little to offend the organizations' powers that be.

The banality of managerial sports media can mean that administrative texts are at risk of going unnoticed and unexamined. Quotidian managerial texts like a Shams Charania tweet or an Adam Schefter segment on *NFL Live* can recall unnecessary work emails—carrying, perhaps, a whiff of importance, but underneath that glimmer of seriousness, very little content of broader significance. As this project has detailed, though, managerial texts not only are worthy of scrutiny but also are perhaps more complex than they may initially appear. As I suggested in the previous chapter on managerial sports video games, there are glimpses of the utopic in managerial sports media. For instance, managerial sports games like *Football Manager* may offer their players a sense of agency and purpose in the same sorts of contexts in which these sensations can so often go lacking. One might apply that same insight to other forms of managerial sports media, too. Some audiences, for instance, might use managerial sports talk as a way of imagining a rare sense of control—vicariously placing themselves in a thriving role at the top of an organizational pyramid instead of being crushed at the bottom. Relatedly, it is possible to imagine managerial sports texts encouraging critiques both of contemporary sport and of contemporary capitalism. In the previous chapter, for instance, I argued that managerial sports games can uniquely illustrate sport's ensnarement in the imperatives of neoliberal capitalism and, in turn, invite questions about the ramifications of that entwinement. Although other forms of managerial sports media may lack the same ability as games to situate audiences within the dizzying sprawl of contemporary sport, one might more broadly suggest that managerial sports media, in so explicitly adopting a financialized, data-driven approach to sport, allow for a remarkably clear-eyed view of contemporary sport's ideological workings.

Managerial sports media's banality, though, can be insidious, helping to overshadow the more troubling aspects of administrative texts. Although there may be glimmers of utopia and clarity within managerial sports media, it is also true that managerial texts generally privilege a deeply hierarchical, dehumanizing view of sport. Across administrative texts, athletes are repeatedly instrumentalized—whether becoming powerless subordinates in managerial sports films, collections of contracts in managerial sports talk, sets of statistics in managerial sports television, or arrays of player ratings in managerial sports games. Moreover, this instrumentalization has gone hand in hand with an ideologically suspect project of elevating administrators in place of these athletes. Within the world of managerial sports media, administrators—mostly men, mostly white—are often the true protagonists of sport in wielding special expertise and skills to shrewdly manage these athletes-cum-investments-cum-data.

Here, too, it can be noted that the ubiquity of managerial sports media helps obscure the more significant sources of power within the sports landscape. Given the sheer volume of managerial texts obsessing over administrators and their maneuvers, it would be easy to assume the executives who effectively serve as middle managers sandwiched between players, coaches, and owners are in total control of their teams. Indeed, some managerial texts, particularly managerial sports games, blur the lines between management and ownership. Only occasionally do managerial texts acknowledge that most executives are themselves under control of another layer of power in serving at the pleasure of the team owners. Conveniently, then, managerial sports texts often allow owners to operate behind something of a veil of secrecy—reaping taxpayer-supported profits while garnering relatively little scrutiny, much less attention. Again, it is no surprise that sports media companies—with a vested interest in pleasing their business partners and, in particular, the team owners who ultimately control their leagues' media rights—might tend toward transactional minutiae as they have looked for ever more hours of content to fill their programming schedules.

The banality of managerial sports media does not just mean that the ideological workings of managerial texts are at risk of being lost amid a flood of marginal details and jargon, but also that any criticism of those workings is likely to be drowned out, too. As mentioned at various points in this project, managerial logics do meet occasional skepticism—recall Fox Sports personality Nick Wright momentarily highlighting the dehumanization inherent in sports talk's financial worldview—but such criticism has generally been submerged underneath the unyielding spread of managerial commonsense. For every comment expressing reservations about administrative content, sports media offers countless more hours of debate and discussion centered around salary negotiations and trade mechanics. One can also recall, then, how even commentators seemingly uncomfortable with an administrative perspective quickly fall back into the familiar managerial patterns of discourse.

More generally, the spread of managerial content—gradually growing into every nook of the sports media landscape—crowds out alternative modes of coverage. As mentioned in the introduction, for instance, sports media

Conclusion   171

outlets have preferred to fill programming schedules with administrative coverage of men's sports rather than additional programming devoted to women's sports. In addition, managerial sports media blocks out alternative methods of interpreting and understanding sport. If managerial texts are primarily centered around a conception of sport as rigidly hierarchical and highly rational, then one might imagine a radically different version of sports media that rejects this orientation—perhaps, for instance, centering the "aesthetic delights" mentioned in the third chapter and, in the process, further highlighting qualities like creativity and playfulness. Such an alternative might, in deemphasizing the financialized, data-driven logics now so familiar across so many outlets, favor process over outcome, cooperation over competition, and athletes as well as fans over administrators.

It is unlikely, though, that such an alternative will appear within mainstream sports media anytime soon. Assuming sports media continues to be one of the most lucrative realms of the media industry—in the process enriching both sports organizations and the media companies that turn to them for content—the symbiotic relationship between sport and media is likely to grow ever tighter. Accordingly, it is also likely that media companies will continue to lean on inoffensive administrative material and that managerial logics will continue to bleed across the entire sports media landscape.

Thinking beyond the managerial, then, requires imagining not just a different type of sports media content, but also an entirely different *form* of sports media: one situated outside the mutually dependent sports/media convergence and, thus, unencumbered by the expectation that media companies move in tight lockstep with teams and leagues. Thus far, this project has been able to offer one text that stands as a sustained critique of the managerial mode: *High Flying Bird*. Notably, *High Flying Bird* is a microbudget independent film that, in apparently forgoing cooperation with the NBA, is able to critically examine the ideological assumptions of professional basketball without worrying about blowback. Another potential model of critical distance is the 1976 teledocumentary *TVTV Goes to the Super Bowl*—a satirical, behind-the-scenes account of that year's Super Bowl. As Brett Kashmere details, *TVTV Goes to the Super Bowl* is a "work of guerrilla television" produced by the alternative video collective Top Value Television (TVTV) and distributed by the Public Broadcasting Service (PBS).[5] Significantly, then, Kashmere argues the work exists outside the "rigidly enclosed, corporate media-sports nexus."[6] Accordingly, he suggests, it is able to offer a "counterhegemonic" depiction of professional sport that avoids sports television's typical tendency toward qualities like "technological mastery" and "technocratic ingenuity"—preferring instead to delve into topics like football's status as dangerous labor and the ongoing exploitation of the sport's players.[7]

Although the costs associated with sports media have historically precluded anything like "independent" sports broadcasting, thereby making outsider experiments like *TVTV Goes to the Super Bowl* few and far between, new distribution and production technologies have made it possible to envision such a sphere finally coming into existence. It is fairly simple, for instance, for anyone with a recording device to create and publish a podcast. Similarly, with a relatively inexpensive camera and a web streaming account, anyone can live stream a sporting event across the world. Indeed, communities surrounding amateur and minor sports have begun taking advantage of these possibilities, in the process creating a new form of sports media outside the traditional sports media apparatus.[8] The question becomes, then, if this new "independent" sports media content will challenge the managerial mode or if, instead, managerial logics have become so ingrained in the presentation of sport they even come to dominate this new realm.

Conclusion   173

Notes

Preface

1. Flannery, "Help Needed, Stat! Is the Sloan Sports Analytics Conference Too Big?"

2. Gay, "Sloan News Day! What Were MIT, ESPN and Obama Hiding?"

3. The Sloan Conference's increasingly hefty registration fees—$425 for students and $850 for non-students for the 2022 edition of the event—have recently attracted criticism, with a number of individuals observing that the sizable cost of registration severely limits who is able to attend the conference and, accordingly, who has access to the event's networking opportunities. For example, Michael Lopez, a National Football League (NFL) executive, comments, "When the preeminent conference is quite challenging to pay for, you end up with people coming from privileged backgrounds." Similarly, John Tobias, a professor and statistician at ESPN, notes how those registration fees stack up with travel costs in saying, "Access creates opportunity. . . . There are so many people in underrepresented communities who want to work in sports and love data as much as anyone but can't pay $1,000." See Funt, "At Sloan Sports Conference, Criticism Mounts over Diversity, Access."

4. Lewis, "The No-Stats All-Star."

5. Lewis, "The No-Stats All-Star."

Introduction

1. "Moneyball (2011)—Financial Information"; Kaufman, "Movie Projector."

2. Murray, "No Money for Moneyball."

3. Brown, "So How Bad Was Soderbergh's Revised Moneyball Script?"

4. McClintock, "Box Office Report"; Fritz, "Oscars 2012."

5. Osterweil, "The Rise of the Sports Management Movie."

6. "Industry Demographics."

7. Rosenthal, "NFL Draft a Reminder LeBron James and NBA Still Far from Overtaking Pro Football."

8. Pollack, "The Cult of the General Manager."

9. Indeed, sociologist Allen Guttmann argues "bureaucratization" is one of the defining characteristics of modern sport. And speaking to the long-important role of executives within professional sport, Robert F. Burk notes that the "rise of the general manager" within baseball was already playing out in the first decades of the twentieth century, with teams—grappling with the transformation of the sport into a "big entertainment business"—adding personnel directors responsible for duties like roster transactions and salary negotiations. Guttman, *From Ritual to Record;* Burk, *Much More Than a Game,* 19.

10. Ginesta and Faedo, "The Influence of North American Ownership on the Business, Management, and Communication Model of Spanish Professional Football," 14.

11. For further analysis of the disparities in coverage, see, for instance, Cooky et al., "One and Done."

12. "Programming."

13. "Programming."

14. Freeman, *ESPN,* 102.

15. Reischel, *100 Things Packers Fans Should Know and Do Before They Die*, 100.

16. King, "Feel the Power—Feel the NFL Draft."

17. Freeman, *ESPN*, 102.

18. For further analysis of the different strategies sports television outlets have used to fill their programming schedules, see Buehler, "Sports Television and the Continuing Search for Alternative Programming."

19. Ourand, "Does Media Rights Bubble Have a Leak?"

20. Karp, "ESPN, ESPN2 In Just Under 100 Million U.S. Homes In August"; Crupi, "Disney to Spend $44.9 Billion on Sports Rights Through 2027."

21. Weprin, "NBCSN Sports Channel to Shutter."

22. Ourand, "Does Media Rights Bubble Have a Leak?"

23. Magder, "Television 2.0: The Business of American Television in Transition," 164.

24. Raphael, "The Political Economic Origins of Reali-TV."

25. Curtis, interview.

26. Curtis, interview.

27. Curtis, interview.

28. Curtis, interview.

29. Favale, "Banana Boats and Emoji Wars."

30. Curtis, interview.

31. Curtis, "The Trade Rumor Era."

32. Curtis, interview.

33. Curtis, interview.

34. Wenner, "Media, Sports, and Society," 15.

35. Curtis, interview.

36. Curtis, interview.

37. Curtis, interview.

38. Curtis, interview.

39. Curtis, interview.

40. Curtis, interview.

41. Dworkin, "The Evolution of Collective Bargaining in Sports," 128.

42. Gilbert, *Expanding the Strike Zone,* 64.

43. Quoted in Goldman, *One Man Out,* 6; Early, *A Level Playing Field.*

44. Mendelsohn, *The Cap,* 128.

45. Smith, *Hard Labor.*

46. Swanson, *Baseball's Power Shift,* xiii.

47. Swanson, *Baseball's Power Shift,* xvi.

48. Ploeg, "A New Form of Fandom," 16.

49. Wong and Deubert, "National Basketball Association General Managers," 6.

50. Mendelsohn, *The Cap,* 278–79.

51. Wong and Deubert, "Major League Baseball General Managers," 101; Deubert, Wong, and Hatman, "National Football League General Managers."

52. Wong and Deubert, "National Basketball Association General Managers," 3.

53. Masteralexis, "Regulating Player Agents," 105.

54. Masteralexis, "Regulating Player Agents," 109.

55. Woike, "Rob Pelinka to Be New Lakers General Manager"; Deb and Stein, "Leon Rose, an Agent, Is Expected to Be the Next Knicks President."

56. Wong and Deubert, "National Basketball Association General Managers," 22–23.

57. Wong and Deubert, "National Basketball Association General Managers," 23.

58. Deubert, Wong, and Hatman, "National Football League General Managers," 430.

59. Deubert, Wong, and Hatman, "National Football League General Managers," 474.

60. Deubert, Wong, and Hatman, "National Football League General Managers," 493.

61. Wong and Deubert, "National Basketball Association General Managers," 23.

62. The NFL's annual television rights, for instance, are worth more than ten billion dollars per year, while the NBA's national rights are worth more than two billion. Belson and Draper, "N.F.L. Signs Media Deals Worth Over $100 Billion"; Young, "NBA Is next up for a Big Rights Increase, and $75 Billion Is the Price."

63. Recent sales have valued the New York Mets at $2.4 billion and the Denver Broncos at $4.65 billion. Thosar, "Steve Cohen officially becomes new sole owner of the Mets ending the Wilpon era"; Legwold, "Denver Broncos reach sale agreement."

64. Deubert, Wong, and Hatman, "National Football League General Managers," 429.

65. Deubert, Wong, and Hatman, "National Football League General Managers," 429.

66. Coffey, "Move Over, Billionaires; the Really Big Money Wants in on Sports."

67. Coffey, "Move Over, Billionaires; the Really Big Money Wants in on Sports."

68. Basak, "SCOOP: Sports as the next Asset Class. A Year after Striking a Deal with the NBA, Investment Firm Dyal Buys a Stake in Its First Franchise—the Phoenix Suns. Executives Give Me Details on How They'll Seek Returns after Team Valuations Have Surged"; see, for instance, Faturechi, Elliott, and Simani, "The Billionaire Playbook" for a discussion of the tax advantages of owning a professional sports team.

69. Torre, "The 76ers' Plan to Win (Yes, Really)."

70. Weitzman, *Tanking to the Top.*

71. Lewis, "The No-Stats All-Star."

72. Reiter, *Astroball,* 229.

73. Lindbergh and Miller, *The Only Rule Is It Has to Work,* 5.

74. Ho, *Liquidated.*

75. Lee, "Inside the Rise of MLB's Ivy League Culture."

76. Ho, *Liquidated,* 40.

77. Lee, "Inside the Rise of MLB's Ivy League Culture."

78. Lee, "Inside the Rise of MLB's Ivy League Culture."

79. Gordon, *Fat and Mean.*

80. Goldstein, "Revenge of the Managers," 273.

81. Goldstein, "Revenge of the Managers," 289.

82. Fleming, *The Mythology of Work,* 95.

83. Klikauer, "What Is Managerialism?" 1107.

84. Fleming, *The Mythology of Work,* 90.

85. Lee, "Inside the Rise of MLB's Ivy League Culture."

86. Haiven, "Culture and Financialization," 347.

87. For a discussion of how the term neoliberalism risks becoming merely a "rhetorical device," see, for instance, Flew, "Michel Foucault's *The Birth of Biopolitics* and contemporary neo-liberalism debates."

88. See, for instance, Kunz, *The Political Economy of Sports Television;* Corrigan, "Digging the Moat."

89. Ouellette and Hay, "Makeover Television, Governmentality and the Good Citizen," 480.

90. Weber, *Makeover TV,* 39.

91. As historian Gabriel Winant explains, "Over the postwar decades, employment in manufacturing underwent a long secular decline. Workers in industry after industry fell prey to some combination of automation, disinvestment, and capital flight, beginning as soon as the 1950s. Surface mining came to coal; decentralization and automation to auto assembly, electronics, and meatpacking; runaway shops to textiles; containerization to shipping; global trade competition to steel." Winant, *The Next Shift,* 16.

92. Graeber, *Bullshit Jobs,* 17.

93. Kendall, *Hanging Out,* 80; Connell, *Masculinities,* 79.

94. Kendall, *Hanging Out,* 81.

95. Salter and Blodgett, *Toxic Geek Masculinity,* 68; Mendick et al., "Geek Entrepreneurs," 10.

96. Taylor, *Raising the Stakes,* 114.

97. Baldwin, *Anxious Men,* 31.

98. Lotz, *Cable Guys,* 88; Nygaard and Lagerwey, *Horrible White People*, 7.

99. See, for instance, Banet-Weiser, *Empowered,* for further analysis of the backlash to popular feminism.

100. Kusz, "'Winning Bigly,'" 116.

101. Kusz, "'Winning Bigly,'" 117.

102. Kusz, "Notes on the uses of sport," 51.

103. Negra and Tasker, "Introduction," 16.

104. Heresco, "Shaping the Market," 10.

105. Fleming, *The Mythology of Work,* 90; As Raymond Boyle and Lisa W. Kelly note, the focus on "troubleshooting" ailing companies has roots in the United Kingdom, as *Troubleshooter*—which ran from 1990 to 1993 on BBC—eventually beget later shows like *Ramsay's Kitchen Nightmares* (Channel 4, 2004–2014). In the United States, the "troubleshooting" focus has found continued success by way of shows like Food Network's *Restaurant: Impossible* (2011–) and *Restaurant Stakeout* (2012–2014), Fox's *Kitchen Nightmares* (2007–2014, adapted from *Ramsay's Kitchen Nightmares*), *Gordon Ramsay's 24 Hours to Hell and Back* (2019–2020), and *Hotel Hell* (2012–2016, also starring Gordon Ramsay), Spike/Paramount Network's *Bar Rescue* (2011–), and Travel Channel's *Hotel Impossible* (2012–2017). Also included in such a list might be the comedic take on the subgenre *Nathan for You* (Comedy Central, 2013–2017). Boyle and Kelly, "The Celebrity Entrepreneur on Television."

106. Tiratelli, "Where Did All the Bullshit Jobs Go?"

107. Graeber, *Bullshit Jobs*.

108. For further discussion of sports media's low cultural value and the related lack of critical analysis, see Buehler, "The Documentary as 'Quality' Sports Television."

Chapter 1. Managerial Sports Films

1. As demonstrated by the labeling of football-centered movies like *Touchdown!* (1931) and *Saturday's Millions* (1933) as "football" films, or by the way *Knute Rockne, All American* (1940) was alternately described as a "football" film and a "biographical" film. See, for instance, "'Ambassador Bill' and 'Touchdown' Take Tops"; "What's New on the Screen"; "Knute Rockne—All American"; "Knute Rockne—All American."

2. Crosson, *Sport and Film,* 43; Babington, *The Sports Film,* 10.

3. Friedman, *Sports Movies,* 15–16.

4. Bonzel, *National Pastimes,* 6; Crosson, *Sport and Film,* 62.

5. Crosson, *Sport and Film,* 62.

6. Friedman, *Sports Movies,* 15; Bonzel, *National Pastimes,* 5.

7. Sutera notes, too, that this interest in the business of sports has also been seen within television, as evidenced by the show *Arliss* (HBO, 1996–2002), which focused on the exploits of a fictional sports agent. More recently, this has also been evidenced by the show *Ballers* (HBO, 2015–2019), which also revolved around a sports agent. See, for instance, Cox, "Broke *Ballers:* The Mediated World of Football and Finance."

8. Sutera, "The Development of the Post-Classical Hollywood Sports Business Film Trend," 81.

9. Sutera, "The Development of the Post-Classical Hollywood Sports Business Film Trend," iii.

10. Boozer, *Career Movies.*

11. Sutera, "The Development of the Post-Classical Hollywood Sports Business Film Trend," 163.

12. Friedman, *Sports Movies,* 24–25.

13. Friedman, *Sports Movies,* 13.

14. Lang, "Disney Throws a Box Office Curve with 'Million Dollar Arm.'"

15. Fleming Jr., "Sony Sparks To 'Million Dollar Arm' Pitch."

16. Fleming Jr., "Sony Sparks To 'Million Dollar Arm' Pitch"; Lang, "Disney Throws a Box Office Curve with 'Million Dollar Arm.'"

17. Aftab, "Steven Soderbergh on #metoo and Making a Movie on His Phone."

18. Schatz, *Hollywood Genres,* 58.

19. Houssart, "The Shifting Cinematic Portrayal of Managers."

20. Bonzel, *National Pastimes,* 6.

21. Friedman, *Sports Movies,* 16.

22. Friedman, *Sports Movies,* 16.

23. Cullen, *American Dream,* 5–6.

24. Bonzel, *National Pastimes,* 81.

25. Cullen, *American Dream,* 7.

26. Friedman, *Sports Movies,* 28.

27. Cullen, *American Dream,* 5.

28. Miller, "Winning It All," 111.

29. Miller, "Winning It All," 117.

30. Miller, "Winning It All," 103–4, 117.

31. Miller, "Winning It All," 112.

32. Miller, "Winning It All," 115.

33. Friedman, *Sports Movies,* 35.

34. Bonzel, *National Pastimes,* 85.

35. Baker, *Contesting Identities,* 24.

36. Bonzel, *National Pastimes,* 94–95.

37. Donalson, *Masculinity in the Interracial Buddy Film,* 60, quoted in Bonzel, *National Pastimes,* 95.

38. Babington, *Sports Film,* 45.

39. Elmwood, "Just Some Bum from the Neighborhood," 49.

40. Bonzel, *National Pastimes,* 112.

41. Kusz, "Remasculinizing American White Guys," 222.

42. Kusz, "Remasculinizing American White Guys," 214.

43. Miller, "Winning It All," 111.

44. Friedman, *Sports Movies,* 16.

45. Miller, "Winning It All," 116.

46. Connor, *Hollywood Math and Aftermath,* 22–23.

47. Lewchuk, "Age of Increased Precarious Employment," 29.

48. Hatton, *Temp Economy,* 82, quoted in Lewchuk, "Age of Increased Precarious Employment," 34.

49. Hyman, *Temp,* 312.

50. Hyman, *Temp,* 52.

51. Hatton, *Temp Economy,* 2, quoted in Lewchuk, "Age of Increased Precarious Employment," 34.

52. Couldry, "Reality TV, or The Secret Theater of Neoliberalism."

53. Negra and Tasker, "Introduction"; Nygaard and Lagerwey, *Horrible White People.*

54. Kelly, "Wounded Man," 2.

55. Hatton, *Temp Economy,* 2, quoted in Lewchuk, "Age of Increased Precarious Employment," 34.

56. Tasker, *Spectacular Bodies;* this is not to say that business attire does not also carry its own connections to hegemonic masculinity (see, for instance, Barry and Weiner, "Suited for Success?") but rather that the connotations attached to business attire—rationality, etc.—have typically not been valorized within the sports film's treatment of masculinity.

57. Kusz, "Remasculinizing American White Guys," 223.

58. Kusz, "Remasculinizing American White Guys," 210.

59. Negra and Tasker, "Introduction," 8.

60. Hunter, "Celluloid Cubicle," 72.

61. Berg, Linden, and Schultz, "Manning Up," 88.

62. Berg, Linden, and Schultz, "Manning Up," 73.

63. Ashcraft and Flores, "Slaves with White Collars," 23.

64. Ashcraft and Flores, "Slaves with White Collars," 6.

65. Tasker, *Working Girls.*

66. Ashcraft and Flores, "Slaves with White Collars," 17.

67. For a breakdown of the riskiness (or ludicrousness) of Weaver's moves, see, for instance, McAtee, "Even in Fiction, the Browns Can't Get It Right."

68. Kusz, "*Jerry Maguire,*" 83.

69. Ashcraft and Flores, "Slaves with White Collars," 23.

70. See, for instance, Friedman, *Sports Movies,* 19–24.

71. Baker, *Contesting Identities,* 49.

72. Miller, "Winning It All," 121.

73. Sutera, "Development of the Post-Classical Hollywood Sports Business Film Trend," 102.

Notes to Chapter 1 181

74. It should be noted, too, there is a long historical precedent for this type of limited characterization. Richard Dyer, for example, draws on the work of Toni Morrison and Edward Said in noting "that white discourse implacably reduces the non-white subject to being a function of the white subject, not allowing her/him space or autonomy, permitting neither the recognition of similarities nor the acceptance of differences except as a means for knowing the white self." Dyer, *White*, 13.

75. Morgenstern, "'Godzilla.'"

76. Dyer, *White*, 45.

77. More, too, might be said about the connections between *Million Dollar Arm* and Dyer's discussion of imperialism and cinema. Discussing the western, for example, Dyer highlights how the genre lays "the land out before the white gaze, so beautiful, so new" but also emphasizes that the land cannot "be possessed without effort, suffering and loss," with that suffering helping to reinforce white masculine identity. Similarly, *Million Dollar Arm* establishes India as new, lucrative terrain for Bernstein to exploit, but also highlights his accompanying struggles against food poisoning, heat, and traffic—struggles all meant to symbolize Bernstein's exceptional perseverance and will power. Dyer, *White*, 34.

78. Ashcraft and Flores, "Slaves with White Collars," 18.

79. Kusz, "Remasculinizing American White Guys," 224.

80. Kusz, "Remasculinizing American White Guys," 223.

81. Cullen, *American Dream*, 7.

82. Connor, *Hollywood Math and Aftermath*, 23.

83. Connor, *Hollywood Math and Aftermath*, 21.

84. Brooks, "Soderbergh's Moneyball Mothballed"; Block, "Brad Pitt Reveals What He, Sony Did to Save 'Moneyball.'"

85. O'Falt, "How Soderbergh Designed His Own Filmmaking Universe."

86. Sheppard, *Sporting Blackness*, 178.

87. Sheppard, *Sporting Blackness*, 179.

88. Perhaps further signaling the relatively minimal importance the film assigns the owner is that it is an uncredited role played by Bobby Kotick, the CEO of major gaming company Activision Blizzard and a friend of the film's director, Bennett Miller. See Good, "In Moneyball, Activision's Bobby Kotick Plays a Familiar Role."

89. See, for instance, Smith and Keeven, "Creating Separation from the On-Field Product."

90. Edwards, *Revolt of the Black Athlete*, 28.

91. To the point about *High Flying Bird* starring another administrative protagonist (rather than athlete), one might also argue that the film suggests Burke's efforts are ultimately about placing himself (rather than athletes) at the top of "the game on top of the game." To that point, Courtney M. Cox suggests that Burke's "actions serve to move him socially and financially closer to sky box rather than realigning power to those on the court." That said, the closing emphasis on Edwards, and particularly Burke's meeting with Edwards, would seem to indicate that the film views Burke's motivations as righteous. See Cox, "Game on Top of the Game."

92. Edwards, *Revolt of the Black Athlete*.

Chapter 2. Managerial Sports Talk

1. See Vogan, *ABC Sports,* on the programming usefulness of anthology shows like *Wide World of Sports.*

2. See Vogan, *ESPN,* on the rapid expansion of ESPN outlets during the multi-channel transition.

3. See Hutchins, Li, and Rowe, "Over-the-Top Sport," on the growing number of sports streaming services.

4. Gullifor, "WFAN and the Birth of All-Sports Radio."

5. Mariscal, "Chicanos and Latinos in the Jungle of Sports Talk Radio," 111.

6. "Programming."

7. Kunz, *Political Economy of Sports Television.*

8. Kunz, *Political Economy of Sports Television,* 87.

9. Mariscal, "Chicanos and Latinos in the Jungle of Sports Talk Radio," 111.

10. Gullifor, "WFAN and the Birth of All-Sports Radio," 63.

11. In an earlier draft of this chapter, I also listed Mike Schmitz as one of ESPN's player evaluation experts. Speaking, though, to the blurry lines between sport and media in matters of management, Schmitz then left ESPN for a front-office job with the Portland Trail Blazers. See Wojnarowski, "Portland Trail Blazers to hire ESPN's NBA draft analyst Mike Schmitz as assistant general manager, sources say."

12. Mader, Mertens, and Zwan, "Financialization," 1.

13. Pellandini-Simányi, "The Financialization of Everyday Life," 281.

14. Martin, *Financialization of Daily Life,* 3.

15. Martin, *Financialization of Daily Life,* 12.

16. Aitken, "'A Machine for Living," 369.

17. Martin, *Financialization of Daily Life,* 75.

18. Fridman, *Freedom from Work,* 13.

19. Heresco, "Shaping the Market," 12.

20. Cormany, "Mediated Affect and Financial News Media."

21. Haiven, *Cultures of Financialization,* 4.

22. Haiven, *Cultures of Financialization.*

23. Andreasen, Frantzen, and Tygstrup, "Finance Fiction," 358.

24. Ouellette and Hay, *Better Living Through Reality TV,* 151.

25. Ouellette and Hay, *Better Living Through Reality TV,* 149.

26. Andreasen, Frantzen, and Tygstrup, "Finance Fiction," 359.

27. Haiven, *Cultures of Financialization,* 11–12.

28. Davis, *Managed by the Markets,* 193.

29. Davis, *Managed by the Markets,* 193–94.

30. Davis, *Managed by the Markets,* 236.

31. Hay, "Too Good to Fail," 382.

32. Shimpach, "Realty Reality," 524.

33. Hardin, "Neoliberal Temporality," 102.

34. Hardin, "Neoliberal Temporality," 105.

35. Heresco, "Shaping the Market," 135.

36. Haiven, "Monsters of the Financialized Imagination," 6.

37. Leary, *Keywords,* 83, 85–86.

38. Leary, *Keywords,* 85.

39. Oates, *Football and Manliness,* 62.

40. Muniesa and Doganova, "The Time That Money Requires," 95.

41. Heresco, "Shaping the Market," 182.

42. Cormany, "Mediated Affect and Financial News Media," 74.

43. Cormany, "Mediated Affect and Financial News Media," 81.

44. Cormany, "Mediated Affect and Financial News Media," 76.

45. Heresco, "Shaping the Market," 211.

46. Real, "Theorizing the Sports-Television Dream Marriage," 21.

47. Heresco, "Shaping the Market," 189.

48. Cormany, "Mediated Affect and Financial News Media," 16.

49. Heresco, "Shaping the Market," 193.

50. Heresco, "Shaping the Market," 173–74.

51. Scott, "You Cannot Be Serious!"

52. Curtis, "All the World's a Studio Show."

53. Heresco, "Shaping the Market," 174, 188.

54. Heresco, "Shaping the Market," 185.

55. Oates, "On the Block," 2.

56. Martin, *Financialization of Daily Life,* 43.

57. Hacker, *The Great Risk Shift.*

58. Langley, "Financialization of Life," 70.

59. Langley, *Everyday Life of Global Finance,* 92.

60. Haiven, *Cultures of Financialization,* 11–12.

61. Maclean, "Gender, Risk and the Wall Street Alpha Male," 10.

62. Neely, *Hedged Out,* 42.

63. Neely, *Hedged Out,* 34.

64. Maclean, "Gender, Risk and the Wall Street Alpha Male," 4.

65. Maclean, "Gender, Risk and the Wall Street Alpha Male," 3.

66. Heresco, "Shaping the Market," 129.

67. Dori-Hacohen and White, "'Booyah Jim.'"

68. Heresco, "Shaping the Market," 127.

69. Dori-Hacohen and White, "'Booyah Jim,'" 182.

70. Neely, *Hedged Out,* 34.

71. Brassett and Heine, "'Men Behaving Badly'?"

72. Salter and Blodgett, *Toxic Geek Masculinity in Media,* 36.

73. Salter and Blodgett, *Toxic Geek Masculinity in Media,* 47–48.

74. Maclean, "Gender, Risk and the Wall Street Alpha Male," 5.

75. Mendick et al., "Geek Entrepreneurs."

76. For further analysis of the broader exclusion of women from commentary/analysis roles within the sports media industry, see Harrison, *On the Sidelines.*

77. Rowe, *Sport, Culture, and the Media,* 147.

78. Morse, "Sport on Television," 44.

79. Morse, "Sport on Television," 44; Rose and Friedman, "Television Sport as Mas(s)Culine Cult of Distraction," 23–24.

80. Johnson, *Sports TV,* 65.

81. Neely, *Hedged Out,* 20 and 30.

82. Lapchick, "The 2021 Racial and Gender Report Card: National Football League"; Lapchick, "The 2021 Racial and Gender Report Card: Major League Baseball."

83. Oates, *Football and Manliness*, 64, 68.

84. Dembinski, *Finance,* 134.

85. Oates, *Football and Manliness,* 72.

86. Oates, *Football and Manliness,* 90.

87. Lee, "Inside the Rise of MLB's Ivy League Culture."

88. Oates, *Football and Manliness,* 88.

89. Oates, *Football and Manliness,* 88.

90. Marchand, "Stephen A. Smith rakes in almost $8M per year on new ESPN megadeal."

91. Roth, "ESPN Has Found the Absolute Worst Way to Talk About The Absolute Coolest Stuff."

92. Leary, *Keywords,* 123.

Chapter 3. Managerial Sports Television

1. Locke and Spender, *Confronting Managerialism,* 181.

2. Alamar and Mehrotra, "Beyond 'Moneyball.'"

3. Caldwell, *Televisuality,* 4.

4. Caldwell, *Televisuality,* 5.

5. Phillips, *Scouting and Scoring,* 41.

6. Hahn, VanDyke, and Cummins, "It's a Numbers Game," 495.

7. Walker and Bellamy, *Center Field Shot;* Lawrence J. Mullen and Dennis W. Mazzocco note, for instance, the significant increase in the number of graphics during Super Bowl telecasts between 1987 and 1997. Mullen and Mazzocco, "Coaches, Drama, and Technology."

8. Sandomir, "Innovation That Grew and Grew."

9. Schwarz, *Numbers Game.*

10. Dachman, "ESPN Commits to K-Zone Live on Every Pitch for MLB Coverage"; Dachman, "MLB 2019 Preview."

11. See, for instance, Lemire, "Australia Leads in Broadcasting Wearables Data as AFL Is Next."

12. Johnson, "Everything New Is Old Again."

13. For further analysis of alternative telecasts, see Buehler, "Alternative Telecasts and the Ongoing Fracturing of Sports Television."

14. Skarka, "ESPN's Exclusive Coverage of the 2018 MLB National League Wild Card Game Presented by Hankook Tire."

15. Caldwell, *Televisuality,* 87.

16. Caldwell, *Televisuality,* 88.

17. Guttmann, *From Ritual to Record,* 15.

18. Phillips, *Scouting and Scoring*; Millington and Millington, "Datafication of Everything." Notably, both Phillips and Millington and Millington reference Ian Hacking's influential argument that nineteenth-century institutions displayed a new enthusiasm for classifying and counting, in the process producing an "avalanche of printed numbers."

19. Goldsberry, "Analytics Illustrated."

20. Millington and Millington, "Datafication of Everything," 150.

21. Schwarz, *Numbers Game.*

22. Schwarz, *Numbers Game,* 164, 128.

23. Phillips, *Scouting and Scoring,* 99. Phillips also emphasizes here (as does Schwarz in *Numbers Game*) that many of the diehard fans that were pioneering intricate statistical analysis had "scientific or technical training."

24. Locke and Spender, *Confronting Managerialism,* 172.

25. Gary L. Anderson and Michael Ian Cohen critique, for instance, the influence of managerialism within education and the related emphasis on numerical metrics. Anderson and Cohen, *New Democratic Professional in Education.*

26. London, "Data-Driven."

27. Willhite, "Baseball Prospectus More than a Diamond in the Rough."

28. London, "Data-Driven."

29. Lewis, "No-Stats All-Star."

30. Lewis, "No-Stats All-Star."

31. Baerg, "Big Data, Sport, and the Digital Divide," 6.

32. Millington and Millington, "Datafication of Everything," 149.

33. Quoted in Futterman, "Baseball After Moneyball."

34. Caldwell, *Televisuality,* 88.

35. Caldwell, *Televisuality,* 7.

36. Lotz, *Television Will Be Revolutionized,* 88.

37. Heresco, "Shaping the Market," 210.

38. Stein, "Playing the Game on Television," 117–18.

39. Stein, "Playing the Game on Television," 118.

40. Stein, "Playing the Game on Television," 132.

41. Robertsson, "Virtual Graphics and Analysis."

42. "FOX Sports Loads Golf Bag with High-Tech Arsenal for Network's First U.S. Open."

43. Nwulu, "For MLS Cup, ESPN Will Deploy an Optical Player Tracking System."

44. "Data Feeds Overview."

45. "Advanced Metrics."

46. Perkins, "State of the Tech."

47. Sandomir, "ESPN Plans to Purchase Sports Wire"; in 2000, ESPN would pur-

chase the remaining 20 percent of the company, as explained in "Dow Jones to Sell Remaining Stake In SportsTicker Enterprises to ESPN."

48. Sandomir, "ESPN Plans to Purchase Sports Wire."

49. "PA Sport Acquires SportsTicker."

50. "PA Sport Acquires SportsTicker."

51. Clark, interview.

52. Roger, interview.

53. As James Andrew Miller, the media reporter who has long chronicled the ups and downs of ESPN, noted upon Walsh's retirement in 2015, Walsh left ESPN "easily ranking as one of the most influential executives in the company's history and as a transformative figure in the larger world of sports journalism." Miller, "John Walsh."

54. Alan, interview.

55. Alan, interview.

56. Roger, interview.

57. Flannery, "Help Needed, Stat!"

58. That maintaining the "Worldwide Leader" reputation would be a priority is not necessarily surprising. As Travis Vogan explains, ESPN has "carefully orchestrated and vigilantly guarded" its "Worldwide Leader" brand, working to claim the sports media "environment as its kingdom and to limit the presence of alternatives that might question or contest its reign." Vogan, *ESPN*, 177.

59. Nick, interview.

60. Clark, interview.

61. Roger, interview.

62. Roger, interview.

63. Alan, interview.

64. Clark, interview.

65. Nick, interview.

66. Alan, interview.

67. Hahn, VanDyke, and Cummins, "It's a Numbers Game," 484.

68. Hahn, VanDyke, and Cummins, "It's a Numbers Game," 484.

69. Notably, too, the relationship between statistical analysis and gambling predates the recent interest in analytics. In an examination of the first years of baseball, for instance, John Thorn argues the link between gambling and quantification helped fuel the early growth of the sport. Thorn, *Baseball in the Garden of Eden*.

70. Wojnarowski and Lowe, "Bob Voulgaris Hired as Mavs' Director of Quantitative Research and Development."

71. Quoted in Guthrie, "ESPN Execs Talk Sports Betting, Growth of Streaming Service."

72. Phillips, *Scouting and Scoring*, 43.

73. Alan, interview.

74. Clark, interview; Roger, interview.

75. Alan, e-mail.

76. Phillips, *Scouting and Scoring,* 7.

77. Phillips, *Scouting and Scoring,* 7.

78. Phillips, *Scouting and Scoring,* 244.

79. Porter, *Trust in Numbers,* ix.

80. Kennedy and Hill, "Feeling of Numbers," 9.

81. Baerg, "Sports, Analytics, and the Number as a Communication Medium," 82.

82. Beer, "Productive Measures," 4.

83. Burroughs, "Statistics and Baseball Fandom," 261.

84. Beer, "Productive Measures," 11.

85. Beer, "Productive Measures," 2.

86. Beer, "Productive Measures," 9.

87. Beer, "Productive Measures," 10.

88. Colás, "Culture of Moving Dots," 345.

89. Colás, "Culture of Moving Dots," 345.

90. Gittell, "Come for the Broadcast, Stay for the Mets Game."

91. Britton, "That's all of us right now."

92. Allen, "Mets' TV broadcast made Edwin Díaz's trumpet entrance look like a movie."

93. Colás, "Culture of Moving Dots," 343.

94. Gumbrecht, *In Praise of Athletic Beauty,* 168.

95. Millington and Millington, "Datafication of Everything," 150.

96. Millington and Millington, "Datafication of Everything," 155.

97. Baerg, "Big Data, Sport, and the Digital Divide."

98. Hutchins, "Tales of the Digital Sublime."

99. boyd and Crawford, "Critical Questions for Big Data," 663.

100. Baerg, "Sports, Analytics, and the Number as a Communication Medium," 77–78.

101. Crawford, Miltner, and Gray, "Critiquing Big Data," 1670.

102. Phillips, *Scouting and Scoring,* 134.

103. Gitelman and Jackson, "Introduction," 12.

104. Kennedy and Hill, "Pleasure and Pain of Visualizing Data in Times of Data Power," 773; Kennedy and Hill, "Feeling of Numbers," 831.

105. Gray et al., "Ways of Seeing Data," 228–29.

106. Drucker, "Humanities Approaches to Graphical Display."

107. Drucker, "Humanities Approaches to Graphical Display."

108. Drucker, "Humanities Approaches to Graphical Display."

109. Kennedy et al., "Work That Visualisation Conventions Do," 729.

110. Kennedy et al., "Work That Visualisation Conventions Do," 731.

111. Drucker, "Non-Representational Approaches to Modeling Interpretation in a Graphical Environment," 252.

112. Drucker, "Graphesis." See also Manovich, "What Is Visualization?"

113. Drucker, "Graphesis."

114. Klein, "Image of Absence," 678.

115. Drucker, "Non-Representational Approaches to Modeling Interpretation in a Graphical Environment," 249, 252.

116. Kennedy and Hill, "Feeling of Numbers," 844.

117. Kennedy and Hill, "Feeling of Numbers," 843.

118. Parks, "Flexible Microcasting," 144.

119. Parks, "Flexible Microcasting," 142.

120. Augustine, "Charles Barkley rants about analytics movement in NBA, labels Rockets GM Daryl Morey an 'idiot.'"

121. Kusz, "Remasculinizing American white guys in/through new millennium American sport films," 223.

122. Chotiner, "Jalen Rose Has a Problem with Basketball Analytics."

123. Leonard, *Playing While White,* 50, 45.

124. Quoted in Chotiner, "Jalen Rose Has a Problem with Basketball Analytics."

Chapter 4. Managerial Sports Games

1. Anable, *Playing with Feelings,* xii.

2. One might point, for example, to the wider resonance of fantasy sports within popular culture, as perhaps most notably exemplified by the success of *The League* (FX, 2009–2015), a sitcom based around a fantasy football league.

3. See, for instance, Burton, Hall, and Paul, "Historical Development and Marketing of Fantasy Sports Leagues."

4. Criblez, "Games about the Game," 131.

5. Ain, "We had no idea."

6. Quoted in Ain, "We had no idea."

7. Billings, Buzzelli, and Fan, "Growing in Tandem with Media," 32.

8. Burton, Hall, and Paul note, for example, the development of services like "Dugout Derby," a phone-based operation launched in 1989. Burton, Hall, and Paul, "Historical Development and Marketing of Fantasy Sports Leagues," 196.

9. Criblez, "Games about the Game," 134.

10. Ruihey, Billings, and Buzzelli, "Ultimate Value-Added Proposition," 254.

11. Burton, Hall, and Paul, "Historical Development and Marketing of Fantasy Sports Leagues," 199.

12. Ploeg, "A New Form of Fandom."

13. Ruihey, Billings, and Buzzelli, "Ultimate Value-Added Proposition," 251.

14. Ruihey, Billings, and Buzzelli, "Ultimate Value-Added Proposition," 251.

15. See, for example, Baumer and Zimbalist, *The Sabermetric Revolution.*

16. Criblez, "Games about the Game," 136.

17. Phillips, *Scouting and Scoring,* 120.

18. Phillips, *Scouting and Scoring,* 121.

19. Walker, *Fantasyland,* 162.

20. Walker, *Fantasyland,* 162.

21. Criblez notes, for instance, that Avalon Hill was the first tabletop sports publisher to begin producing digital simulations. Criblez, "Games about the Game," 135.

22. Bagley, "Coaching Neoliberal Citizen/Subjects, Fulfilling Fundamental Fantasies," 281; Hoxworth, "Football Fantasies," 156.

23. Jagoda, *Experimental Games,* 12.

24. Rose, "Governing 'Advanced' Liberal Democracies," 43.

25. Rose, "Governing 'Advanced' Liberal Democracies," 61.

26. Ouellette and Hay, *Better Living through Reality TV,* 3.

27. Rose, "Governing 'Advanced' Liberal Democracies," 58.

28. Hoxworth, "Football Fantasies," 157.

29. Hoxworth, "Football Fantasies," 163.

30. Baerg, "Classifying the Digital Athletic Body," 144.

31. Baerg, "Classifying the Digital Athletic Body," 144.

32. Baerg, "Neoliberalism, Risk, and Uncertainty in the Video Game."

33. Baerg, "Draft Day," 113.

34. Baerg, "Draft Day," 114.

35. Hoxworth, "Football Fantasies," 174.

36. Oates, "New Media and the Repackaging of NFL Fandom," 31.

37. Oates, "New Media and the Repackaging of NFL Fandom," 31.

38. Oates, "New Media and the Repackaging of NFL Fandom," 44.

39. Baerg, "It's (Not) in the Game," 220.

40. Oates, *Football and Manliness,* 145–46.

41. Oates, *Football and Manliness,* 150.

42. Oates, *Football and Manliness,* 144.

43. Bagley, "Coaching Neoliberal Citizen/Subjects, Fulfilling Fundamental Fantasies"; Oates, *Football and Manliness.*

44. Bogost, *Persuasive Games,* ix; Galloway, *Gaming,* 3.

45. Friedman, "Civilization and Its Discontents."

46. Friedman, "Civilization and Its Discontents."

47. Friedman, "Making Sense of Software."

48. Friedman, "Making Sense of Software."

49. Friedman, "Making Sense of Software."

50. Friedman, "Civilization and Its Discontents."

51. Jagoda, *Experimental Games,* 28.

52. Ruberg, *Video Games Have Always Been Queer,* 137.

53. Ruberg, *Video Games Have Always Been Queer,* 136.

54. Ruberg, *Video Games Have Always Been Queer,* 143.

55. Friedman, "Making Sense of Software."

56. Jagoda, *Experimental Games,* 25.

57. Schleiner, *Player's Power to Change the Game,* 134, 10.

58. Schleiner, *Player's Power to Change the Game,* 11.

59. Jagoda, *Experimental Games,* 30, 67.

60. Oates, "New Media and the Repackaging of NFL Fandom," 31.

61. Jagoda, *Experimental Games,* 256.

62. Crawford, "Is it in the Game?" 581, 585.

63. Ervine, "Football Videogames," 146.

64. Crawford, "Is it in the Game?" 587.

65. See, for example, Stein, "Playing the Game on Television."

66. See, for instance, Fiske and Watts, "Video Games."

67. Yee, "Labor of Fun," 70.

68. Yee, *Proteus Paradox,* 74.

69. Yee, "Labor of Fun," 70.

70. Lukacs, Embrick, and Wright, "Managed Hearthstone," 175.

71. Rettberg, "Corporate Ideology in World of Warcraft," 20.

72. Rettberg, "Corporate Ideology in World of Warcraft," 26.

73. Kuo, Lutz, and Hiler, "Brave New World of Warcraft," 501.

74. Csikszentmihalyi, *Flow and the Foundations of Positive Psychology,* 142.

75. Kuo, Lutz, and Hiler, "Brave New World of Warcraft," 501.

76. Kuo, Lutz, and Hiler, "Brave New World of Warcraft," 501.

77. Iversen, "Paradox and Pleasure," 101.

78. Iversen, "Paradox and Pleasure," 114.

79. Kuo, Lutz, and Hiler, "Brave New World of Warcraft," 503.

80. Calleja, "Digital Games and Escapism," 349.

81. Chess, "Going with the Flo," 91.

82. Chess, "Going with the Flo," 96.

83. Chess, "Going with the Flo," 88.

84. Chess, "Going with the Flo," 88.

85. Graeber, *Bullshit Jobs,* 134.

86. Tiratelli, "Where Did All the Bullshit Jobs Go?"

87. Graeber, *Bullshit Jobs,* 17.

88. Graeber, *Bullshit Jobs,* 134.

89. Anable, "Casual Games, Time Management, and the Work of Affect."

90. Graeber, *Bullshit Jobs,* 135.

91. Brown, *Enjoying It.*

92. Ruberg, *Video Games Have Always Been Queer,* 126.

93. Ruberg, *Video Games Have Always Been Queer,* 126.

94. Anable, "Casual Games, Time Management, and the Work of Affect."

95. Anable, "Casual Games, Time Management, and the Work of Affect."

96. Hoxworth, "Football Fantasies," 165.

97. Brown, *Enjoying It.*

98. Brown, *Enjoying It.*

99. Anable, *Playing with Feelings,* 132.

100. Stuelke, *Ruse of Repair,* 17.

101. Stuelke, *Ruse of Repair,* 218.

Conclusion

1. For a historical account of this long-standing relationship, see, for instance, Bryant and Holt, "A Historical Overview of Sports and Media in the United States." For an account of the continuing significance of this relationship today, see, for instance, Serazio, "The Irreverent Life and Uncompromising Death of Deadspin."

2. Something of a converse example involves baseball journalist Ken Rosenthal. For more than a decade, Ken Rosenthal served as one the MLB Network's "insiders" and, like insiders at other outlets, played a prominent role in coverage of items like free agency signings and trade rumors. Despite, though, being one the sport's most prominent reporters, Rosenthal was left off the MLB Network for much of 2020 and then saw his contract go unrenewed at the end of the 2021. The primary alleged reason for this fate? "Light criticism" of the league's commissioner in Rosenthal's columns for *The Athletic,* as reported in Marchand, "Ken Rosenthal out at MLB Network over Rob Manfred Criticism."

3. In the case of *Moneyball,* cinematographer Wally Pfister comments that MLB was "pretty powerful" while describing the relationship between the league and the production, also noting the league had a "certain degree of script approval." Quoted in Ditzian, "'Moneyball' Filmmakers Getting 'Phenomenal' Support From MLB And Oakland Athletics."

4. Florio, "NFL has clear financial incentive in Draft Day"; Rothman, "How the NFL Helped Make Draft Day a Super Accurate Sports Movie."

5. Kashmere, "Running the Wrong Pattern," 35.

6. Kashmere, "Running the Wrong Pattern," 35.

7. Kashmere, "Running the Wrong Pattern," 42.

8. Buehler, "Independent Sports Television in the Networked Era."

Bibliography

Aaronson, Charles A. "Knute Rockne—All American." *Motion Picture Daily,* October 7, 1940. Media History Digital Library.

"Advanced Metrics." https://www.optasports.com/services/analytics/advanced-metrics/.

Aftab, Kaleem. "Steven Soderbergh on #metoo and Making a Movie on His Phone." inews.co.uk, March 22, 2018. https://inews.co.uk/culture/steven-soderbergh-interview-unsane-director-claire-foy-daniel-kaluuya-weinstein-metoo-137338.

Ain, Morty. "We Had No Idea." ESPN.com, February 23, 2010. https://www.espn.com/mlb/insider/news/story?id=4939543.

Aitken, Rob. "'A Machine for Living': The Cultural Economy of Financial Subjectivity." In *The Routledge International Handbook of Financialization,* edited by Philip Mader, Daniel Mertens, and Natascha van der Zwan, 369–79. London: Routledge, 2020.

Alamar, Benjamin, and Vijay Mehrotra. "Beyond 'Moneyball': The Rapidly Evolving World of Sports Analytics." *Analytics,* October 2011. http://analytics-magazine.org/beyond-moneyball-the-rapidly-evolving-world-of-sports-analytics-part-i/.

Allen, Scott. "Mets' TV Broadcast Made Edwin Díaz's Trumpet Entrance Look like a Movie." *Washington Post,* August 11, 2022. https://www.washingtonpost.com/sports/2022/08/11/edwin-diaz-entrance/.

Anable, Aubrey. "Casual Games, Time Management, and the Work of Affect." *Ada: A Journal of Gender, New Media, and Technology* no. 2 (2013).

Anable, Aubrey. *Playing with Feelings: Video Games and Affect.* Minneapolis: University of Minnesota Press, 2018.

Anderson, Gary L., and Michael Ian Cohen. *The New Democratic Professional in Education: Confronting Markets, Metrics, and Managerialism.* New York: Teachers College Press, 2018.

Andreasen, Torsten, Mikkel Krause Frantzen, and Frederik Tygstrup. "Finance Fiction." In *The Routledge Handbook of Critical Finance Studies,* edited by Christian Borch and Robert Wosnitzer, 358–79. New York: Routledge, 2020.

Ashcraft, Karen Lee, and Lisa A. Flores. "'Slaves with White Collars': Persistent Performances of Masculinity in Crisis." *Text and Performance Quarterly* 23, no. 1 (January 2003): 1–29.

Augustine, Bernie. "Charles Barkley Rants about Analytics Movement in NBA, Labels Rockets GM Daryl Morey an 'Idiot.'" *New York Daily News,* February 11, 2015. https://www.nydailynews.com/sports/basketball/don-talk-charles-barkley-nba-analytics-article-1.2110764.

Babington, Bruce. *The Sports Film: Games People Play*. New York: Columbia University Press, 2014.

Baerg, Andrew. "Big Data, Sport, and the Digital Divide: Theorizing How Athletes Might Respond to Big Data Monitoring." *Journal of Sport and Social Issues* 41, no. 1 (February 2017): 3–20. https://doi.org/10.1177/0193723516673409.

Baerg, Andrew. "Classifying the Digital Athletic Body: Assessing the Implications of the Player-Attribute-Rating System in Sports Video Games." *International Journal of Sport Communication* 4, no. 2 (January 2011): 133–47.

Baerg, Andrew. "Draft Day: Risk, Responsibility, and Fantasy Football." In *Fantasy Sports and the Changing Sports Media Industry: Media, Players, and Society,* edited by Nicholas David Bowman, John S. W. Spinda, and Jimmy Sanderson, 99–120. Lanham, Md.: Lexington Books, 2016.

Baerg, Andrew. "'It's (Not) in the Game': The Quest for Quantitative Realism and the Madden Football Fan." In *Sports Mania: Essays on Fandom and the Media in the 21st Century*, edited by Lawrence W. Hugenberg, Paul M. Haridakis, and Adam C. Earnheardt, 218–28. Jefferson: McFarland & Company, 2008.

Baerg, Andrew. "Neoliberalism, Risk, and Uncertainty in the Video Game." In *Capital at the Brink: Overcoming the Destructive Legacies of Neoliberalism,* edited by Jeffrey R. Di Leo and Uppinder Mehan, 186–214. Ann Arbor, Mich.: Open Humanities Press, 2014.

Baerg, Andrew. "Sports, Analytics, and the Number as a Communication Medium." In *Routledge Handbook of Sport Communication,* edited by Paul Mark Pedersen, 75–83. London: Routledge, 2013.

Bagley, Meredith M. "Coaching Neoliberal Citizen/Subjects, Fulfilling Fundamental Fantasies: Cultural Discourse of Fantasy Football." In *Sports and Identity,* edited by Barry Brummett and Andrew Ishak, 280–304. New York: Routledge, 2013.

Baker, Aaron. *Contesting Identities: Sports in American Film*. Urbana: University of Illinois Press, 2003.

Baldwin, Clive. *Anxious Men: Masculinity in American Fiction of the Mid-Twentieth Century*. Edinburgh: Edinburgh University Press, 2020.

Banet-Weiser, Sarah. *Empowered: Popular Feminism and Popular Misogyny*. Durham, N.C.: Duke University Press, 2018.

Barry, Ben, and Nathaniel Weiner. "Suited for Success? Suits, Status, and Hybrid Masculinity." *Men and Masculinities* 22, no. 2 (June 2019): 151–76.

Basak, Sonali. "SCOOP: Sports as the next Asset Class. A Year after Striking a Deal with the NBA, Investment Firm Dyal Buys a Stake in Its First Franchise—the Phoenix Suns. Executives Give Me Details on How They'll Seek Returns after Team Valuations Have Surged." Twitter, July 6, 2021. https://twitter.com/sonalibasak/status/1412401540179148800.

Baumer, Benjamin, and Andrew Zimbalist. *The Sabermetric Revolution: Assessing the Growth of Analytics in Baseball.* Philadelphia: University of Pennsylvania Press, 2014.

Beer, David. "Productive Measures: Culture and Measurement in the Context of Everyday Neoliberalism." *Big Data & Society* 2, no. 1 (June 2015).

Belson, Ken, and Kevin Draper. "N.F.L. Signs Media Deals Worth Over $100 Billion." *New York Times,* March 18, 2021. https://www.nytimes.com/2021/03/18/sports/football/nfl-tv-contracts.html.

Berg, Adam, Andrew D. Linden, and Jaime Schultz. "Manning Up: Modern Manhood, Rudimentary Pugilistic Capital, and Esquire Network's White Collar Brawlers." *Journal of Sport and Social Issues* 44, no. 1 (February 2020): 70–92.

Billings, Andrew C., Nicholas R. Buzzelli, and Minghui Fan. "Growing in Tandem with Media: Fantasy Sport, Media Use, and the Formation of an Industry Giant." *International Journal of the History of Sport* 38, no. 1 (2021): 28–40.

Block, Alex Ben. "Brad Pitt Reveals What He, Sony Did to Save 'Moneyball.'" *Hollywood Reporter,* December 16, 2011. https://www.hollywoodreporter.com/news/general-news/moneyball-making-brad-pitt-bennett-miller-274738/.

Bogost, Ian. *Persuasive Games: The Expressive Power of Videogames.* Cambridge, Mass.: MIT Press, 2007.

Bonzel, Katharina. *National Pastimes: Cinema, Sports, and Nation.* Lincoln: University of Nebraska Press, 2020.

Boozer, Jack. *Career Movies: American Business and the Success Mystique.* Austin: University of Texas Press, 2010.

Bown, Alfie. *Enjoying It: Candy Crush and Capitalism.* Winchester, U.K.: Zero Books, 2015.

boyd, danah, and Kate Crawford. "Critical Questions for Big Data." *Information, Communication & Society* 15, no. 5 (June 2012): 662–79.

Boyle, Raymond, and Lisa W. Kelly. "The Celebrity Entrepreneur on Television: Profile, Politics and Power." *Celebrity Studies* 1, no. 3 (2010): 334–50.

Brassett, James, and Frederic Heine. "'Men Behaving Badly'? Representations of Masculinity in Post-Global Financial Crisis Cinema." *International Feminist Journal of Politics* 23, no. 5 (2021): 763–84.

Britton, Tim. "'That's All of Us Right Now': How a Mets Fan and Her Face-Palm Captured the Worst Stretch of New York's Season." *The Athletic,* August 10, 2021. https://theathletic.com/2761567/2021/08/10/thats-all-of-us-right-now-how-one-mets-fan-and-her-face-palm-captured-the-worst-stretch-of-new-yorks-season/.

Brooks, Xan. "Soderbergh's Moneyball Mothballed." *The Guardian,* July 3, 2009. https://www.theguardian.com/film/2009/jul/03/steven-soderbergh-brad-pitt-moneyball-mothballed.

Brown, Lane. "So How Bad Was Soderbergh's Revised Moneyball Script?" *Vulture,* June 23, 2009. http://www.vulture.com/2009/06/so_how_bad_was_soderberghs_rev.html.

Bryant, Jennings, and Andrea M. Holt. "A Historical Overview of Sports and Media in the United States." In *Handbook of Sports and Media,* edited by Arthur A. Raney and Jennings Bryant. New York: Routledge, 2006.

Buehler, Branden. "Alternative Telecasts and the Ongoing Fracturing of Sports Television." *Journal of Sports Media* 15, no. 2 (Fall 2020): 117–35.

Buehler, Branden. "Independent Sports Television in the Networked Era." *Television & New Media* 23, no. 4 (May 2022): 352–67.

Buehler, Branden. "Sports Television and the Continuing Search for Alternative Programming." *International Journal of Sport Communication* 13, no. 3 (September 2020): 566–74.

Buehler, Branden. "The Documentary as 'Quality' Sports Television." In *Sporting Realities: Critical Readings of the Sports Documentary,* edited by Samantha N. Sheppard and Travis Vogan, 11–34. Lincoln: University of Nebraska Press, 2020.

Burk, Robert F. *Much More Than a Game: Players, Owners, and American Baseball Since 1921.* Chapel Hill: University of North Carolina Press, 2001.

Burton, Rick, Kevin Hall, and Rodney Paul. "The Historical Development and Marketing of Fantasy Sports Leagues." *Journal of SPORT* 2, no. 2 (2013): 185–215.

Caldwell, John Thornton. *Televisuality: Style, Crisis, and Authority in American Television.* New Brunswick, N.J.: Rutgers University Press, 1995.

Calleja, Gordon. "Digital Games and Escapism." *Games and Culture* 5, no. 4 (October 2010): 335–53.

Chess, Shira. "Going with the Flo." *Feminist Media Studies* 12, no. 1 (2012): 83–99.

Chotiner, Isaac. "Jalen Rose Has a Problem with Basketball Analytics." *New Yorker,* June 6, 2019. https://www.newyorker.com/news/q-and-a/jalen-rose-has-a-problem-with-basketball-analytics.

Coffey, Brendan. "Move Over, Billionaires; the Really Big Money Wants in on Sports." Sportico, July 27, 2020. https://www.sportico.com/business/finance/2020/sports-team-ownership-billionaires-investment-funds-private-equity-1234609947/.

Colás, Yago. "The Culture of Moving Dots: Toward a History of Counting and of What Counts in Basketball." *Journal of Sport History* 44, no. 2 (Summer 2017): 336–49.

Connell, Raewyn. *Masculinities.* Second Edition. Berkeley: University of California Press, 2005.

Connor, J. D. *Hollywood Math and Aftermath: The Economic Image and the Digital Recession.* New York: Bloomsbury, 2018.

Cooky, Cheryl, LaToya D. Council, Maria A. Mears, and Michael A. Messner. "One and Done: The Long Eclipse of Women's Televised Sports, 1989–2019." *Communication & Sport* 9, no. 3 (June 2021): 347–71.

Cormany, Diane L. "Mediated Affect and Financial News Media: The Closing Bell, Marketplace and the Wall Street Journal." Ph.D. diss., University of Minnesota, 2016.

Corrigan, Thomas F. "Digging the Moat: The Political Economy of ESPN's Cable Carriage Fees." In *The ESPN Effect: Exploring the Worldwide Leader in Sports*, edited by John McGuire, Greg G. Armfield, and Adam Earnheardt, 37–52. New York: Peter Lang, 2015.

Couldry, Nick. "Reality TV, or The Secret Theater of Neoliberalism." *Review of Education, Pedagogy, and Cultural Studies* 30, no. 1 (2008): 3–13.

Cox, Courtney M. "Broke Ballers: The Mediated World of Football and Finance." *InMedia* 6 (2017).

Cox, Courtney M. "'The Game on Top of the Game': Navigating Race, Media, and the Business of Basketball in High Flying Bird." Flow, February 22, 2019. https://www.flowjournal.org/2019/02/game-on-top-of-the-game/.

Crawford, Garry. "Is It in the Game? Reconsidering Play Spaces, Game Definitions, Theming, and Sports Videogames." *Games and Culture* 10, no. 6 (November 2015): 571–92.

Crawford, Kate, Kate Miltner, and Mary L. Gray. "Critiquing Big Data: Politics, Ethics, Epistemology." *International Journal of Communication* 8 (2014): 1663–72.

Criblez, Adam. "Games about the Game: A History of Tabletop Baseball." *NINE: A Journal of Baseball History and Culture* 29, no. 1–2 (Fall–Spring 2020–2021): 125–41.

Crosson, Seán. *Sport and Film*. London: Routledge, 2013.

Crupi, Anthony. "Disney to Spend $44.9 Billion on Sports Rights Through 2027." Sportico, November 30, 2022. https://www.sportico.com/feature/disney-to-invest-44-9-billion-on-sports-rights-through-2027-1234697032/.

Csikszentmihalyi, Mihaly. *Flow and the Foundations of Positive Psychology: The Collected Works of Mihaly Csikszentmihalyi*. Dordrecht, Netherlands: Springer, 2014.

Cullen, Jim. *The American Dream: A Short History of an Idea That Shaped a Nation*. Oxford, U.K.: Oxford University Press, 2004.

Curtis, Bryan. "All the World's a Studio Show." The Ringer, June 21, 2017. https://www.theringer.com/2017/6/21/16041610/adrian-wojnarowski-yahoo-web-show-nba-draft-studio-tv-29bb03dd78de.

Curtis, Bryan. Interview by Branden Buehler. Phone, May 9, 2016.

Curtis, Bryan. "The Trade Rumor Era." Grantland, July 7, 2014. https://grantland.com/features/nba-trade-rumors-espn-yahoo-new-york-post-lebron-james-jason-kidd-offseason-trade-signing/.

Dachman, Jason. "ESPN Commits to K-Zone Live on Every Pitch for MLB Coverage." Sports Video Group, April 3, 2015. https://www.sportvision.com/news/espn-commits-k-zone-live-every-pitch-mlb-coverage-0.

Dachman, Jason. "MLB 2019 Preview: ESPN Continues to Up Its Virtual Game with More K-Zone 3D, Statcast Graphics." Sports Video Group, March 28, 2019. https://www.sportsvideo.org/2019/03/28/mlb-2019-preview-espn-continues-to-up-its-virtual-game-with-more-k-zone-3d-statcast-graphics/.

Davis, Gerald F. *Managed by the Markets: How Finance Re-Shaped America*. Oxford, U.K.: Oxford University Press, 2009.

Deb, Sopan, and Marc Stein. "Leon Rose, an Agent, Is Expected to Be the Next Knicks President." *New York Times,* February 6, 2020. https://www.nytimes.com/2020/02/06/sports/basketball/leon-rose-knicks-president.html.

Dembinski, Paul H. *Finance: Servant or Deceiver? Financialization at the Crossroads*. Translated by Kevin Cook. London: Palgrave Macmillan, 2009.

Deubert, Christopher R., Glenn M. Wong, and Daniel Hatman. "National Football League General Managers: An Analysis of the Responsibilities, Qualifications, and Characteristics." *Jeffrey S. Moorad Sports Law Journal* 20, no. 2 (2013): 427–94.

Ditzian, Eric. "'Moneyball' Filmmakers Getting 'Phenomenal' Support From MLB And Oakland Athletics." MTV News, July 20, 2010. https://www.mtv.com/news/cl9p4r/moneyball-filmmakers-getting-phenomenal-support-from-mlb-and-oakland-athletics.

Donalson, Melvin. *Masculinity in the Interracial Buddy Film*. Jefferson, N.C.: McFarland, 2006.

Dori-Hacohen, Gonen, and Timothy T. White. "'Booyah Jim': The Construction of Hegemonic Masculinity in CNBC 'Mad Money' Phone-in Interactions." *Discourse, Context & Media* 2, no. 4 (2013): 175–83.

Drucker, Johanna. "Graphesis." *Poetess Archive Journal* 2, no. 1 (December 10, 2010).

Drucker, Johanna. "Humanities Approaches to Graphical Display." *Digital Humanities Quarterly* 5, no. 1 (2011).

Drucker, Johanna. "Non-Representational Approaches to Modeling Interpretation in a Graphical Environment." *Digital Scholarship in the Humanities* 33, no. 2 (June 2018): 248–63.

Dworkin, James B. "The Evolution of Collective Bargaining in Sports." In *Research Handbook of Employment Relations in Sport*, edited by Michael Barry, James Skinner, and Terry Engelberg, 127–48. Cheltenham, U.K.: Edward Elgar Publishing, 2016.

Dyer, Richard. *White: Essays on Race and Culture*. London: Routledge, 1997.

Early, Gerald Lyn. *A Level Playing Field: African American Athletes and the Republic of Sports*. Cambridge, Mass.: Harvard University Press, 2011.

Edwards, Harry. *The Revolt of the Black Athlete: 50th Anniversary Edition*. Urbana: University of Illinois Press, 2017.

Elmwood, Victoria A. "'Just Some Bum from the Neighborhood': The Resolution of Post-Civil Rights Tension and Heavyweight Public Sphere Discourse in Rocky (1976)." *Film & History* 35, no. 2 (2005): 49–59.

Ervine, Jonathan. "Football Videogames: Re-Shaping Football and Re-Defining Fandom in a Postmodern Era." In *Digital Football Cultures: Fandom, Identities and Resistance,* edited by Stefan Lawrence and Garry Crawford, 139–53. London: Routledge, 2018.

ESPN employee "Alan." Interview by Branden Buehler. Phone, September 3, 2015.

ESPN employee "Alan." Email, August 12, 2022.

ESPN employee "Clark." Interview by Branden Buehler. Phone, August 21, 2015.

ESPN employee "Greg." Interview by Branden Buehler. Phone, September 8, 2015.

ESPN employee "Nick." Interview by Branden Buehler. Phone, August 25, 2015.

ESPN employee "Roger." Interview by Branden Buehler. Phone, September 4, 2015.

Faturechi, Robert, Justin Elliott, and Ellis Simani. "The Billionaire Playbook: How Sports Owners Use Their Teams to Avoid Millions in Taxes." *ProPublica,* July 8, 2021. https://www.propublica.org/article/the-billionaire-playbook-how-sports-owners-use-their-teams-to-avoid-millions-in-taxes?token=mp-L3ieFIJqb1z 31KSB10HyiAgnJ_V0z.

Favale, Dan. "Banana Boats and Emoji Wars: The Day DeAndre Jordan Turned Twitter Upside Down." Bleacher Report, July 7, 2017. https://bleacherreport.com/articles/2719108-banana-boats-and-emoji-wars-the-day-deandre-jordan-turned-twitter-upside-down.

Fiske, John, and Jon Watts. "Video Games: Inverted Pleasures." *Australian Journal of Cultural Studies* 3, no. 1 (1985): 89–104.

Flannery, Paul. "Help Needed, Stat! Is the Sloan Sports Analytics Conference Too Big?" *Boston Magazine,* February 25, 2014. https://www.bostonmagazine.com/news/2014/02/25/mit-sloan-sports-analytics-conference/.

Fleming, Mike, Jr. "Sony Sparks To 'Million Dollar Arm' Pitch." *Deadline,* April 29, 2010. https://deadline.com/2010/04/sony-sparks-to-million-dollar-arm-pitch-36786/.

Fleming, Peter. *The Mythology of Work: How Capitalism Persists Despite Itself.* London: Pluto Press, 2015.

Flew, Terry. "Michel Foucault's The Birth of Biopolitics and Contemporary Neo-Liberalism Debates." *Thesis Eleven* 108, no. 1 (February 2012): 44–65.

Florio, Mike. "NFL Has Clear Financial Incentive in Draft Day." *ProFootballTalk,* April 11, 2014. https://profootballtalk.nbcsports.com/2014/04/11/nfl-has-clear-financial-incentive-in-draft-day/.

FOX Sports Press Pass. "FOX Sports Loads Golf Bag with High-Tech Arsenal For Network's First U.S. Open." Press Release, June 10, 2015. https://www.foxsports.com/presspass/blog/2015/06/10/fox-sports-loads-golf-bag-with-high-tech-arsenal-for-networks-first-u-s-open/.

Freeman, Michael. *ESPN: The Uncensored History.* Lanham, Md.: Taylor Trade Publishing, 2000.

Fridman, Daniel. *Freedom from Work: Embracing Financial Self-Help in the United States and Argentina.* Stanford, Calif.: Stanford University Press, 2016.

Friedman, Lester D. *Sports Movies.* New Brunswick, N.J.: Rutgers University Press, 2020.

Friedman, Ted. "Civilization and Its Discontents: Simulation, Subjectivity, and Space." In *On a Silver Platter: CD-ROMs and the Promises of a New Technology,* edited by Greg M. Smith, 132–50. New York: New York University Press, 1999.

Friedman, Ted. "Making Sense of Software: Computer Games and Interactive Textuality." In *CyberSociety: Computer-Mediated Communication and Community,* edited by Steven G. Jones, 73–89. Thousand Oaks, Calif.: Sage Publications, 1995.

Fritz, Ben. "Oscars 2012: 'The Help,' 'Moneyball' among Those Snubbed." *Los Angeles Times,* February 27, 2012. https://www.latimes.com/la-et-oscars-snubs-20120227 -story.html.

Funt, Danny. "At Sloan Sports Conference, Criticism Mounts over Diversity, Access." *Washington Post,* June 13, 2022. https://www.washingtonpost.com/sports/ 2022/06/13/sloan-sports-conference-diversity/.

Futterman, Matthew. "Baseball After Moneyball." *Wall Street Journal,* September 30, 2011. http://www.wsj.com/articles/SB1000142405311190379150457658469 1683234216.

Galloway, Alexander R. *Gaming: Essays on Algorithmic Culture.* Minneapolis: University of Minnesota Press, 2006.

Gay, Jason. "Sloan News Day! What Were MIT, ESPN and Obama Hiding?" *Wall Street Journal,* March 1, 2018. https://www.wsj.com/articles/sloan-news-day-what -were-mit-espn-and-obama-hiding-1519942362.

Gilbert, Daniel A. *Expanding the Strike Zone: Baseball in the Age of Free Agency.* Amherst: University of Massachusetts Press, 2013.

Ginesta, Xavier, and Nahuel I. Faedo. "The Influence of North American Ownership on the Business, Management, and Communication Model of Spanish Professional Football: A Case Study of Real Club Deportivo Mallorca (2016–2021)." *Communication & Sport,* OnlineFirst (2022).

Gitell, Noah. "Come for the Broadcast, Stay for the Mets Game." *New York Times,* August 16, 2022. https://www.nytimes.com/2022/08/16/sports/baseball/sny-mets -diaz.html.

Gitelman, Lisa, and Virginia Jackson. "Introduction." In *Raw Data Is an Oxymoron,* edited by Daniel Rosenberg and Travis D. Williams. Cambridge, Mass.: MIT Press, 2013.

Goldsberry, Kirk. "Analytics Illustrated." Presented at the MIT Sloan Sports Analytics Conference, Boston Convention and Exhibition Center, Boston, February 28, 2015.

Goldstein, Adam. "Revenge of the Managers: Labor Cost-Cutting and the Paradoxical Resurgence of Managerialism in the Shareholder Value Era, 1984 to 2001." *American Sociological Review* 77, no. 2 (April 2012): 268–94.

Good, Owen. "In Moneyball, Activision's Bobby Kotick Plays a Familiar Role." Kotaku, September 27, 2011. https://kotaku.com/in-moneyball-activisions-bobby -kotick-plays-a-familiar-5844105.

Gordon, David M. *Fat and Mean: The Corporate Squeeze of Working Americans and the Myth of Managerial "Downsizing."* New York: The Free Press, 1996.

Graeber, David. *Bullshit Jobs: A Theory.* New York: Simon and Schuster, 2018.

Gray, Jonathan, Liliana Bounegru, Stefania Milan, and Paolo Ciuccarelli. "Ways of Seeing Data: Toward a Critical Literacy for Data Visualizations as Research Objects and Research Devices." In *Innovative Methods in Media and Communica-*

tion Research, edited by Sebastian Kubitschko and Anne Kaun, 227–51. Cham, Switzerland: Palgrave Macmillan, 2016.

Gullifor, Paul F. "WFAN and the Birth of All-Sports Radio: Sporting a New Format." In *Sports-Talk Radio in America: Its Context and Culture,* edited by Frank Hoffmann, Jack M. Dempsey, and Martin J. Manning, 53–64. New York: Routledge, 2006.

Gumbrecht, Hans Ulrich. *In Praise of Athletic Beauty.* Cambridge, Mass.: Harvard University Press, 2006.

Guthrie, Marisa. "ESPN Execs Talk Sports Betting, Growth of Streaming Service." *Hollywood Reporter,* May 14, 2019. https://www.hollywoodreporter.com/news/espn-2019-upfront-presentation-sports-betting-espn-1210461.

Guttmann, Allen. *From Ritual to Record: The Nature of Modern Sports.* New York: Columbia University Press, 1978.

Hacker, Jacob S. *The Great Risk Shift: The New Economic Insecurity and the Decline of the American Dream.* Second Edition. Oxford, U.K.: Oxford University Press, 2019.

Hahn, Dustin A., Matthew S. VanDyke, and R. Glenn Cummins. "It's a Numbers Game: Change in the Frequency, Type, and Presentation Form of Statistics Used in NFL Broadcasts." *International Journal of Sport Communication* 11, no. 4 (December 2018): 482–502.

Haiven, Max. "Culture and Financialization: Four Approaches." In *The Routledge International Handbook of Financialization,* edited by Philip Mader, Daniel Mertens, and Natascha van der Zwan. London: Routledge, 2020.

Haiven, Max. *Cultures of Financialization: Fictitious Capital in Popular Culture and Everyday Life.* London: Palgrave Macmillan, 2014.

Haiven, Max. "Monsters of the Financialized Imagination: From Pokémon to Trump." *State of Power.* Transnational Institute, 2017.

Hardin, Carolyn. "Neoliberal Temporality: Time-Sense and the Shift from Pensions to 401(k)s." *American Quarterly* 66, no. 1 (2014): 95–118.

Harrison, Guy. *On the Sidelines: Gendered Neoliberalism and the American Female Sportscaster.* Lincoln: University of Nebraska Press, 2021.

Hatton, Erin. *The Temp Economy: From Kelly Girls to Permatemps in Postwar America.* Philadelphia: Temple University Press, 2011.

Hay, James. "Too Good to Fail: Managing Financial Crisis Through the Moral Economy of Reality TV." *Journal of Communication Inquiry* 34, no. 4 (October 2010): 382–402.

Heresco, Aaron. "Shaping the Market: CNBC and the Discourses of Financialization." Ph.D. diss., Pennsylvania State University, 2014.

Ho, Karen. *Liquidated: An Ethnography of Wall Street.* Durham, N.C.: Duke University Press, 2009.

Hollywood. "What's New on the Screen," January 1934. Media History Digital Library.

Houssart, Mark. "The Shifting Cinematic Portrayal of Managers in the United States Post-2008." *European Journal of American Culture* 37, no. 3 (September 2018): 223–39.

Hoxworth, Kellen. "Football Fantasies: Neoliberal Habitus, Racial Governmentality, and National Spectacle." *American Quarterly* 72, no. 1 (March 2020): 155–79.

Hunter, Latham. "The Celluloid Cubicle: Regressive Constructions of Masculinity in 1990s Office Movies." *Journal of American Culture* 26, no. 1 (March 2003): 71–86.

Hutchins, Brett. "Tales of the Digital Sublime: Tracing the Relationship between Big Data and Professional Sport." *Convergence: The International Journal of Research into New Media Technologies* 22, no. 5 (October 2016): 494–509.

Hutchins, Brett, Bo Li, and David Rowe. "Over-the-Top Sport: Live Streaming Services, Changing Coverage Rights Markets and the Growth of Media Sport Portals." *Media, Culture & Society* 41, no. 7 (October 2019): 975–94.

Hyman, Louis. *Temp: The Real Story of What Happened to Your Salary, Benefits, and Job Security*. New York: Penguin Books, 2018.

Fantasy Sports and Gaming Association. "Industry Demographics." https://thefsga.org/industry-demographics/.

Iversen, Sara Mosberg. "Paradox and Pleasure." *Mediekultur. Journal of Media and Communication Research* 56 (2014): 100–116.

Jagoda, Patrick. *Experimental Games: Critique, Play, and Design in the Age of Gamification*. Chicago: University of Chicago Press, 2020.

Johnson, Victoria E. "Everything New Is Old Again: Sport Television, Innovation, and Tradition for a Multi-Platform Era." In *Beyond Prime Time: Television Programming in the Post-Network Era,* edited by Amanda D. Lotz, 114–37. New York: Routledge, 2009.

Johnson, Victoria E. *Sports TV*. New York: Routledge, 2021.

Karp, Austin. "ESPN, ESPN2 In Just Under 100 Million U.S. Homes In August." *Sports Business Journal,* August 4, 2011. https://www.sportsbusinessjournal.com/Daily/Issues/2011/08/04/Research-and-Ratings/Cable-nets.aspx.

Kashmere, Brett. "Running the Wrong Pattern: TVTV Goes to the Super Bowl." *The Velvet Light Trap* 87, no. 1 (Spring 2021): 35–49.

Kelly, Casey Ryan. "The Wounded Man: Foxcatcher and the Incoherence of White Masculine Victimhood." *Communication and Critical/Cultural Studies* 15, no. 2 (2018): 161–78.

Kendall, Lori. *Hanging Out in the Virtual Pub: Masculinities and Relationships Online*. Berkeley: University of California Press, 2002.

Kennedy, Helen, and Rosemary Lucy Hill. "The Feeling of Numbers: Emotions in Everyday Engagements with Data and Their Visualisation." *Sociology* 52, no. 4 (August 2018): 830–48.

Kennedy, Helen, and Rosemary Lucy Hill. "The Pleasure and Pain of Visualizing Data in Times of Data Power." *Television & New Media* 18, no. 8 (December 2017): 769–82.

Kennedy, Helen, Rosemary Lucy Hill, Giorgia Aiello, and William Allen. "The Work That Visualisation Conventions Do." *Information, Communication & Society* 19, no. 6 (2016): 715–35.

King, Bill. "Feel the Power—Feel the NFL Draft." *Sports Business Journal*, April 24,

2000. http://www.sportsbusinessdaily.com/Journal/Issues/2000/04/20000424/No-Topic-Name/Feel-The-Power-151-Feel-The-NFL-Draft.aspx.

Klein, Lauren F. "The Image of Absence: Archival Silence, Data Visualization, and James Hemings." *American Literature* 85, no. 4 (December 1, 2013): 661–88.

Klikauer, Thomas. "What Is Managerialism?" *Critical Sociology* 41, no. 7–8 (November 2015): 1103–19.

Kunz, William M. *The Political Economy of Sports Television*. New York: Routledge, 2020.

Kuo, Andrew, Richard J. Lutz, and Jacob L. Hiler. "Brave New World of Warcraft: A Conceptual Framework for Active Escapism." *Journal of Consumer Marketing* 33, no. 7 (2016): 498–506.

Kusz, Kyle W. "Jerry Maguire: Reading the Politics of the White Male Redemption." *International Review for the Sociology of Sport* 36, no. 1 (March 2001): 83–88.

Kusz, Kyle W. "Notes on the Uses of Sport in Trump's White Nationalist Assemblage." *Review of Nationalities* 9 (2019): 39–59.

Kusz, Kyle W. "Remasculinizing American White Guys in/through New Millennium American Sport Films." *Sport in Society* 11, no. 2–3 (May 2008): 209–26.

Kusz, Kyle W. "'Winning Bigly': Sporting Fantasies of White Male Omnipotence in the Rise of Trump and Alt Right White Supremacy." *Journal of Hate Studies* 14, no. 1 (2017): 113–36.

Lang, Brent. "Disney Throws a Box Office Curve with 'Million Dollar Arm.'" *Variety*, May 14, 2014. https://variety.com/2014/film/news/disney-throws-a-box-office-curve-with-million-dollar-arm-1201180903/.

Langley, Paul. *The Everyday Life of Global Finance: Saving and Borrowing in Anglo-America*. Oxford, U.K.: Oxford University Press, 2008.

Langley, Paul. "The Financialization of Life." In *The Routledge International Handbook of Financialization*, edited by Philip Mader, Daniel Mertens, and Natascha van der Zwan, 68–78. London: Routledge, 2020.

Lapchick, Richard E. "The 2021 Racial and Gender Report Card: Major League Baseball." The Racial and Gender Report Card. The Institute for Diversity and Ethics in Sport, 2020.

Lapchick, Richard E. "The 2021 Racial and Gender Report Card: National Football League." The Racial and Gender Report Card. The Institute for Diversity and Ethics in Sport, 2020.

Leary, John Patrick. *Keywords: The New Language of Capitalism*. Chicago: Haymarket Books, 2019.

Lee, Joon. "Inside the Rise of MLB's Ivy League Culture: Stunning Numbers and a Question of What's Next." ESPN.com, June 30, 2020. https://www.espn.com/mlb/story/_/id/29369890/inside-rise-mlb-ivy-league-culture-stunning-numbers-question-next.

Legwold, Jeff. "Denver Broncos Reach Sale Agreement; Price Tag Is $4.65 Billion, Sources Say." ESPN.com, June 8, 2022. https://www.espn.com/nfl/story/_/id/34055696/denver-broncos-reach-agreement-sale-walton-penner-family-ownership-group.

Lemire, Joe. "Australia Leads in Broadcasting Wearables Data As AFL Is Next." SportTechie, August 1, 2017. https://www.sporttechie.com/afl-becomes-third-australian-sports-league-to-broadcast-wearable-tech-data/.

Leonard, David J. *Playing While White: Privilege and Power on and Off the Field.* Seattle: University of Washington Press, 2017.

Lewchuk, Wayne. "The Age of Increased Precarious Employment: Origins and Implications." In *Working in the Context of Austerity: Challenges and Struggles,* edited by Donna Baines and Ian Cunningham, 29–47. Bristol, U.K.: Bristol University Press, 2020.

Lewis, Michael. "The No-Stats All-Star." *New York Times,* February 13, 2009. https://www.nytimes.com/2009/02/15/magazine/15Battier-t.html.

Lindbergh, Ben, and Sam Miller. *The Only Rule Is It Has to Work: Our Wild Experiment Building a New Kind of Baseball Team.* New York: Henry Holt, 2016.

Locke, Robert R., and J. C. Spender. *Confronting Managerialism: How the Business Elite and Their Schools Threw Our Lives Out of Balance.* London: Zed Books, 2011.

London, Jay. "Data-Driven: MIT Infuses the Rise of Sports Analytics." MIT News, February 26, 2014. http://news.mit.edu/2014/data-driven-mit-infuses-the-rise-of-sports-analytics.

Lotz, Amanda D. *Cable Guys: Television and Masculinities in the 21st Century.* New York: New York University Press, 2014.

Lotz, Amanda D. *The Television Will Be Revolutionized.* Second Edition. New York: New York University Press, 2014.

Lukacs, Andras, David G. Embrick, and Talmadge Wright. "The Managed Hearthstone: Labor and Emotional Work in the Online Community of World of Warcraft." In *Facets of Virtual Environments: First International Conference, FaVE 2009, Berlin, Germany, July 27–29, 2009, Revised Selected Papers,* edited by Fritz Lehmann-Grube and Jan Sablatnig, 165–77. Berlin: Springer, 2010.

Maclean, Kate. "Gender, Risk and the Wall Street Alpha Male." *Journal of Gender Studies* 25, no. 4 (2016): 427–44.

Mader, Philip, Daniel Mertens, and Natascha van der Zwan. "Financialization: An Introduction." In *The Routledge International Handbook of Financialization,* edited by Philip Mader, Daniel Mertens, and Natascha van der Zwan, 1–16. London: Routledge, 2020.

Magder, Ted. "Television 2.0: The Business of American Television in Transition." In *Reality TV: Remaking Television Culture,* edited by Susan Murray and Laurie Ouellette, 141–64. New York: New York University Press, 2009.

Manovich, Lev. "What Is Visualization?" *Visual Studies* 26, no. 1 (2011): 36–49.

Marchand, Andrew. "Ken Rosenthal out at MLB Network over Rob Manfred Criticism." *New York Post,* January 3, 2022. https://nypost.com/2022/01/03/ken-rosenthal-out-at-mlb-network-over-rob-manfred-criticism/.

Marchand, Andrew. "Stephen A. Smith Rakes in Almost $8M per Year on New ESPN Megadeal." *New York Post,* November 7, 2019. https://nypost.com/2019/11/07/stephen-a-smith-rakes-in-almost-8m-per-year-on-new-espn-megadeal/.

Mariscal, Jorge. "Chicanos and Latinos in the Jungle of Sports Talk Radio." *Journal of Sport and Social Issues* 23, no. 1 (February 1999): 111–17.

Martin, Randy. *Financialization of Daily Life*. Philadelphia: Temple University Press, 2002.

Masteralexis, Lisa Pike. "Regulating Player Agents." In *Research Handbook of Employment Relations in Sport,* edited by Michael Barry, James Skinner, and Terry Engelberg, 99–124. Cheltenham, U.K.: Edward Elgar Publishing, 2016.

McAtee, Riley. "Even in Fiction, the Browns Can't Get It Right." The Ringer, July 20, 2016. https://www.theringer.com/2016/7/20/16043548/even-in-fiction-the-browns-cant-get-it-right-da822577b30e.

McClintock, Pamela. "Box Office Report: Brad Pitt's 'Moneyball' Tops Friday; Taylor Lautner's 'Abduction' Lands at No. 4." *Hollywood Reporter,* September 24, 2011. https://www.hollywoodreporter.com/movies/movie-news/box-office-brad-pitt-moneyball-taylor-lautner-abduction-239869/.

Mendelsohn, Joshua. *The Cap: How Larry Fleisher and David Stern Built the Modern NBA*. Lincoln: University of Nebraska Press, 2020.

Mendick, Heather, Andreas Ottemo, Maria Berge, and Eva Silfver. "Geek Entrepreneurs: The Social Network, Iron Man and the Reconfiguration of Hegemonic Masculinity." *Journal of Gender Studies* (September 2021).

Miller, Andrew. "Winning It All: The Cinematic Construction of the Athletic American Dream." In *American Dreams: Dialogues in U.S. Studies,* edited by Ricardo Miguez, 103–21. Newcastle, U.K.: Cambridge Scholars Press, 2007.

Miller, James Andrew. "John Walsh: His Own Unique Self." *Sports Business Journal,* May 11, 2015. https://www.sportsbusinessjournal.com/Journal/Issues/2015/05/11/Media/John-Walsh.aspx.

Millington, Brad, and Rob Millington. "'The Datafication of Everything': Toward a Sociology of Sport and Big Data." *Sociology of Sport Journal* 32, no. 2 (January 2015): 140–60.

Morgenstern, Joe. "'Godzilla': Delay Before Large-Scale Dazzle." *Wall Street Journal,* May 15, 2014. https://online.wsj.com/article/SB10001424052702304547704579563570504683020.html.

Morse, Margaret. "Sport on Television: Replay and Display." In *Regarding Television: Critical Approaches,* edited by E. Ann Kaplan, 44–66. Frederick, Md.: American Film Institute, 1983.

Movie Age. "'Ambassador Bill' and 'Touchdown' Take Tops," December 1, 1931. Media History Digital Library.

Mullen, Lawrence J., and Dennis W. Mazzocco. "Coaches, Drama, and Technology: Mediation of Super Bowl Broadcasts from 1969 to 1997." *Critical Studies in Media Communication* 17, no. 3 (2000): 347–63.

Muniesa, Fabian, and Liliana Doganova. "The Time That Money Requires: Use of the Future and Critique of the Present in Financial Valuation." *Finance and Society* 6, no. 2 (2020): 95–113.

Murray, Noel. "No Money for Moneyball." The A.V. Club, June 22, 2009. http://www.avclub.com/article/no-money-for-emmoneyballem-29476.

Neely, Megan Tobias. *Hedged Out: Inequality and Insecurity on Wall Street.* Berkeley: University of California Press, 2022.

Negra, Diane, and Yvonne Tasker. "Introduction: Gender and Recessionary Culture." In *Gendering the Recession: Media and Culture in an Age of Austerity,* edited by Diane Negra and Yvonne Tasker, 1–30. Durham, N.C.: Duke University Press, 2014.

The Numbers. "Moneyball (2011)—Financial Information." https://www.the-numbers.com/movie/Moneyball-(2011).

Nwulu, Mac. "For MLS Cup, ESPN Will Deploy an Optical Player Tracking System." ESPN Front Row, December 6, 2014. http://www.espnfrontrow.com/2014/12/for-mls-cup-espn-will-deploy-an-optical-player-tracking-system/.

Nygaard, Taylor, and Jorie Lagerwey. *Horrible White People: Gender, Genre, and Television's Precarious Whiteness.* New York: New York University Press, 2020.

Oates, Thomas P. *Football and Manliness: An Unauthorized Feminist Account of the NFL.* Urbana: University of Illinois Press, 2017.

Oates, Thomas P. "New Media and the Repackaging of NFL Fandom." *Sociology of Sport Journal* 26, no. 1 (2009): 31–49.

Oates, Thomas P. "On the Block: Race, Gender and Power in the NFL Draft." Ph.D. diss., University of Iowa, 2004.

O'Falt, Chris. "How Soderbergh Designed His Own Filmmaking Universe—The 'High Flying Bird' Interview." IndieWire, February 15, 2019. https://www.indiewire.com/2019/02/steven-soderbergh-high-flying-bird-interview-netflix-iphone-1202044279/.

Opta. "Data Feeds Overview." http://www.optasports.com/services/media/data-feeds/opta-data-feeds-overview.aspx.

Osterweil, Vicky. "The Rise of the Sports Management Movie." Al Jazeera America, April 27, 2014. http://america.aljazeera.com/opinions/2014/4/sports-management moviemilliondollararmmoneyball.html.

Ouellette, Laurie, and James Hay. *Better Living Through Reality TV: Television and Post-Welfare Citizenship.* Malden, Mass.: Blackwell Publishing, 2008.

Ouellette, Laurie, and James Hay. "Makeover Television, Governmentality and the Good Citizen." *Continuum* 22, no. 4 (2008): 471–84.

Ourand, John. "Does Media Rights Bubble Have a Leak?" *Sports Business Journal,* May 2, 2016. http://www.sportsbusinessdaily.com/Journal/Issues/2016/05/02/In-Depth/Media-rights.aspx.

Parks, Lisa. "Flexible Microcasting: Gender, Generation, and Television-Internet Convergence." In *Television after TV: Essays on a Medium in Transition,* edited by Lynn Spigel and Jan Olsson, 133–56. Durham, N.C.: Duke University Press, 2004.

Pellandini-Simányi, Léna. "The Financialization of Everyday Life." In *The Routledge Handbook of Critical Finance Studies,* edited by Christian Borch and Robert Wosnitzer, 278–99. New York: Routledge, 2020.

Perkins, Brian. "State of the Tech: The Top Graphics Technology Trends of 2019."

Presented at the SVG Sports Graphics Forum, Microsoft Technology Center, New York, March 6, 2019.

Phillips, Christopher. *Scouting and Scoring: How We Know What We Know about Baseball*. Princeton, N.J.: Princeton University Press, 2019.

Ploeg, Andrew J. "A New Form of Fandom: How Free Agency Brought about Rotisserie League Baseball." *International Journal of the History of Sport* 38, no. 1 (2021): 7–27.

Pollack, Neal. "The Cult of the General Manager." *Slate,* August 29, 2005. https://slate.com/culture/2005/08/the-cult-of-the-general-manager.html.

Porter, Theodore M. *Trust in Numbers: The Pursuit of Objectivity in Science and Public Life*. Princeton, N.J.: Princeton University Press, 1995.

PR Newswire. "PA Sport Acquires SportsTicker," May 10, 2006. http://www.prnewswire.com/news-releases/pa-sport-acquires-sportsticker-69975047.html.

"Programming," ca 1981. NFL draft clippings file. Ralph Wilson Jr. Pro Football Research and Preservation Center, Canton, Ohio.

Raphael, Chad. "The Political Economic Origins of Reali-TV." In *Reality TV: Remaking Television Culture,* edited by Susan Murray and Laurie Ouellette, 123–40. New York: New York University Press, 2009.

Real, Michael. "Theorizing the Sports-Television Dream Marriage: Why Sports Fit Television So Well." In *Sports Media: Transformation, Integration, Consumption,* edited by Andrew C. Billings, 19–39. New York: Routledge, 2011.

Reischel, Rob. *100 Things Packers Fans Should Know and Do Before They Die*. Chicago: Triumph Books, 2013.

Rettberg, Scott. "Corporate Ideology in World of Warcraft." In *Digital Culture, Play, and Identity: A World of Warcraft Reader,* edited by Hilde Corneliussen and Jill Walker Rettberg, 19–38. Cambridge, Mass.: MIT Press, 2008.

Robertsson, Tomas. "Virtual Graphics and Analysis." Presented at the SVG Sports Graphics Forum, HBO Theater, New York, February 25, 2015.

Rose, Ava, and James Friedman. "Television Sport as Mas(s)Culine Cult of Distraction." *Screen* 35, no. 1 (Spring 1994): 22–35.

Rose, Nikolas. "Governing 'Advanced' Liberal Democracies." In *Foucault and Political Reason,* edited by Andrew Barry, Thomas Osborne, and Nikolas Rose, 37–64. London: Routledge, 1996.

Rosenthal, Phil. "NFL Draft a Reminder LeBron James and NBA Still Far from Overtaking Pro Football." *Chicago Tribune,* April 30, 2018. https://www.chicagotribune.com/sports/ct-spt-nfl-draft-ratings-vs-nba-lebron-james-20180430-story.html.

Roth, David. "ESPN Has Found The Absolute Worst Way To Talk About The Absolute Coolest Stuff." *Defector,* July 13, 2021. https://defector.com/espn-has-found-the-absolute-worst-way-to-talk-about-the-absolute-coolest-stuff/.

Rothman, Lily. "How the NFL Helped Make Draft Day a Super Accurate Sports Movie." *Time,* April 11, 2014. https://time.com/56594/draft-day-nfl-agreement/.

Rowe, David. *Sport, Culture and the Media*. Second Edition. Maidenhead, U.K.: Open University Press, 2004.

Ruberg, Bo. *Video Games Have Always Been Queer*. New York: New York University Press, 2019.

Ruihley, Brody J., Andrew C. Billings, and Nicholas R. Buzzelli. "The Ultimate Value-Added Proposition: How Fantasy Sport Evolved to Accommodate the Changing Social Needs of Sports Fans." In *Sports Media History: Culture, Technology, Identity*, edited by John Carvalho, 251–61. London: Routledge, 2020.

Salter, Anastasia, and Bridget Blodgett. *Toxic Geek Masculinity in Media: Sexism, Trolling, and Identity Policing*. London: Palgrave Macmillan, 2017.

Sandomir, Richard. "ESPN Plans To Purchase Sports Wire." *New York Times*, November 8, 1994. http://www.nytimes.com/1994/11/08/business/the-media-business -espn-plans-to-purchase-sports-wire.html.

Sandomir, Richard. "The Innovation That Grew and Grew." *New York Times*, June 12, 2014. http://www.nytimes.com/2014/06/13/sports/the-tv-score-box-that-grew -and-grew.html.

Schatz, Thomas. *Hollywood Genres: Formulas, Filmmaking, and The Studio System*. Philadelphia: Temple University Press, 1981.

Schleiner, Anne-Marie. *The Player's Power to Change the Game: Ludic Mutation*. Amsterdam: Amsterdam University Press, 2017.

Schwarz, Alan. *The Numbers Game: Baseball's Lifelong Fascination with Statistics*. New York: Thomas Dunne Books, 2004.

Scott, David. "You Cannot Be Serious! New SportsCenter Set Seriously Debuts Sunday." ESPN Front Row, June 18, 2014. https://www.espnfrontrow.com/2014/06/ serious-new-sportscenter-set-seriously-debuts-sunday/.

Serazio, Michael. "The Irreverent Life and Uncompromising Death of Deadspin: Sports Blogging as Punk Journalism." *Journalism* 23, no. 2 (February 2022): 461–78.

Sheppard, Samantha N. *Sporting Blackness: Race, Embodiment, and Critical Muscle Memory on Screen*. Berkeley: University of California Press, 2020.

Shimpach, Shawn. "Realty Reality: HGTV and the Subprime Crisis." *American Quarterly* 64, no. 3 (2012): 515–42.

Skarka, Michael. "ESPN's Exclusive Coverage of the 2018 MLB National League Wild Card Game Presented by Hankook Tire." ESPN Press Room, September 27, 2018. https://espnpressroom.com/us/press-releases/2018/09/espns-exclusive-coverage -of-the-2018-mlb-national-league-wild-card-game-presented-by-hankook-tire/.

Smith, J. Scott, and Danny Keeven. "Creating Separation From the On-Field Product: Roger Goodell's Image Repair Discourse During the Ray Rice Domestic Violence Case." *Communication & Sport* 7, no. 3 (June 2019): 292–309.

Smith, Sam. *Hard Labor: The Battle That Birthed the Billion-Dollar NBA*. Chicago: Triumph Books, 2017.

Stein, Abe. "Playing the Game on Television." In *Sports Videogames*, edited by Mia Consalvo, Konstantin Mitgutsch, and Abe Stein, 115–37. New York: Routledge, 2013.

Stuelke, Patricia. *The Ruse of Repair: US Neoliberal Empire and the Turn from Critique*. Durham, N.C.: Duke University Press, 2021.

Sutera, David M. "The Development of the Post-Classical Hollywood Sports Business Film Trend: A Socio-Historic Approach." Ph.D. diss., University of Kansas, 2016.

Swanson, Krister. *Baseball's Power Shift: How the Players Union, the Fans, and the Media Changed American Sports Culture*. Lincoln: University of Nebraska Press, 2016.

Tasker, Yvonne. *Spectacular Bodies: Gender, Genre, and the Action Cinema*. London: Routledge, 1993.

Tasker, Yvonne. *Working Girls: Gender and Sexuality in Popular Cinema*. London: Routledge, 1998.

Taylor, T. L. *Raising the Stakes: E-Sports and the Professionalization of Computer Gaming*. Cambridge, Mass.: MIT Press, 2012.

Thorn, John. *Baseball in the Garden of Eden: The Secret History of the Early Game*. New York: Simon and Schuster, 2012.

Thosar, Deesha. "Steve Cohen Officially Becomes New Sole Owner of the Mets Ending the Wilpon Era." *New York Daily News,* November 6, 2020. https://www.nydailynews .com/sports/baseball/mets/ny-steve-cohen-officially-mets-owner-20201106 -mjaluvelrrfovkgbxmkykblqb4-story.html.

Tiratelli, Matteo. "Where Did the Bullshit Jobs Go?" *Catalyst* 6, no. 3 (Fall 2022): 128–61.

Torre, Pablo. "The 76ers' Plan to Win (Yes, Really)." ESPN.com, January 26, 2015. https://www.espn.com/nba/story/_/id/12318808/the-philadelphia-76ers-radical -guide-winning.

Vogan, Travis. *ABC Sports: The Rise and Fall of Network Sports Television*. Berkeley: University of California Press, 2018.

Vogan, Travis. *ESPN: The Making of a Sports Media Empire*. Urbana: University of Illinois Press, 2015.

Walker, James R., and Robert V. Bellamy. *Center Field Shot: A History of Baseball on Television*. Lincoln: University of Nebraska Press, 2008.

Walker, Sam. *Fantasyland: A Sportswriter's Obsessive Bid to Win the World's Most Ruthless Fantasy Baseball*. New York: Penguin Books, 2007.

Wall Street Journal. "Dow Jones to Sell Remaining Stake in SportsTicker Enterprises to ESPN," June 16, 2000. http://www.wsj.com/articles/SB96117234941783381.

Weaver, William R. "Knute Rockne—All American." *Motion Picture Herald,* October 12, 1940. Media History Digital Library.

Weber, Brenda R. *Makeover TV: Selfhood, Citizenship, and Celebrity*. Durham, N.C.: Duke University Press, 2009.

Weitzman, Yaron. *Tanking to the Top: The Philadelphia 76ers and the Most Audacious Process in the History of Professional Sports*. New York: Grand Central Publishing, 2020.

Wenner, Lawrence A. "Media, Sports, and Society: The Research Agenda." In *Media, Sports, and Society,* edited by Lawrence A. Wenner, 13–48. Newbury Park, Calif.: Sage Publications, 1989.

Weprin, Alex. "NBCSN Sports Channel to Shutter." *Hollywood Reporter,* January 22,

2021. https://www.hollywoodreporter.com/tv/tv-news/nbcuniversal-to-shutter-its-nbcsn-sports-channel-4120480/.

Willhite, Lindsey. "Baseball Prospectus More than a Diamond in the Rough." *Daily Herald,* June 16, 2009.

Winant, Gabriel. *The Next Shift: The Fall of Industry and the Rise of Health Care in Rust Belt America.* Cambridge, Mass.: Harvard University Press, 2021.

Woike, Dan. "Rob Pelinka to Be New Lakers General Manager." *Los Angeles Times,* February 22, 2017. https://www.latimes.com/sports/lakers/la-sp-lakers-gm-pelinka-20170221-story.html.

Wojnarowski, Adrian. "Portland Trail Blazers to Hire ESPN's NBA Draft Analyst Mike Schmitz as Assistant General Manager, Sources Say." ESPN.com, May 26, 2022. https://www.espn.com/nba/story/_/id/33989997/portland-trail-blazers-hire-espn-nba-draft-analyst-mike-schmitz-assistant-general-manager-sources-say.

Wojnarowski, Adrian, and Zach Lowe. "Bob Voulgaris Hired as Mavs' Director of Quantitative Research and Development." ESPN.com, October 5, 2018. https://www.espn.com/nba/story/_/id/24897221/bob-voulgaris-hired-dallas-mavericks-director-quantitative-research-development.

Wong, Glenn M., and Chris Deubert. "Major League Baseball General Managers: An Analysis of Their Responsibilities, Qualifications, and Characteristics." *NINE: A Journal of Baseball History and Culture* 18, no. 2 (2010): 74–121.

Wong, Glenn M., and Chris Deubert. "National Basketball Association General Managers: An Analysis of the Responsibilities, Qualifications and Characteristics." *Villanova Sports & Entertainment Law Journal* 18, no. 1 (2011): 213–66.

Yee, Nick. "The Labor of Fun: How Video Games Blur the Boundaries of Work and Play." *Games and Culture* 1, no. 1 (January 2006): 68–71.

Yee, Nick. *The Proteus Paradox: How Online Games and Virtual Worlds Change Us—And How They Don't.* New Haven, Conn.: Yale University Press, 2014.

Young, Jabari. "NBA Is next up for a Big Rights Increase, and $75 Billion Is the Price." CNBC, March 22, 2021. https://www.cnbc.com/2021/03/22/nba-is-next-up-for-a-big-rights-increase-and-75-billion-is-the-price.html.

Index

ABC, 64, 127

ACC Network, 6

Acho, Emmanuel, 88

Age of Empires, 146

aggression (as financial logic), 87–88, 92–93, 100. *See also* financialization; risk management (as financial logic)

Ainge, Danny, 101

Alexander, Leslie, 19

All-Star Baseball, 143. *See also* tabletop sports simulations

alternative telecasts, 23, 109–12, 138

American Beauty, 51

American Dream, 27, 33–34, 38–49, 56, 62

American Professional Baseball Association (APBA), 143. See also *APBA Baseball*; tabletop sports simulations

Anable, Aubrey, 166–67

analytics (sports analytics), xi–xiii, 16–17, 23, 29–30, 103–39, 144–45. *See also* quantification; tracking systems

Any Given Sunday, 35, 60

APBA Baseball, 144

The Apprentice, 26, 48, 77

Arliss, 17, 180n7

Around the Horn, 7

Ashcraft, Karen Lee, 51–54

Astroball, 19

Auerbach, Red, 17

augmented reality. *See* television graphics

Avalon Hill, 146

Babington, Bruce, 34, 41

Baerg, Andrew, 55, 116, 129, 131–33, 147–49

Bagley, Meredith M., 146, 149

Baker, Aaron, 40, 53

Ball Park Baseball, 145. *See also* tabletop sports simulations

Ballers, 17, 180n7

Barkley, Charles, 138

baseball. *See* Major League Baseball (MLB)

Baseball Encyclopedia, 114

Baseball Prospectus, 115

basketball. *See* National Basketball Association (NBA); Women's National Basketball Association (WNBA)

Bayless, Skip, 81

Beane, Billy, 1, 113–15, 145. See also *Moneyball*

Beer, David, 129–30

Big Brother, 48

big data, 23, 30, 105, 108, 116, 131–35. *See also* analytics; quantification; tracking systems

Big Ten Network, 6

The Bill Simmons Podcast, 2, 3, 80

biometric data, 108, 116, 131. *See also* analytics; quantification; tracking systems

Blodgett, Bridget, 24, 93–95

Bonzel, Katharina, 34–35, 38–41

Brady, Tom, 14, 26

Brinson, Will, 89

Brooks, Bucky, 88

Bull Durham, 35–36
The Busher, 39
business attire, xii, 33, 50, 181n56
business career movies, 35–36
business schools, xii, 22, 70, 115–16

calculation (as financial logic), 86–87, 92, 103. *See also* financialization; risk management (as financial logic)
Caldwell, John, 106, 113, 117
Carlos, John, 61
casual games, 162–66
CBS, 64, 89, 119, 135
CBS Sports HQ, 80
CBS Sports Network, 6
CBS Sports Spectacular, 64
The Champion, 34
Championship Manager, 144. See also *Football Manager*
Charania, Shams, 67, 170. *See also* "insider" journalists
Chess, Shira, 162–66
Chris Simms Unbuttoned, 89
ChryonHego, 118
Cinderella Man, 41
Civilization series, 146, 150, 153
CNBC. *See* financial television
Coach Carter, 41
college football, 67, 110, 112, 118, 126
Company Men, 26
completion probability, 134–35
Connor, J. D., 46, 57
Cormany, Diane, 72, 76, 81–82, 84
Costner, Kevin, 2, 36. See also *Draft Day*
Cramer, Jim, 72–73, 93
Crane, Jim, 19
Crawford, Kate, 132–33
Creed, 34, 36, 41
Criblez, Adam, 143–45
Crosson, Seán, 34–35
Cullen, Jim, 39, 56
Curtis, Bryan, 8–13, 85

Daily Wager, 126–27
The Dan Patrick Show, 66
data-driven decision-making. *See* analytics; quantification
data visualization. *See* television graphics
Deal or No Deal, 72
"The Decision," 14
DeMarsico, John, 131
Deubert, Christopher, 15, 17–18

Diamond Mind Baseball, 144–45
digital work, 10, 24, 31, 157–67
Diner Dash series, 162–66
Disney, 37. *See also* ESPN; *Million Dollar Arm*
Dodgeball: A True Underdog Story, 41, 50
Dow Jones & Company, 122
Draft Day, 2, 8, 26–28, 33–62, 169–70
Dragons' Den, 77
Drucker, Johanna, 134–36
Drucker, Peter, 21
Durant, Kevin, 14
Defense-adjusted Value Over Average (DVOA), 130
Dyer, Richard, 55, 182n74, 182n77

Edwards, Harry, 61–62, 182n91
entry drafts. See *Draft Day*; National Basketball Association (NBA); National Football League (NFL)
escapism, 159–63
ESPN: draft coverage, 5–6, 67, 127, 183n11; ESPN+, 7, 65; and fantasy sports, 69, 144, 149; and financialization, 74–84, 91, 94, 100; free agency coverage, 4–14, 67, 79; "insider" journalists, 8, 10–11, 16, 67, 85, 170; and media convergence, 8; and "media rights bubble," 7; NBA trade deadline coverage, 12, 16, 82–83; and sports gambling, 126–27; statistical analysis of sport, xi, 16, 104–11, 120–27, 133, 137–44; use of talk programming, 64–69
European Super League, 155–56
Executive Suite, 36
Expected Assists (xA), 121
Expected Goals (xG), 121
The Express, 41

Falling Down, 51
fandom. *See* sports fandom
fantasy sports, 2, 11–12, 30–31, 69, 125, 141–68
Fareed, Ahmed, 89
Farming Simulator, 164
Fast Money, 72
Field of Dreams, 36
Fields, Justin, 80–81
FIFA, 2, 141–42, 147–48. *See also* sports video games
Fight Club, 51
financial crisis (2007–2008), 93. *See also* Great Recession

212   Index

financial industry, 18–22, 72–73; culture, 19–20

financial television, 26, 71–73, 76, 81–85, 92–93, 117

financialization, 22–23, 28–29, 63–103, 149, 153–55, 170–72

Finke, Nikki, 10

First Take, 14, 64, 66, 79–81, 100, 109

First Things First, 67, 101

Flash Boys, 93

Flood, Curt, 13–14, 37

Flores, Lisa A., 51–54

football. *See* college football; National Football League (NFL)

Football Manager, 2, 4, 24–27, 141–67, 170. *See also* sports video games

Football Power Index (FPI), 123

Ford vs. Ferrari, 36

42 (film), 36, 41

Fox, 67, 110, 120–22, 138

Fox Business. *See* financial television

Foxcatcher, 49

Foxworth, Domonique, 79

Franchise Hockey Manager, 142

free agency: history, 4–5, 13–15; media coverage, 4–14, 37, 67, 79, 88, 100; and sports fandom, 15

The Freshman, 34, 40

Friedman, Andrew, 19

Friedman, Lester, 34–36, 39

Friedman, Ted, 150–51, 153, 165

FS1, 6, 66–67, 79–81, 88, 101, 110

FS2, 6

game modifications (mods), 155–56

Gamson, William, 143, 145

Gaudelli, Fred, 6

Get Up, 14, 64

Gill, Mike, 76

Givony, Jonathan, 67

The Gladiator, 40

Glover, Richard, 122

Goff, Jared, 87

golf, 6, 108, 120–21

Golf Channel, 6

Golf on NBC, 108

Good Morning America, 66

Goodell, Roger, 170

Gordon, David, 21

gossip, 10–11

Graeber, David, 24, 164

Grantland, 8

Great Recession, 25–26, 49–50

Griffin, David, 77

Guttmann, Allen, 113, 176n9

Haiven, Max, 22, 72–73, 77

The Half Back, 39–40

Hamm, Jon, 2, 45–46. See also *Million Dollar Arm*

Harper, Bryce, 14

Harris, Josh, 18–19

Hay, James, 72–74, 147

The Herd with Colin Cowherd, 87

Heresco, Aaron, 26, 71–72, 76, 81–85, 92–93, 117

HGTV, 74–75

High Flying Bird, 17; as a critique of the managerial mode, 34, 57–61, 99, 172, 182n91; and the sports film genre, 33–34, 36–38, 45

Hill, Rosemary Lucy, 129, 134, 136–37

Hinkie, Sam, 18–20, 22, 116

Ho, Karen, 19–20

hockey. *See* National Hockey League (NHL)

Hot Stove, 67

House, Joe, 80

Hoxworth, Kellen, 146–47, 167

Hudrick, Paul, 76, 78, 94

Hunter, Latham, 50–51

Icahn, Carl, 21

Iguodala, Andre, 15

"in house" sports media, 124

independent sports media, 173

"insider" journalists, 8, 10, 67, 169, 192n2

Instagram, 8

investment (as financial logic), 73–78, 92, 97. *See also* financialization

investment banking, 19. *See also* financial industry

Irving, Kyrie, 94

It's a Wonderful Life, 92

Ivy League, 20, 22, 94, 98

The Jackie Robinson Story, 4

Jagoda, Patrick, 146, 152, 155–56

James, Bill, 114, 145

James, LeBron, 14

Jazayerli, Rany, 115

Jefferson, Richard, 80

Jerry Maguire, 17, 33, 35–38, 42–43, 46, 52–54

Index   213

Johnson, Keyshawn, 74
Jones, Jerry, 88
Jordan, DeAndre, 9, 11
Judge, Aaron, 109
The Jump, 16, 77–78, 80, 91, 123

Kellerman, Max, 79
Kennedy, Helen, 129, 134–37
Keyshawn, JWill & Zubin, 74
Kiyosaki, Robert, 71
Knute Rockne, All American, 39
Kotick, Bobby, 182n88
Kusz, Kyle, 26, 41, 50, 53, 56

labor relations (sports industry), 13–15, 17
Lambre, Wosny, 74, 101–2
Langley, Paul, 86–88
Leary, John Patrick, 78, 102
Lemonis, Marcus, 26
Leonard, Kawhi, 100, 102
Lewis, Michael, 2, 19, 114–16. See also *Flash Boys*; *Moneyball*
liveness, 83–85
Lowe, Zach, 2, 83–84, 112
The Lowe Post, 2, 94
Luhnow, Jeff, 19–20

Madden, 2, 8, 141–44, 147–49, 152, 164. *See also* sports video games
Mad Money, 72–73, 93
Major League, 35, 60
Major League Baseball (MLB), 3–6, 12–20, 96, 98, 192nn2–3; free agency, 13–15, 67, 144; and statistical analysis of sport, 1, 104–16, 126, 128, 132–33. See also *Million Dollar Arm*; *Moneyball*; *Out of the Park Baseball*
Major League Baseball Players Association (MLBPA), 13–14
Major League Soccer (MLS), 116, 155
management consulting, xii, 19, 21–22, 48
managerialism, 21–22, 153, 157; and quantification, 103, 115; and sports films, 28, 33–34, 44–45
Mangini, Eric, 79
The Man in the Gray Flannel Suit, 25, 50
Margin Call, 93–94
market movement (as financial logic), 79–85, 92. *See also* financialization
Marks, Bobby, 67–68, 94
Martin, Randy, 71–72, 86, 103
masculinity, 24–26; and digital sports games, 149, 167; financial masculinity,

91–99; geek masculinity, 24–26, 29, 93–95, 138–39, 149; and race, 25–29, 40–41, 50–56, 90–99, 137–39, 149; and sports films, 28, 34, 40–41, 49–55; and sports talk, 29, 63–64, 90–99; and sports television, 63–64, 90–99, 138–39
Massively Multiplayer Online Role-Playing Games (MMORPGs), 159–60
Mayhew, Martin, 91
McShay, Todd, 67
media convergence, 8
media rights, 6–9, 18, 23, 60, 155, 177n62
Megacasts, 110, 112. *See also* alternative telecasts
Microsoft Flight Simulator, 164
Microsoft Office, 31, 157, 161
Mid-Atlantic Sports Network (MASN), 7
Mike and the Mad Dog, 65
Miller, Andrew, 39–40, 42
Millington, Brad, 113, 116, 131
Millington, Rob, 113, 116, 131
Million Dollar Arm, 2, 17, 25, 27, 33–55, 182n77
Miracle, 41
Massachusetts Institute of Technology (MIT), xi–xii, 22, 93, 115. *See also* Sloan Sports Analytics Conference
Mitchell, Donovan, 57–58, 61
MLB Network, 6, 65–68, 121, 132, 192n2
MLB Tonight, 65, 132–33
MMORPGs (Massively Multiplayer Online Role-Playing Games), 159–60
mods. *See* game modifications
Monday Night Football, 127
Moneyball: book version, 1, 114–15, 127–28, 144–45, 189n15; cultural and societal impact, 25, 27, 114–15, 127–28, 144–45, 189n15; film version, 1–2, 33–62, 90, 94, 182n88, 192n3. *See also* analytics
Morey, Daryl, xii–xiii, 19–23, 76–80, 90–99, 116, 138
"Moreyball," 116
Motorsport Manager, 142
MSG Network, 66

National Basketball Association (NBA): entry draft, 2, 6, 17; free agency, 9, 11, 14–15, 67, 79, 100; prominent executives, xii–xiii, 19–23, 76–80, 90–99, 116, 125–26, 138; and origins of managerial mode, 5–20; salary cap, 15–17, 70, 94; and sports films, 57–61, 172; and sports talk/financialization, 67–70, 74–80,

83–84, 94, 97, 100–2; and sports television/quantification, 110–12, 116, 125–26, 136–37; and statistical analysis of sport, 110, 112, 116, 125–26, 138; trades/trade deadline, 10, 12, 83–84. See also *High Flying Bird*

National Basketball Players Association (NBPA), 14

National Football League (NFL): and digital sports games, 146–52, 164; entry draft, 2–9, 37, 57, 67, 80–81, 96–98; free agency, 9, 14, 79, 88; and origins of managerial mode, 5–20; and sports films, 2, 33–62, 169–70; and sports talk/financialization, 67–74, 79–80, 85–89, 91, 96–102; and sports television/quantification, 106–7, 116, 118–19, 134–35. See also *Draft Day*; *Jerry Maguire*; *Madden*

National Hockey League (NHL), 5–6, 14, 116

National Women's Soccer League (NWSL), 5, 116

NBA on ESPN, 112

NBA Today, 16, 66–67

NBA TV, 6

NBA 2K, 2, 8, 141. See also sports video games

NBC, 7, 64, 87, 89, 108, 119

Neely, Megan Tobias, 92, 96

Negra, Diane, 26, 49–50

neoliberalism, 23–25; and digital sports games, 30–31, 141–68, 170; and sports films, 37, 48; and sports talk/financialization, 86; and sports television/quantification, 130

New England Sports Network (NESN), 66

NFL Live, 66, 91, 170

NFL Network, 6, 9, 67–68, 89

NFL on CBS, 119, 134–35

NFL Total Access, 89

NHL Network, 6

North Dallas Forty, 4, 35

Number One, 4, 35

Oates, Thomas, 55, 80, 86, 96–99, 148–49, 156

O'Brien, Bill, 89

O'Dowd, Dan, 132, 138

office movies, 51–52, 54

Office Space, 51–52

Okrent, Daniel, 143

On-base Plus Slugging (OPS), 23, 104, 107–9, 114–16, 123, 126

On-base Plus Slugging Plus (OPS+), 104, 107, 109

Opta, 120

The Organization Man, 50

Ouellette, Laurie, 72–73, 147

Out of the Park Baseball, 24, 26–27, 141–42, 153–54, 157–58, 161–62. See also sports video games

overwhelm, 165–66

Pac-12 Network, 6

Paramount+, 7

Pardon the Interruption, 66

Parlor Base-Ball, 143

Patrick, Dan, 66, 130

Peacock, 7

Pelinka, Rob, 17

Perkins, Brian, 121

PFT Live, 87

Phillips, Christopher, 113–14, 126–28, 133, 145, 186n18, 186n23

Picker, Gregg, 131

Pick Six, 89

"player empowerment," 100–2

podcasting. See sports radio and podcasting

Pollack, Neal, 3

portfolios (as financial logic), 88–89. See also financialization; risk management (financial logic)

postindustrialization, 24–25, 28, 31, 54, 157. See also digital work

postmodernity, 153

precariousness, 48–52, 55–57, 165–67. See also social class

Prescott, Dak, 79, 88

Presti, Sam, 77–78, 91

Pride of the Yankees, 39–40

private equity, 18–19. See also financial industry

The Profit, 26

Project Scoresheet, 145

Public Broadcasting Service (PBS), 172

QBR (Total Quarterback Rating), 123

quantification, 23–25, 29–30, 103–39, 144–52, 170–72. See also analytics

Race, 41

race and representation, 25–26; and digital sports games, 149, 167; and sports films, 27–28, 50–56; and sports talk/financialization, 90–99; and sports television/

race and representation (*continued*)
quantification, 137–39. *See also* masculinity

Rapoport, Ian, 67, 89. *See also* "insider" journalists

re-gamification, 165–66

reality television, 7–8, 26, 48–49, 51, 72–75, 77

Reds, 57

regional sports networks (RSNs), 7, 66, 106, 130–31

Reiter, Ben, 19

reserve systems/clauses, 13–14. *See also* labor relations (sports industry)

The Revolt of the Black Athlete, 61–62

The Rich Eisen Show, 66

Rickey, Branch, 4

Riddick, Louis, 67

The Ringer, 8, 74, 80, 101

The Ringer NBA Show, 74, 101

risk management (as financial logic), 85–90, 92–93, 96, 100, 102–3. *See also* financialization

Robertson, Oscar, 14

Rocky series, 40–42, 52–53

Rollercoaster Tycoon, 27, 146

Rose, Jalen, 139

Rose, Leon, 17

Rosenthal, Ken, 67, 192n2. *See also* "insider" journalists

Roth, David, 100

Rotisserie League Baseball (Roto), 15, 143–44. *See also* fantasy sports

Rozelle, Pete, 6

Ruberg, Bo, 152, 165–66

Rudy, 45

Russillo, Ryen, 80

Ruth, Babe, 3, 13

The Ryen Russillo Podcast, 80

Salter, Anastasia, 24, 93–95

Schefter, Adam, 8, 10–11, 67, 85, 170. *See also* "insider" journalists

Schell, Connor, 126

Schmitz, Mike, 183n11

Schneider, Jon, 89

SEC Network, 6

second screens, 8, 109, 144

Second Spectrum, 110

shareholder value principle, 21

Shark Tank, 26

Sharpe, Shannon, 81

shot charts, 112, 136–37

Silicon Valley, 19, 115

Silverman, Matthew, 19

SimCity, 150–51, 153

Simmons, Ben, 69, 74–77, 80, 97, 101–2

Simmons, Bill, 2–3

Simmons, Chet, 6

Simms, Chris, 87, 89

The Sims series, 160–62

Sklar, Robert, 143

Sky, 4

Slap Shot, 60

Sloan Sports Analytics Conference, xi–xiii, 16, 29, 123, 125, 175n3. *See also* analytics

Smith, Sam, 14

Smith, Stephen A., 74, 81, 100

Smith, Tommie, 61

SMT, 118

soccer, 108, 118. See also *FIFA*; Major League Soccer (MLS); National Women's Soccer League (NWSL)

social class, 25–26, 39–40, 45–50, 52. *See also* precariousness

social media, 8–9

Soderbergh, Steven, 57. See also *High Flying Bird*

Southpaw, 34

Speak for Yourself, 79–80, 88

spin rate, 132–33, 138

Sportradar, 120

sports agents, 16–17, 37, 58, 169, 180n7. See also *High Flying Bird*; *Jerry Maguire*; *Million Dollar Arm*

The Sports Bash with Mike Gill, 76, 78, 94

sports betting. *See* sports gambling

SportsCenter, 8, 14, 64–65, 74–76, 84–85, 106

sports fandom, 10, 15, 125, 129–32, 144–45

sports film (genre), 27–28, 33–62, 91

sports gambling (sports betting), 11–12, 69, 125–27, 187n69

SportsNet New York (SNY), 130–31

sports radio and podcasting, 2–3, 5–12, 16, 22–23, 28–29, 63–102

sports streaming services, 7, 64–65, 110

sports talk, 16, 28, 29, 63–102, 170–71

sports television, 1–12, 14, 16, 18, 23, 169–73; and financialization, 27–28, 63–102; and quantification, 23, 29–30, 103–140

SportsTicker, 122

sports video games, 2, 8, 23–24, 30–31, 141–67. *See also* fantasy sports

Spotify, 74, 80, 101

Stadium (network), 67
Stafford, Matthew, 87, 89
Stark, Tony, 94
Statis-Pro, 143. *See also* tabletop sports simulations
statistical analysis of sport. *See* analytics; quantification
Steeg, Jim, 6
Strat-O-Matic, 143, 145. See also *Strat-O-Matic Computer Baseball*; tabletop sports simulations
Strat-O-Matic Computer Baseball, 144
Sunday Night Baseball, 104–6, 111
Sunday Night Football, 119
Sutera, David, 35, 37, 54
swimming, 118
symbiotic relationship (between sport and media), 169, 172, 192n1

tabletop sports simulations, 4, 143–46
Tasker, Yvonne, 26, 49–51
Taubman, Brandon, 19
Tavares, John, 14
Taylor, Joy, 87
television graphics, 30, 82, 91, 104–12, 117–20, 134–37; critiqued as data visualizations, 134–37; relationship with video games, 118, 120; virtual graphics (augmented reality), 118–20, 136
televisuality, 106, 113, 117
temporality, 10, 75–76, 81–85
Tennis Channel, 6
Tin Cup, 36
Tippett, Tom, 145
Today, 66
Total Quarterback Rating (QBR), 123
Towns, Karl-Anthony, 57
tracking systems, 108, 110, 116–17, 121, 127–28, 131–35. *See also* analytics; big data; quantification
Trotter, Jim, 89
Trouble with the Curve, 35
Tunsil, Laremy, 89
TVTV Goes to the Super Bowl, 172–73
Twitter, 8–9

Uehara, Koji, 132–33
Undercover Boss, 26
Undisputed, 81
unions (player unions). *See* labor relations (sports industry)
Up in the Air, 26

Value Over Replacement Player (VORP), 115
Vizrt, 118
Voulgaris, Haralabos, 126

Wagner-McGough, Sean, 89
Wall Street, 36, 92
Walks and Hits per Inning Pitched (WHIP), 130
Walsh, John, 123, 187n53
WAR (Wins Above Replacement), 23, 109
weighted On-Base Average (wOBA), 110, 126
Welch, Jack, 21
WFAN, 65
WHIP (Walks and Hits per Inning Pitched), 130
White Collar, 50
White Collar Brawlers, 51
white-collar work. *See* postindustrialization
Whitlock, Jason, 79
Who Wants to Be a Millionaire, 138
Wide World of Sports, 64
Wife Swap, 72–73
Wiley, Marcellus, 79, 88
Wilson, Sloan, 25, 50
Windhorst, Brian, 76
win probability, 123
Wins Above Replacement (WAR), 23, 109
wOBA (weighted On-Base Average), 110, 126
Wojnarowski, Adrian, 2, 8, 10–11, 16, 67, 83–85. *See also* "insider" journalists
The Woj Pod, 2
Wolf of Wall Street, 77
Women's National Basketball Association (WNBA), 5, 116
Wong, Glenn, 15, 17–18
Woolner, Keith, 115
World of Warcraft, 159–62
The Wrestler, 49
Wright, Nick, 101–2, 171

xA (Expected Assists), 121
xG (Expected Goals), 121

Yahoo, 122, 144
Yankees Entertainment and Sports Network (YES), 7

BRANDEN BUEHLER is an assistant professor of visual and sound media at Seton Hall University.

Studies in Sports Media

Six Minutes in Berlin: Broadcast Spectacle and Rowing Gold at the Nazi Olympics
  Michael Socolow
Fighting Visibility: Sports Media and Female Athletes in the UFC
  Jennifer McClearen
The Digital NBA: How the World's Savviest League Brings the Court to
  Our Couch   *Steven Secular*
Front Office Fantasies: The Rise of Managerial Sports Media   *Branden Buehler*

The University of Illinois Press
is a founding member of the
Association of University Presses.

———————————————————

University of Illinois Press
1325 South Oak Street
Champaign, IL 61820-6903
www.press.uillinois.edu